THE WORLD OF

ADRIENNE VON SPEYR

THE WORLD OF PRAYER

WITH A FOREWORD BY
HANS URS VON BALTHASAR

Translated by Graham Harrison

IGNATIUS PRESS   SAN FRANCISCO

Title of the German original:
Die Welt des Gebetes
© 1951 Johannes Verlag
Einsiedeln, Switzerland

Cover by Victoria Hoke

© 1985 Ignatius Press, San Francisco
ISBN 0–89870–033–7
Library of Congress catalogue number 84–080904
Printed in the United States of America

CONTENTS

FOREWORD

The uniqueness of Adrienne von Speyr's writings makes it appropriate for the editor to give a brief word of explanation. Most of the works which have appeared so far were meditations on Holy Scripture, an endeavor to hear and interpret the Word of God afresh verse by verse. The effort involved in this tireless determination to "begin afresh" will make sense to the reader at each step only if he undertakes the same effort just as tirelessly, seeing what is presented to him, not as a connected treatise, but as an intellectual stimulus, an invitation to his own meditation. The same is true of this volume, despite its external form. The editor has selected some of the author's numerous observations on the subject of prayer, putting them together like flowers in a bouquet. Like all bouquets, there is something arbitrary about it: It could have been larger, smaller or differently arranged. The reader should pay less attention to the external arrangement, which, including the titles and headings, is the work of the editor—and which would probably be incomplete in whatever form it were presented—than to the substance and value of the individual pieces, which reveal an unmistakably unified style of thought and approach to prayer and indeed to the whole of Christian life. Strange as it may seem, it hardly matters where one opens this book and begins to read: All paths lead straight to the center like sectors of a circle. The reader's attention should be directed in all respects to the inner, not the outer, unity.

Initially we can say that this unity lies in the fact that every human perspective needs to be traced to and grounded in an ecclesial perspective, every ecclesial perspective within a christological one and every christological perspective within a trinitarian one. Here we find the fundamental idea of the book, audacious and yet entirely logical: Like everything that comes to man through God's self-revelation in Christ (such as grace, faith, hope and love, the relationship between Christ and the Church), prayer is ultimately rooted in God himself and in his triune exchange of life. Beyond all purely creaturely motives and needs, Christian prayer is a participation in the inner life and prayer of the Divinity, which is revealed, prepared and accomplished in the world by Jesus Christ our Lord and by him made available for us to take part in. Since this idea is the core of the book, the section dealing expressly and most completely with the trinitarian basis of prayer has been placed at the beginning, in spite of various reasons against this plan. Readers who are less inclined to follow demanding theological trains of thought would be advised, after having read the Introduction, to skip over this section initially, along with the chapter on the prayer of Christ, and to begin with either the chapter on the prayer of Mary (a chapter which is complete in itself, since it was written for a particular occasion) or the one on the development of prayer in man. In reading those later chapters, readers will continually encounter related trinitarian and christological ideas, since they are part of the book's innermost substance. These later passages, however, will provide an easier approach to the earlier chapters, which, in certain respects, might have come at the end of the book.

Notwithstanding the wealth of themes presented here, the book does not intend to offer a complete doctrine of prayer. The author has dealt in detail with other areas of this doctrine (questions of action and contemplation, the nature and methods of contemplative prayer, the prayer of faith and mystical prayer, particular forms of prayer of the individual saints), partly in previous books and partly in works still to be published; hence it is not yet possible to arrive at a definitive appraisal of her views. But what has been offered so far is rich enough to rekindle genuine prayer life in the Church and to give a powerful impetus to the theology of prayer.

Hans Urs von Balthasar
Epiphany 1951

I

INTRODUCTION

On the Nature of Prayer

No real definition of prayer can be given, for it is a mysterious life with God, a participation in the center of his being and in his divine, triune love. Certainly those forms which are furthest from the center are, in their isolation, also the most clearly delineated; thus they are to some extent amenable to description and definition. In order to understand the real nature of prayer, however, one must begin with that prayer in which man is most perfectly joined to God, i.e., full contemplation, wherein he is completely conformed to the will of God by God himself, wherein God places man in that state which he desires for him, wherein man has become an untarnished mirror of the divine will, a clear response to divine revelation. At this point the word of God has become so powerful that it requires no other words for its expression. God reveals, and man no longer needs to translate what has been revealed into alien images; he is absorbed in being part of what belongs to God. Just as a child at play, completely caught up in what he is doing, must first build a bridge from his world to the outside world if he has to explain his game to the uninitiated, so it is with the person who has been perfected in prayer when he is called upon to explain to others what he does.

***

At the root every conversation with God is an embarrassment, a substitute for a much deeper mutual understanding. If we had not sinned it would have been natural to love God and respond to him. In Paradise God asks no questions of Adam; Adam lives simply in God's sight in faith and happiness, and everything he does corresponds to God's purposes. "You shall have dominion", God says to him; no answer from Adam is recorded. It is natural for him to understand God's word and carry it out. It does not occur to him to ask, "O God, how can I have dominion over the animals, and how shall I set about it?" God does not question man until after the Fall: "Adam, where are you?" Only now begins the dialogue as between two estranged subjects, which we today call prayer: something which, at some point or another, has its basis in a bad conscience, which draws the best conclusions still possible from a baneful fact, which aims to bring those who are estranged back to God again. Thus, in the Our Father, the Son takes sin into consideration. If there were no sin we would not need to say "Hallowed be thy name", for God's name would always be hallowed; nor "Thy kingdom come", for it would be here; nor "Thy will be done on earth as it is in heaven", for God's will would be carried out equally on earth and in heaven. It would be superfluous to ask for daily bread, for all that God had created for man, even before creating him, would be available. And the remaining petitions would not apply.

In prayer God enables man to *approach* him once more. Most people live so estranged from God that prayer's first task must be to make them aware of their distance from God. In the light of prayer they should recognize what their life thus far has amounted to, what they owe to God the Father, Son and Spirit for which they have not thanked him. In contrition that opens the heart they ought to try to bridge the abyss which separates them from God; they are to begin their prayer by bringing to a halt the movement that estranges them from God and so turning back toward him. Prayer is first of all *conversion*.

But perhaps they no longer know what prayer is; and they start praying as if it were the most natural thing in the world, as if it went without saying that God is ready to listen to them, to answer them and to carry out their wishes. Or they have a slight apprehension of their estrangement but try not to let it enter their consciousness too forcefully or become real in their prayer. They present themselves to God as they are and leave it to God to forget the estrangement, as they have done. But prayer cannot be built on an untruth. Every believer who tries to live by his faith will try at least once a day to consider his sin and estrangement so that he can ask God's pardon for it. He need not make this awareness the content of his prayer; indeed he must not, otherwise he will have too little time for the real approach to God, adoration and thanksgiving. But he may only dare to approach God in the recognition of his distance from him, in sorrow for his sin and in the humility of the prodigal son who accepts every grace the Father bestows on him as the most undeserved gift. Not until the pain of his estrangement burns in his soul can the divine fire of grace really burn within him.

In turning to God and returning home from our estrangement, we discover that we are entering the existent world of prayer, which is the world of God. We no longer imagine that prayer is something we fashion arbitrarily, to be started and broken off as we wish, one human activity among others that have no necessary connection to it. Now we understand that we had dropped out of something which in itself is connected and continuous, that prayer, as God offers it to the believer, ought really to have begun at his birth, to end at his death. Entering once more into the life of prayer, man must feel how much he has missed of this life and how incapable he is of making up for it himself; for he cannot begin his life all over again at the day of his birth. But at conversion, with the realization of this hopeless incapacity, God grants the genuine possibility of a rebirth, and we may stand before God as newborn men and women each day of our lives, endeavoring to stay faithful to him to the end.

Understood in this way, we could define prayer as standing constantly before God, our unobstructed fellowship with him, our will to hear and follow him despite all the hindrances existing within us. It is a deep, fundamental *readiness*, therefore, that provides the foundation for all particular dialogues and acts of prayer. This readiness must accompany us through all our daily work, condensing at certain times into what we are accustomed to call prayer in the restricted sense: that state in which there is no room left in us for anything but God's voice, our listening to it and our acknowledgment.

Vocal prayers have their place in this restricted area. They are summed up in the Our Father taught to us by the Son of God; it expresses his own attitude of prayer before the Father and his perfect readiness to serve the Father. We endeavor to say these words as the Son meant them and as he wishes to hear them from us. We know that God the Father first heard this prayer upon the lips of his Son and that therefore it is his gracious will to listen and receive the prayer from us as well. And we understand that these words contain everything that the Son recommends us to say to the Father and that they would never have occurred to us in this richness and simplicity—they bear the stamp of the Son. We also know that the Son places his Holy Spirit at our disposal so that we can utter these words with his filial disposition. When we begin, "Our Father", we are reminded that he is both the Son's Father and our Father and that he hears the word of both as a unity. Consequently,

16

we strive in every phrase and every petition for the original meaning imparted to them by the Son, so that he may come to life in us, so that God may hear our words as living and so that we may discover, through this life, a new way of approach to him. For the person praying does not need to have found already what he seeks; each prayer is a search, and each of God's answers to prayer always implies a new fulfillment, a discovery—the fulfillment of an expectation that we have not even recognized as such and that God formed perhaps out of our readiness. In every genuine prayer a new nearness to God is created, through which we are remade.

The person who endeavors to pray vocal prayers in the spirit of the Lord, always attentive to this spirit, will discover that every word has a context. Every petition of the Our Father echoes through the rest of the gospel. Each is related to other words of the Lord, is made comprehensible by his actions and ultimately is interpreted by the whole of Scripture and the whole of God's revelation. No word of the Lord's is isolated; each is related to all. It is precisely in prayer that these connections become visible. Each word of the Lord (and his actions too are lessons and words) has the power to reveal further connections to the person at prayer and to initiate him into the mysteries of the Son's earthly life and of his eternal life in the Father. The person who has grasped this will begin to search for such connections in the same spirit in which he sought to pray the Lord's words. This search will imply a deepening and lengthening of prayer and thus will require the person to remain longer in the attitude of prayer. He may have little time for prayer; in that case he will take one or more words from his prayer to accompany him through his day, repeating these words in his free moments and renewing their connection with his prayer. The words will incite him to *read* more; he will delight to dwell upon the Lord's words in the gospel, to read Holy Scripture and so be drawn deeper into the life and nature of the eternal Word. In all this he will not forget his point of departure and fall into a worldly, inquisitive investigation but will keep in mind that he began with prayer and that only the attitude of prayer can give him true information about the depths of the Word.

Once he has learned to live with the Word of God, keeping the Lord's words within him and never becoming estranged from them, having them so near that he can recall them at any time, he will discover how to live in a *continual attitude of prayer*, without ever slipping from it. By the Lord's grace he will learn how to be forever in the presence of the Word, as the Son was in the Father's presence, in a continual intercourse with him which for the most part does not need words to express it, and in a constant attentiveness to what the Father does and desires. Prayer will result in an attitude of obedience. And as prayer gradually becomes an activity controlling the whole of life, all the events of daily life will be seen, perhaps unconsciously at first, in connection with God: All things become signposts mysteriously leading to God, revealing proofs of his existence and presenting ways of drawing closer to him. This experience will further encourage the one praying to strive for an uninterrupted attitude of prayer. His own self will be less and less a single, isolated, unconnected entity in relation to people and things: It will become inseparable from the connections revealed in prayer. His manner of seeing the world and of judging things will spring from his attitude of prayer. Conversely, things will no longer seem alien and unintelligible to him: They are God's world, to which God continually provides the key in prayer.

From this, *contemplative prayer* develops, with its definite time for contemplation. When someone realizes that a relation to God can be discovered in everything, then at the same time he will understand, if he is a believer, that he can only attain the correct view of things if he beholds and evaluates everything with the eyes and dispositions of the Son who reveals. Thus, in both prayer and reading, his approach will become more markedly contemplative, i.e., he will try to comprehend everything as the Lord meant it while he dwelt on earth, as he regards it now in heaven and ultimately as the Son, who is the eternal Word, was and is in the Father's presence. He will become aware of the Word in both his incarnate form and his eternal being: By realizing the former as concretely as possible he will attain the most vivid awareness of the latter. The self, which had already retired into the background at an earlier stage of prayer, is now even more stripped and abandoned; now the only important thing is the word of God, its truth and its realization. This word grows in the soul until it takes charge entirely, until the meaning of God has become the meaning of life, until the soul has been refashioned totally into the handmaid of the Lord. This fruit of contemplation will not grow, however, unless the one who prays reserves a definite time for contemplation in his daily life. Certainly there may and must be meeting points between daily work and contemplation where the latter streams forth into activity. But in order to arrive at this, the Christian needs times in which he devotes himself exclusively to contemplation. He cannot be content to glance now and again at God's connections with the world, maintaining only a fleeting contact with them, dependent on mood or whim. The life of the believer in God is not a superficial, vague matter. It demands just as much effort, decision and discipline from man as God took upon himself when he set about recovering the world and bringing it home, in his orderly, decisive turning toward mankind.

This redemptive turning is served by contemplation, by every prayer, by man himself. In contemplation he should not be removed into an aesthetic mood that distances him from the urgency of Christian life. Rather, he should be trained in the *service* of faith. In prayer the Christian receives assurance about everything that God requires and expects of him. He understands that he is to remain uninterruptedly in the presence of God, ready to do his will and to receive his word as fully as he can. This assurance is one with the certainty of knowing that God is concerned for him, that nothing in his daily life is an accident, that everything has its meaning in God and that, as a believer, he is called to seek this meaning and to help the things around him to attain their own meaning. In both ways he becomes a servant and an instrument of God; he must never lose sight of his position of service. Prayer and service are an indivisible unity, a unity of watchfulness, readiness, self-offering and the attempt to bear and to carry out what one has received.

Hence prayer becomes an expression of *faith*. No one can believe without being in constant contact with God. God established this bond at creation and bestowed it upon the first man, who obscured and weakened it through the fall into sin. Prayer reconstitutes the interrupted contact of faith with God. Indeed, faith is not merely an objective, conceptual content to be accepted and applied to life: The content of faith lives in the believer as genuine divine life and makes possible in him the act and state of faith. Faith is what man has grasped of God, for in faith God reveals himself and allows himself to be grasped by man. Man is situated in the midst of faith; he lives and moves in it, and faith continually is at work on him and presents new challenges to his intelligence and awareness. So he must continually come to terms with this faith, or rather with the God who communicates himself to him in faith. This contact with God that is the sign of an alert faith is called prayer. It is the exchange, the give and take, between God and man in faith. It is man's Yes to God in response to God's constant readiness with regard to man. And the one who prays knows that God's readiness exists, that the realm of prayer is permanently open to him, that if the bond with God is broken, it is he who is at fault and not God, whose readiness is constant. Man can refuse prayer as he can refuse nourishment. But as the body dies without food, so the soul perishes without prayer, which brings God's bread to it. This nourishment is always offered. God never shuts the door against the one who knocks. The man who never enters his father's house cannot complain that he is an orphan. And God is there at all times to welcome his child. Through the Son's redeeming work, prayer has acquired a new form. The meaning is the same as it was in Paradise: fellowship with God. But now mankind has seen *the Son at prayer*, witnessed his death on the Cross and learned from his own attitude of prayer how much God the Father has taken upon himself for their sake. They have not seen the Son's divine nature in the Father, but they could always discern in his prayer his human nature in the Father; and now, looking to the Son, they know how to reach the Father by prayer and how, in this same prayer, they are entrusted by the Father to the Son. This, then, is the meaning of prayer: We are in the presence of the Father, the Son and the Holy Spirit, and in and through them we strive to become what the Father created us to be—his children.

* * *

Everything good, and that means everything selfless and loving, is transparent to God. Its transparency is not simply like that of glass which is inert, so that all the effort of looking through it is our own: This transparency is active, compelling the observer to look and come into contact with God. One cannot meet the Son in faith without being brought by him to the Father, coming into contact with the Father and being drawn into the attitude of prayer. A believer cannot have a merely theoretical relation to him. It is in and through him that we must encounter the real God who, as soon as he appears, compels us to adore, to thank and to surrender ourselves to him. And it is the Son's love—for the Father and for us—which puts him (and us through him) in the immediate presence of God. His love for us is the reflection of his love for the Father. Even before we hear his express words of love, it is his very nature and conduct which awaken in us this movement toward God. The Word of the Father, prayer in the Father—this is his nature, and it leads us irresistibly into the world of prayer. His nature as Word and prayer is contagious: One cannot watch him at prayer to the Father without being drawn into the same prayer.

What is true of God in the highest degree is true of all who live in his grace and participate in his love. Human love, when it is genuine and selfless, enables one to come nearer the love of God. This is true not only intellectually, as when a person comes to understand, through the love of another, something of the way God loves him, nor only emotionally, as when a person begins to catch a sense of wonder from someone who marvels at divine things and points them out: Human love leads to God in an even more radical sense. Suddenly, repeatedly, here and there, a beloved person may become quite obviously transparent, opening up a path to God without being aware of it. Perhaps by his manner of self-giving he unwittingly reveals in a flash something of his relationship to God, or perhaps simply through his nature he compels one to pray, without one's knowing why. One can express in words the love one feels. One can also live in love wordlessly because everything that there was to say has already been said, or because it is so simple that nothing more needs to be said and being together itself becomes prayer. Living with the beloved becomes a way of living with God, of speaking with him as with the loved one, with or without words, in a prayer of being. But in this speechless communion it is the beloved who creates the atmosphere of transparency and access to God, and the response is joy and silence. Involuntarily and without being aware of it, the person who loves God is continually opening doors of prayer for everyone who loves him and shares his life; just as a good musician opens the whole realm of music with the very first note, so the person who loves God opens heaven. A musical person may be not very accomplished technically, yet his playing will lead one most directly into music, much further than the soulless playing of a virtuoso. Thus love spurs one on to prayer, whereas mere virtue without love leaves one cold. The genuine musician simply plunges into the music like a swimmer into water; he does not put on airs or make apologies but simply serves his music without reflecting on his ability or lack of it. He does not live in himself, he lives in the notes; he is concerned, not with the effect that *he* will produce, but with that of the music. And the listener is captivated, not by his playing, but by the greatness of the music. In the same way, the one who loves lives in God; he reveals God and brings those who know him into a living fellowship with God.

In the love between man and woman, God has given human nature a rich analogy of heavenly love. Where this love is cultivated according to God's will, in purity and in the self-lessness of faith, it becomes an introduction to prayer. The woman is the surrendered one; if she really loves, she is always ready to respond to the man, always reaching beyond herself as she listens to discover whether the man will reply to her readiness or not. She embodies the love which is receptive.

The man is the love which does not calculate, which stoops, lets itself be used, gives itself more and more and in its prodigality makes something comprehensible of the Lord's Body in the Eucharist. And as the bodily act of love immediately opens into an overwhelming state of love, so each individual prayer bursts into a wealth of contemplation. And just as the lovers' constant readiness for the act of love may be fulfilled now or at some other time or much later, without their love being diminished, so in prayer our availability for God is fulfilled by the approaches which God makes in his own time and which cannot be brought about or hastened by any means. But between physical love and prayer there is not only a comparison but a connection: The woman is brought to God by the man and the man by the woman, and each sees in the other a parable and a representation of God's incarnate love. If their love is pure, they glimpse beyond and within this physical form a fuller embodiment of God's love, and they are led to adoration, thanksgiving, surrender and submission.

***

Between the individual and God there is the personal relationship established by prayer. But notwithstanding this direct relationship there is, in and through prayer, a kind of intermediate level between man and God, the locus for what God makes out of the prayer. God may answer a personal prayer, a petition for instance, in a thoroughly creative, transforming way. This transformation will be partly dependent on the community of all praying people and particularly on the Church's treasury of prayer. God's answer is not only his direct, private action in reply to an isolated request; it is drawn from and inspired by the concern of all those who pray, especially the saints. This level is actually the place where the saints exercise their influence, particularly those saints whose office is to pray; indeed, it is largely the fruit of their prayer. It is like the dwelling place which every person has in God, the security which is part of his mission. It is the place where the believer is together with God, where perhaps he can ponder with his Lord some difficult case which he cannot solve on his own. It is where, in the weariness that makes thought or prayer about some question impossible, one can hand it over to God, relying not only on his grace but also on the support that can be expected from every prayer. Here it is almost immaterial whether the issue is commended to God himself or confided to one of his saints so that he or she may bring it before God and set it aright, so long as everything takes place within the connection with God, the Christian vocation. Having glimpsed the intermediate realm, man loses his perspective on the power and effect of his own praying; but at the same time he understands that, because of this realm, he and all his concerns are much safer than if he were dependent on purely personal effort.

When the Son of God on earth does some particular work, like a miracle, it does not interrupt his constant contact with the Father. His works are not only fruits of his prayer; they are a direct expression of his union with God. They arise from the Son's world of prayer. At any moment the Son can ask the Father for the power to perform such a work. This illuminates something of the Christian treasury of prayer. It is the entire Church's uninterrupted conversation with God. It makes no difference whether at any particular moment hundreds of thousands are praying, or a few, or perhaps no one: The dialogue is never broken off, and the relation of love between the Bride and the heavenly Bridegroom is always fresh and flowing. What the Church receives as grace, as prayer, as dialogue, is put at the disposal of all who pray as a support to their prayer; it is also laid up in God and is thus open in both directions, never subject to growing cold, never threadbare, worn out or dead, but always full of life and ready for use. This is equally true for the individual and the community, since it originates in the same source as both of these. Everyone has a claim to it, not only to the fruit of his own prayers, but also because of the catholicity of all praying, to a share in the fruit of all prayer. The individual who prays knows that the effect of his prayer always contributes to the effect of the universal prayer. The limits of his achievement in prayer, be it weak or strong, cannot be determined: In genuine prayer and surrender to God and in sacrifice together with the Son, he is certain of participating in something greater than himself. Indeed, it is greater than the voices of all the individual prayers of men because it is joined to the practice and the fruit of the Church's prayer in her unity with the Son's prayer before God. Since this prayer taps a divine (and hence infinite) fountain, all finite relations between achievement and fruit, between what is deposited in the treasury with what is taken out, are abolished. Everything is founded upon the accomplishment of the Son, and this in turn streams from his infinite vision of the Father.

In its availability for all men, the Church's treasury of prayer is by no means made any less available to God. The ultimate reason for this lies in the Son's generation by the Father: The Son knows that he is eternally begotten, but he does not arrogate to himself the power of knowing how. Similarly in the procession of the Spirit: The Spirit knows that he is the fruit of the spiration of Father and Son, yet he does not seek to control his own source, precisely because it is his source, and he is passively brought forth, not actively bringing forth. In virtue of his eternal generation, the Son has a kind of right to ask for the fulfillment of his wishes through the Father's generative power. Yet this power is also the will of the Father, and as such the Son will not infringe upon it. Similarly, God has his will for each person, which must be accepted by the person and cannot be altered at its source. Within this plan man's relationship with God unfolds; he commends his praying and entrusts his creative endeavors to the divine will, so that they can be shaped by God's abundant creativity. Man's activity is so hidden within this all-embracing majesty that it achieves infinitely more than it could ever have done by itself.

In the treasury of prayer there is a going forth that corresponds to the Son's going forth from the Father, an exchange that corresponds to the exchange of the Spirit between Father and Son, and a source, an origin, that corresponds to the Father. The treasury exists as the Father exists; it is made manifest as the Son is made manifest; and it is nourished and exchanged in the same way that the Spirit is eternal life, which nourishes, changes and transforms.

II

SOURCES OF PRAYER

1. PRAYER IN THE TRINITY

Expectation and Fulfillment

Prayer has no beginning because Father, Son and Spirit have been in conversation from all eternity, united in an eternal expectation and an eternal decision. The Father possesses one Word—the Son. The Son is his Word, and the Father is continually bringing forth this one Word, who is always being fulfilled in him and in the Spirit. All that the Father intends, thinks and utters is always expressed in the Son as Word, intelligible and understood. And the Word of the Father is prayer, since he is simultaneously a conversation with the Father and the Spirit. The uttered, emitted Word of the Father replies in his own words, his own speech, always in accord with the expectation that lies in the Father's will. It is no meaningless conversation, no superfluous disclosure of what is already fixed and settled. In this dialogue, plans are continually being proposed and carried out. Every word spoken is both adoration and commitment: It is adoration of the God who is addressed, but it is a fulfilled adoration, for the word lays a divine commitment on the speaker. A commitment of this kind can be seen in the decision to proceed with the Incarnation, for the Son is committed to the Father's will, the Father to the path the Son has set before him, and the Spirit to both. What has been promised will be performed: Every guarantee has been furnished.

From all eternity the Father has needed to love perfectly.

And since, in God, need and fulfillment are one, this need caused him from all eternity to beget the Son. The first thing they do together is to send forth the Spirit from them both, thus extending this love of theirs which has achieved a divine objectivity. And as it was the Father's nature so to love that he must beget the Son, so too this extension is so much part of the Father's nature that both Spirit and Son possess that nature. They are not afterthoughts or adopted strangers: Their origin is directly from the Father, and they share his nature. And the first thing the Son and Spirit do is to thank the Father. They thank him for having begotten them and breathed them forth, for having allowed them to be of the same nature as himself and for endowing them, in the act of bringing them forth, with a divinity that develops freely in his love. They thank him that they are eternally bound to him through sharing the one nature but also that they may eternally meet him in contrast and confrontation, so that reciprocal exchange is possible. And the Father accepts these thanks because he is perfect love, of his nature bestowing love, and thus cannot seek to avoid their thanks. But he does not accept their gratitude in order to hide it within himself; instead, he passes it on to them again, grateful that they have undertaken to share his nature with him. Eternally brought forth, eternally becoming, they correspond to his will, expectation and love.

Thanks is the first declaration of this love which has come to be. The Father wishes to beget the Son and expects him to be as he wants him to be. And in coming forth, the Son perfectly fulfills the Father's expectation from the outset, so that the Father feels bound to him in gratitude from that first moment. The Father's perfection begets the Son's perfection, and yet at that moment when he is before the Father it is as though the Son has exceeded the Father's boldest expectations. For he is not a lifeless replica but a living Thou with the infinite fullness of divinity. In the result of the begetting of the Son we see for the first time the excess, the "greater-than", of the divine being. The Son is the overfulfillment of the Father's expectation. But there is no time when the Father is alone in God, still planning the Son—no time prior to the begetting. So the expectation does not precede the overfulfillment but is one with it. Similarly, there is no time in God when the Son was still becoming and not yet really fully in being (as a human child develops after conception and only later wakens into consciousness): Rather, right at his origin in the Father's begetting of him, the Son participates in his own begetting. Thus fulfillment is never separated from expectation but rather is one with it; and at the same time there is room within this unity for the infinite "greater-than" of the fulfillment. A person in love who is waiting for the beloved knows who is coming, and yet the actual arrival of the beloved brings a fulfillment greater than the expectation. Instead of a correspondence between them, there is a relation of superabundance. Even when love knows what it may expect, namely, "more", the "more" of fulfillment is not simply a replica of the expected "more". The Son is the Father's first expectation and his first fulfillment, and for eternity he remains what he was and is: expectation and fulfillment, expectation which, though unsurpassable, is surpassed by the fulfillment. The Son is for the Father the perpetual proof that in God there are no limits, no disappointments. Far from a minimal fulfillment that is just enough to vindicate the expectation, here we have a prodigality outstripping the most daring hopes. This superabundance occurs again in the procession of the Holy Spirit, when Father and Son see their mutual love surpassed as it issues forth from them as a third Person, standing bodily before them and expressing their innermost being.

In this "more" of God's nature lies prayer's ultimate root: in the fruitfulness of the divine nature, containing the threeness of Persons in the oneness of nature. In the divine love which unites them they adore each other with the entire spirit of God. God stands in the presence of God. God the Father stands before God the Son and God the Spirit, perceiving God in each of them. But what the Father adores in them is not the nature which is his but that which is distinctively theirs. And the Son and Spirit adore the Father in the same way. Though they share in a divine nature, they are distinct; each sees in the other what is uniquely his. All three are one in their origin from the Father but distinct through their different relation to the origin. They are related as Persons fundamentally united by the divine love, yet who carry on a conversation among themselves from the primal beginning and for all ages, a conversation whose nature is prayer. Nothing they expect of, perform for or communicate to one another is outside of divine love and thus outside of prayer.

The Father's expectation lay in his infinite intention to create an object for his perfect, divine love. Since he was Almighty God, divinely perfect in himself, his will knew no greater yearning than to give his love an object like himself. And since the Father knows and sees everything from eternity, he knows eternally that, beside the Son, he will create creatures who are to love him but who, because they are creatures and not of one nature with God but different from him, will disappoint him. But since he begets the eternal Son prior to all creation, he sees that he will never be disappointed by his love and that neither of them will be so disappointed in the creation that their love will grow cold, for this love has been cultivated from all eternity. From the Son, who never disappoints, the Father draws strength, as it were, to bear all the coming disappointments from creatures. And in the conversation which they carry on from eternity, which is prayer, they lay the foundation for all coming conversations between God and creatures and for all the prayers which are to arise from the world to God.

The eternal dialogue is prayer first and foremost because it is divine vision: vision as the core of contemplation, as a silent listening, a reciprocal beholding, being led, adjusting to the other and getting to know him more, a reciprocal expectation and response. This abundant life streams from one Person to another, since each one always stands in view of the others. There is no self-concealment or reserve between them, only a constant acceptance and surrender, self-opening and self-disclosure, showing and loving.

As soon as Father and Son are together, they cause the Spirit to proceed as the witness to their living bond, to the life which consists of their being in unity. And at once, at the very origin of his procession, the Spirit takes on this role of witness to their life. From the very beginning the dialogue between Father and Son sees the signs of fruitfulness in the Spirit, and from the beginning the Spirit, bearing witness, receives a share in their fruitfulness. To the Father he bears witness to the Son's equality of nature; to the Son he testifies to the Father's equality. And the Spirit so fulfills and overfills the expectations of Father and Son that they see more in him than they looked for: In him they experience a totally unsuspected proof of their love. So they are bound to him in gratitude, just as he to them. Immediately and without any rehearsal he is in the midst of their prayer and dialogue, sharing in their knowledge, discernment, speech, obedience and silence, ensuring that this prayer is a constant adoration and fulfillment. It is adoration because God is in the presence of God; it is fulfillment because God may expect everything from God.

So great is their joy in the reciprocity of their going forth and being that, in a certain respect, the Father cannot cease begetting the Son, and Father and Son cannot cease from causing the Spirit to proceed; and in a more passive manner the Son and Spirit cannot but place themselves at the disposal of their generation in a process of becoming which always exhibits all the qualities of being. And this eternal, amazing relationship of joy lays the foundation for the world and mankind to be taken up one day into the divine joy, just as the communion of true lovers is always a preparation for the adoption into the relationship of others who do not yet love.

Believing, Beholding, Loving

God the Father stands eternally vis-à-vis the Son and the Spirit. Their features have always been known to him. Yet in his fellowship with them it is as though he is always positing a new beginning, a beginning rooted in himself and partaking of that primal foundation in him which, beyond time, gives rise to faith, hope and love. Faith, because God the Father knows and expects himself and in this knowledge and expectation continually discovers afresh God the Son and God the Spirit; faith, since he continually finds his expectation fulfilled in the others; faith which is never disappointed in God the Son and God the Spirit because his expectation corresponds exactly with the result, since their superabundant response is perfect. This fulfilled knowledge and expectation contain in themselves the origin of faith, for the relationship of trust is always totally new, and the response to it comes fresh each time. The Father's prior knowledge is never an obstacle to his love relationship with the Son and Spirit, causing the Father to find in himself the fulfillment which the Son and Spirit offer him. Rather, he finds this fulfillment in them as their continual gift to him. His infinite knowledge does not impede him if he wishes to be in a state of perpetual expectation. The moment he wishes to put his knowledge at love's service—and he does this from eternity, since he eternally begets the Son and sends forth the Spirit—knowledge, faith and trust become one in him. This faith is anchored in divine love, which guarantees that there can be no disappointment because divine love is always perfect and, in its perfection, participates in God's perfect nature. What in God and in the Father can be called faith and trust is there only to provide love with every opportunity for development, to give it the room which it would lack if everything were stale foreknowledge—room which it needs, for it cannot exist without self-surrender, movement and flight. Love always has this element of trust, this kind of yearning, this reverent waiting upon the other's freedom, waiting for his spontaneous disclosure, his incalculable gift. To try to remove this element is to kill love. This reverent, divine waiting contains the source, the first cell of hope, that hope which the Father puts in the Son and the Spirit. He gives them such a full participation in his nature that they are equal in nature to him. Thus the Father's hope, love and faith are found the same and undiminished in the Son and Spirit, so that even though the Father remains Father eternally, just as the Son and Spirit remain themselves forever, they encounter each other in an equal power and intensity of divine experience, expectation and fulfillment. The participation of each in what the other has is undiminished; in every relationship and surpassing response there is an equal strength, equally transmitted.

Among men, where two equally gifted people love each other, one partner will still be stronger and one weaker at different times in the exchange of love; a negative element will meet a positive one. And the exchange of love will grow and improve to the extent that these supportive movements occur. Not so in God: In God the tension arises not only through the heterogeny but also through the homogeny, where the one discovers and fulfills himself in his equal. No tedium arises because the tension does not slacken; it always springs fresh from its source bearing all the characteristics of the divine: perfect, self-surpassing correspondence. In God, therefore, one can no more speak of a faith prior to sight than of an expectation prior to fulfillment. In God, faith is always fulfilled in sight; yet, since it is based on love, it continually renews itself from contemplation.

Certainly there is something unsatisfactory and misleading in speaking of an element, in God, of faith. And yet the concept is indispensable, particularly when we speak of prayer in God. If we were to give up the concept of faith in order to clarify our idea of the divine life, then that life would no longer be at all accessible to us. In initiating us into his inner-divine world of love, showing us ways to his trinitarian nature and guiding us into the "greater-than" of his being, God lets us keep our human concept with all its inadequacy because it can be transformed through grace. And precisely those highest gifts of God which come directly from his inner-divine life, faith, love and hope, are far better adapted to reveal his nature than any powers of our creaturely nature as such. We must use what experience we as Christians have of God as access to his nature, as a means of interpreting his being. To renounce this would be to shut ourselves in our earthly world and reject the most precious gifts which give access to God. It would be to hold the strange opinion that God had given us something perfectly good which, on entering heaven, we found to be earthly, temporal, ephemeral and useless. Of course our faith will be transformed when we enter heaven. God will fulfill it beyond our boldest expectations, for God, when he reveals himself, will be the One who is always greater. And the direct vision he then will give us will be a much more concrete, proven and evident form of faith. But far from destroying faith, this vision will fulfill it. Faith will be the root from which vision arises. Now faith is revealed and sight is concealed; then sight will be revealed and faith will be its hidden precondition.

A kind of transitional state, connecting on earth both links of the chain, is mystical contemplation.[1] Mysticism is always an expression of faith; it can only take place within faith. Faith loses its abstract, speculative character in order to take into itself an element of experience of divine reality. But one cannot use vision in order to take a rest from faith. Moreover, the faith which does not see cannot be defined as a state of loss of vision. Faith after a vision is not very different from faith before it; perhaps it is not even different from faith during the vision. And it is certainly not the case that the more a mystic sees, the less he has to believe. The truth is that in mysticism faith and sight form a unity in tension which is emphasized in the one or other direction at different times, according to how God fashions the given situation.

Something of the simultaneity of faith and sight in earthly mysticism is taken up into the beatific vision in heaven, just as something of our earthly life of faith, of the most personal aspect of our Christian existence—this absolutely special gift of God's grace—will enter into our eternal vision. The little child wants to delight his father by bringing him the little things he finds; his love means it very seriously. Later, when the child is grown up, he can give "valuable" gifts; but this does not mean that the love and devotion have also grown.

---

[1] To be joined in this way, the links must first be open. Thus even in God there is an opening which is the precondition for the eternal closing. Father and Son are not parallel, and they do not merely touch like two rings; they are in one another, penetrating and encompassing one another. To do this, however, they must have an open place. The Father's opening is in begetting and conceiving the Son, and the Son's opening is in his cooperation in being begotten and in his return to the Father. Something analogous can be said of faith and vision.

The father accepts both with equal love. Thus God will not despise the fruits of our faith and accept only the fruits of our vision. And the fruits are not separable from the act. When the Lord was a child on earth he possessed vision (as *comprehensor*) and faith (as *viator*). If he had only seen and known and not *also* believed, he would not have been the first Christian and everything would have gone much too easily. He possessed a boundless, childlike trust in the Father's guidance. He had the will to accept everything the Father offered him without examining whether it was hard or easy, intelligible or unintelligible. He did not want to play the grown-up, judging everything himself, but to accept everything from the Father, sight unseen. And he kept this attitude all his life. So too for the mystic, much more perfectly for the Son on earth, and ultimately for the blessed in heaven, there can be a simultaneity of seeing and believing. (Just as on earth true love knows a simultaneity of penitence and joy, of being caressed and being humbled. We human beings are accustomed to experience in succession things which in reality can exist entwined in a unity, in love, in the Christian life, in mysticism, in Christ, in heaven.) This simultaneity proves that there is something eternal in faith and that, by analogy, one can speak of a faith in the midst of the vision of the trinitarian God.

* * *

There is in God the point at which his vision begins. The Father begets the Son as the expression of his love, and he wishes him to share in all he possesses from the very first. The moment the Father sees the Son, the Son also sees the Father. And the Father's love for the Son that he sees is perfectly simultaneous with the Son's love on seeing the Father. Divine love is so strong that it cannot bear to deprive the beloved of

37

what belongs to love, even for an instant. Where a human being loves another and yet lets him remain in uncertainty about it, he shows that his love is not perfect. Love has an impatience which will not tolerate any postponement. The one who loves never has enough of his love, can never have enough of the joy it brings him; he must straightway act as one who is loved and communicate himself and his love to the other. This communication succeeds where he awakes the lover in his beloved. Thus, at the outset vision is so connected with love that one cannot say whether vision is an expression of love or love an expression of vision. It is like a sudden revelation, an unexpected encounter fulfilling all hopes, as if two things were suddenly to coincide simultaneously at the deepest level: that the Father expected the Son in the very way he now sees him, and yet that he would never have dared to hope for his love to be so confirmed, to have such a Son who is God as perfectly as he is himself. And while everything takes place in such detailed correspondence and the highest fulfillment, the eternal moment is effective retrospectively and prospectively, including everything from all eternity and for all eternity. What is "now" always was, and it is so full that it is unsurpassable: not in such a way that the present moment stifles freedom of action, but in such a way that expectation and fulfillment exactly coincide. And at the same moment that the impression the Son makes on the Father is shown to be perfect truth, the Son too finds in the Father the confirmation of his eternal expectation. It is as if, from his prototypical existence, he had always lived in his Father's eternal expectation and has now, at the end of this eternal waiting, *at last* appeared: as if he too, now that *at last* he sees the Father, finds his expectation satisfied. Though he, the Eternal One, has had no time in which to wait, he still experiences this fulfillment as the result of an eternal expectation. Indeed, through this

38

fulfillment, both become aware of the presence of an eternal expectation and, through it, of the presence of the fulfillment. And in the perpetual immediacy of this sudden moment, without limits of time, without sequence in their reciprocal vision, both of them know in perfect simultaneity of their reciprocal love. In their communion, which was from eternity and yet is created afresh at every instant, they know of their ineffable, expectant love for the Spirit, who at this precise moment is proceeding from them both as the expression of their common purpose and expectation. So now the Father sees the Son he has always loved and expected, and he and the Son see the Spirit, loved and expected from eternity; and the Spirit knows that he is eternally expected by Father and Son, and in his own being he sees them both as the perfect fulfillment of what he had eternally expected. It is as if from eternity he had felt the need to bear witness to their love, as if he had always been looking for such a Father and Son so that he can be what he is: the Spirit, possessing a divine, connatural relationship with both of them. And it is as if he also knows how welcome his procession is, causing the intimacy of his breathing to pass between Father and Son. He is desired no less than the Son was desired by the Father; thus he can bring them the complete fulfillment they were expecting, just as they give him the fulfillment he needed in order to be Spirit.

In this origin of their reciprocal vision are determined the relations between them, distinguishing and uniting them, causing fulfillment and yet again expectation, as if in some everlasting game. Here they experience a perfect, divine love; and yet within this fulfilled love there is room for what we can only call faith and hope, something that stimulates and reveals the freedom of each to do as seems best to him, a freedom that is nowhere better expressed than in the words, "The Spirit blows where he will", and that has its correlative in the being of the Father and the being of the Son. In fact, this "blowing" provides something like a substance for the reciprocal divine faith and hope, which are both eternally surpassed, veiled and fulfilled by reciprocal love, and yet can be traced wherever God is and into all eternity.

In eternal vision and love, consequently, two things are united which in the earthly vision and love are separate, namely, *act and state*. In sexual love, for instance, the encounter of man and woman is a process in which elements of state and act alternate; state is emphasized more in the case of the woman, act more in the man's case. In God both are present in principle: The Father begets and loves the Son without interruption, and yet this love and begetting is event at every point; at every point he brings forth the Spirit together with the Son. One can say that God's state is that of an eternal, personal love which acquires a certain actuality in the acts of begetting, breathing and beholding; or, equally, that his state is his eternal begetting and beholding, and within this state the reciprocal love of the Persons is what has the character of act.

Love between man and woman can be inspired and shaped from two sides: by prior experiences that brought fulfillment and by present needs and expectations, not by each partner making his or her own plans, but in mutual accommodation. In this way a rich texture arises through the interplay of fulfillment and expectation, what is present and what is yet to be discovered, state and act—an interplay that creates love's vitality and inexhaustibility. True love can never be boring; it is self-renewing. But this continual motion of human love is only a reflection of the infinite movement of divine love. For instance, a man may plan for himself, but in the center of his planning his expectation of the woman's response plays a role. The Father also plans, as it were, with regard to what he expects from his Son, but he leaves room for the Son's response. And the Son's response will always be totally divine and therefore totally personal. In the scope between the divine and the personal, divine love shows itself in its fruitfulness and wealth of creativity. The woman responds both as a lover and as a woman to the man's expectation, which is both loving and masculine. Again, if he is not only a man but also a lover, the man's masculine expectation is quite different from the same expectation in the absence of love. In one way it is more sensitive, nuanced, discerning and appropriate, and in another way more differentiated and more characteristically masculine: as if only love's unity could bring out the true differences of sexes and persons.

Finally, sexual love provides us with another analogy in the fact that the lovers know exactly what they are doing and at the same time do not know at all. The man already knows the nature of their union, but he does not know how the woman will receive him on this occasion; he can only hope that it will happen in love, awakening in her an even greater love for him. The point of departure is a solitary planning; the fulfillment of these plans becomes more and more a mutual affair and at the same time robs the two individuals of absolute power and control. The man does retain a certain primacy, yet in such a way that he only takes the lead by surrendering and losing himself. In an analogous way, all processes in God are based on an initial vision: the Father's plan, ordering all things. The act of begetting the Son is as if included in this primal vision, as is the Son's act of cooperation in his begetting and the Spirit's procession, like an action within an all-embracing contemplation. In the same way, Mary's assent to the angel is an act within an all-embracing assent of contemplation. The difference is that in God there can be no moment which is only planning and vision, without action and begetting: The Father's vision is the begetting of the Son, and the vision of

Father and Son is the spiration of the Spirit. It is as if this vision is so overpowering that it constitutes, in itself, the bringing forth of what it envisages, and thus the overwhelming and inundation of the observer by the reality of the beloved and the mutuality of love.

Action springs from vision, but vision immediately acquires new substance through action and its result. Thus God is infinite to himself: Every infinity of his being opens new doors to the infinity of his understanding, which in turn is the creative source of new infinity of his being. It is one of the laws of love that the lover cannot completely fathom the essence of the beloved. No human being can calculate or possess another's reactions in advance, or count on them as if they were not the expression of a free personal nature. If anyone could do this, the other person would instantly cease to be a spiritual being. Love is built up essentially on the incalculability of the beloved. He must always disclose and surrender himself afresh, continually surprising and overwhelming the lover. If ever this movement were to stop, to be replaced by a conclusive knowledge of each other, love would come to an end. What seemed to be complete knowledge would be the sign of a real finitude. But in God nothing is finite.

Action and Contemplation

Since in God everything takes place in a perfect unity, the Son's being begotten is already present in the Father's begetting as the answer to the Father's act, an answer which resides from all eternity in the divine will of both Son and Father. The Son's divinity is already perfect and finished in the very act of begetting. In being begotten, the Son comprehends the Father's perfect generative intention and puts himself at its disposal in a passivity which is itself action. Action and passivity are one in the Trinity because the one acted upon so comprehends the one acting that the former—the one begotten, breathed forth—cooperates with him who begets and breathes forth, since he shares his nature and hence his understanding and will. Apprehending the Father's will, the Son immediately understands what it is and what its purpose is, and adopts it from eternity as his own. Thus, in the single act of begetting and being begotten, we see a perfect unity of active deed and passive agreement which admits no separation. In this unity everything is completely compact: Activity and passivity embrace, comprehend and cooperate with each other entirely.

That is the original unity of action and contemplation, their unity of birth, of origin, of being. It is a unity that is a core, a primal cell. If things had stayed like that, we should scarcely have come up with these two concepts to characterize the divine process. But then there are acts of beholding—in God himself and, communicated by him, in creatures—which can only be shown to be contemplative on the basis of this origin. In themselves they would seem isolated and hard to understand, but related to this origin they show the unity which resides in the Father's will. Similarly, there are divine contemplations which can only be shown to be active—and not the mere content of a vision with no results—in virtue of this core in which the two are one. So God's act of creation introduces no surprises or changes into his vision. Even before the world was created, chaos was ordered and divided in the Father's will and intention because his will to create was at the service of his almighty power. No unforeseen obstacle ever intrudes between his will and his action, his intention and realization, to bring about a change or a disruption. Contemplating the work he had planned, he already saw it as he would bring it about. His act of creation was already complete in the eternal contemplation of his will. In no point is the created world different from the world envisaged. For the world itself, its realization is something entirely new, unexpected, undeducible; but for God its actual existence is only the perfectly natural, tangible answer to what sprang to life in his eternal contemplation. It is as though all the effort of doing and creating had already been accomplished in contemplation. If action is the consequence of contemplation, contemplation already perfectly contains the expected action.

God rests on the seventh day as a sign that the action of creating meant a certain amount of work. But this was not something extraneous to the effortlessness of contemplation. It was always contained in it, just as God's contemplation was always contained in his act of creation but appeared visibly to us on the seventh day. The active element is not visible in God's eternal contemplation, since no world had yet been created and hence there was no time; in the eternity of heaven with its total simultaneity, there was no possibility of a rhythmical alternation of work and rest. It was purely for the needs of creatures that the unity of action and contemplation, work and rest, which exists in God, was translated from eternity into time and separated out. This separation occurs so that we may understand something of God and his eternal life, and of the unity of intention and realization which exists there. It is like a slow-motion camera analyzing some movement so that one can see how it is made, or like a person teaching someone a new skill, performing each action very slowly and deliberately.

Like creation, the Incarnation is also an act of God, an action on the part of the Father which is completely rooted in contemplation. From eternity he sees the Son before him with all the qualities of divinity and omnipotence. And in his omniscience he knows from eternity and not only at the moment of the Fall, when mankind is irretrievably lost, that it can only be saved and brought back by a God. Contemplating the divinity of the Son, he sees from eternity that it fulfills all the requirements for performing the task of redemption. So that from the moment when the Son, begotten, stands before him (that is, from eternity), he appears as the bearer of redemption. From eternity the Son shares the Father's knowledge: He knows that he can do it; he knows this in gratitude to the Father and in intimacy with him, and for him this knowledge is a gift given by the Father which he can return to the Father as thanks for his divinity. Thus the Father knows from eternity that the Son will carry out the Incarnation out of love for him and that in being man he will not lose his divinity, for both human nature and divine nature come from the Father, and all that the Father gives the Son is final and is adopted totally by the Son. He will not throw away his divinity in becoming man, nor his humanity when he returns to heaven (and so he will take with him that most precious gift given to man by God—namely, faith—when he reenters heaven and the heavenly vision). The Father's eternal vision and redemption and the Son's eternal offer are wholly contemplative; but the Father will give the seed and the Son will permit himself to be borne by the Holy Spirit into the womb of the Virgin, and this will be their divine, unified action, which is already a living reality within their contemplation. Once again, no obstacle can intrude between the intention in contemplation and its realization in action. Father, Son and Spirit, as God, are omnipotent, and nothing they intend and do can be subject to vicissitude. Omnipotent, they are also immutable. "No sooner said than done"—here we have the perfect case.

What is true of the Son is also true of the Spirit. Father and Son, seeing the Spirit before them as they breathe him forth, know how equipped he is to represent their reciprocal love, how in this capacity he puts himself completely at the disposal of their plans for creation, because as God and Spirit he has the power and characteristic of carrying God's seed into the world, or even earlier, at creation, of communicating fresh revelations of God's spirit to the world. Right from the beginning, from eternity, he has given evidence of possessing everything that Father and Son can, may and must expect of a God who is Holy Spirit. And simply by his very being he has already fulfilled and overfulfilled every requirement made of him by Father and Son—and by himself too, for each not only knows of the other's divinity; he lives equally in his own divinity which he sees and knows, so that he does not need to separate the requests made to and by the others from the demands on himself. There is a unity of requirements, just as there is a unity of reciprocal availability.

The actions which proceed from divine contemplation give it certain contours which are intelligible to us. There are features of this eternal interplay which God in his grace shows us and even imparts to us, giving us a sense of what is going on in the Trinity and an understanding of the nature of every contemplation or action which takes place in the world; ultimately they give us a fundamental understanding of our fellowmen. Starting from the relationship of God with God, from one divine Person's understanding of the others, God opens our understanding of our fellows. No mystery of the Trinity is so hidden in God that it is unnecessary to the Christian, so that he is absolved from trying to understand it: He is involved in it and must relate it to his life. Contemplating as God does, the Christian learns to contemplate. Observing how God lives with God, the Christian learns how to live with his fellowman. It is not enough for every action and every contemplation on earth to aspire to heaven in the vague hope of arriving somewhere and being accepted. Action and contemplation must also participate spiritually and cognitively in God's way, using it as a guide and a plumbline for earthly life in God. The human being is not only the observer of God: He contemplates God's contemplation, and he sees God's vision, a vision that embraces contemplation and action in a unity.

If two people who love each other were compelled un-interruptedly to share the same room night and day, alone and with no other occupation, the time would come when their love could no longer stand this togetherness. It would decline and die. If their love is to remain alive, each person must have his sphere of freedom and be able to pursue his interests, in order to return to the beloved with new discoveries, results and achievements. To remain fulfillment, love must be freighted with new expectancy. That is why purely human love can scarcely imagine the eternal communion of the divine Persons. In human love's view, there must be times of distance and separation in God too, so that his love remains alert. To help men and women avoid tedium in love, God has given them two things. First he offers them the gift of sex with its possibility of bodily fruitfulness, of having children who, by their growth and development and by their own life, enrich the life of their parents, so that the latter acquire a renewed vigor as the years progress and child succeeds child. But beyond this, God has given a far greater gift: He has granted human love a share in his own divine love. He offers himself in his inexhaustible wealth, so that human life and love too receive a new, deeper and inexhaustible meaning. Now there is a new seeking and finding, both supported by God's nearness and by participation in him. There is a fresh and unsuspected richness, with all possible transformations and ways of complementing and corresponding to one another, which are an expression of the "greater-than" of supernatural

47

love. For the Christian who lives out of this wealth, human distances and absences become largely superfluous; he lives more in God than in nature, and the way love now conceals and reveals, the way it surprises and overwhelms, renewing and refreshing his life in God, relieves him of the anxiety of having to revivify his love by artificial distance. In this way, from his own experience, he suddenly realizes that, in God, love is the opposite of tedium, that everything that moves us away from tedium is divine, and that in God unity and distance are not opposites but full and eternally fruitful unity. Thus God does not need to engage in action in order to renew his contemplation. Because his love bridges unity and distance, it likewise joins action and contemplation.

In the Father, the Son always beholds the One who is able to beget God. And the almighty and all-knowing Son knows that the Father brings forth this omnipotent and omniscient being in begetting him, and that the Father attains the fullness of his greatness and fatherhood through the Son's begetting. As begetter the Father shows the Son the distance which separates the begetter from the begotten. But this distance is not one-sided; it determines not only the Son's reverence for the Father but also the Father's reverence for the Son, who, as the One eternally begotten, continually reveals his characteristic of allowing himself to be begotten, and begotten precisely as the omniscient and omnipotent One. And as both of them behold the Spirit, they see in him the One who proceeds from them to reunite them in love across the distance between them. It is as if the Spirit is witness that the distance between them can never be separation because he constantly bridges the permanent, perpetual distance with the love of him who proceeds. Thus in triune being, distance and union are motive forces which can only increase and which are rooted so deeply in the life of God that they keep it forever new and fruitful.

48

One can get some notion of the infinite multiplicity of relations in God by contemplating the world: If the world's variety is so colorful, fascinating, exciting and inexhaustible, how rich must the source of this variety be! And if God delights in man whom he has caused to live in his grace, never tiring of taking pleasure in man's joys, man's love, and the millions of possibilities open to him of relationships with God and his fellows, how much greater must be his delight in the infinity of his own omnipotence and the inventive love of his eternal intercourse! The Father sees all that the incarnate Son undertakes together with his brothers; the Son sees the plans the Father has for mankind and how he is carrying them out; and both observe how the Spirit carries out the most surprising initiatives and miracles in the world. It is all such a spectacle that even a God cannot see enough of it. And yet all that God undertakes in the world is a drop in the ocean of the divine tensions, distances and unions within the one divine love.

In this way, eternal presence replaces all absences. Despite his omniscience, God loves in such a way that he always lets himself be surpassed and surprised by the beloved. Children love hiding something in order to have the delight of searching for it. In the fairy story the prince dresses as a peasant in order to win the princess; or else he is a peasant and only at the end, to everyone's surprise including his own, turns out to be a prince. Two friends, experts in different fields, will not try to dominate each other with their expertise; rather, each will initiate the other into his field, thus discovering more and more in common, viewed and understood in different but complementary ways. The child who hides the ball from himself must pretend in order to have the pleasure of looking for it; if two play hide-and-seek, however, there is no pretence. God is not alone but triune. Each Person shows his qualities to the others and lets the others discover them. And the Father shows the Son less his total knowledge than his total love, which conceals something whose concealment lets love radiate even more brightly. He lets love predominate and omniscience retire to the background, since the central thing in eternal fellowship is love, which even knowledge serves. Everything we can describe as "surprise" in God always occurs according to the law of the other: The Father will never seek to change or override the law of the Son's filial stature, but fulfill it. Every gift is such that it can be given again in return, a gift of which the joy of giving is a part, a gift specially devised with a view to the recipient's distinctive otherness. It is never a private gift to a private Person but a gift in the service of inner-divine communion, and thus in the service of the divine triune Personality. Ultimately each of the Father's actions is aimed at revealing him in a new and different light in order to stir up the Son's love afresh, offering it new targets. Each action creates new distances and vistas, in order to give the contemplating Son new delight in the Father. And so it is with the other Persons. It applies to all forms of divine activity, within the divine nature or in creation: Every divine action is always equally rooted in the other Person, and its ultimate purpose is to increase divine love. Thus the Father created the world as a gift for the Son, and the Son replied to this action of creation with his action of Incarnation, in order to demonstrate his love and to delight the Father through redeeming and recovering the world. Of course they do all things together, but this does not preclude each action exhibiting personal features; in performing a particular work, the Person whose work it is grants the others, through love, an equal share in it.

From all this it is again clear how united are action and contemplation in God. The distance between the Persons, a distance that is ever greater but ever bridged, is the foundation of contemplation and is in turn founded upon it. Each determines the other. And yet it is equally true that contemplation acquires its shape through the action which lies within it and through the nature of the Persons contemplating one another. God, who contemplates himself within this eternal contemplation, is both subject and object of contemplation and fashions himself for this purpose in such a way that he continually reveals contrasts to promote the triune love. So too, corresponding to this mode of being and of contemplation, we see that the forms of eternal life are not always the same: They are always fresh in their manifestations.

Worship

God can recognize himself in another. It is as if being God is a matter of indifference to the Father: as if he first sees the stupendous magnitude and sublimity of divinity in the moment when he gives it as a gift to the Son. It is as if the Son through his presence discloses the infinity of the divine being to the Father. This is so because the love which joins Father and Son in the Spirit reveals to the Father the greatness of the Son, to the Son the greatness of the Father, to the Spirit the greatness of both, and to both the greatness of the Spirit. Love is the basis for this discovery, and love unites with each of the divine attributes. So the Father sees that the Son is God; he sees that he is God because he is full of love, that he is true because he is full of love, that he is ready to redeem the world because he is full of love; he sees that the Spirit blows because his blowing is in love, and so on. Love causes each to see the divine primarily in the other. In the love which is God's nature, and which is equally the nature of the God whom he sees before him, God discovers anew, as it were, what God is: He sees God's sublimity, feels God's love, is continually transfixed by God's nature. And since God sees the other's divine nature in truth, worship immediately flows from this recognition. Worship is the expression of God's encounter with God in love. Only in worship can God encounter God, when he confronts himself as Father, Son and Spirit. Consequently worship can only be correct in the context of love, in the imitation of God. Hence, in love, it will always be a worship which experiences and understands. When the incarnate Son manifests his love to the Father in the form of worship, he is doing nothing new. He is doing what he has done from all eternity. His innermost attitude toward God has not changed through the Incarnation: His human nature should express the divine, the heavenly. Praying on earth, the Son experiences the Father as he has known him as God from eternity: as the God whom he worships. He says that he is greater than himself (Jn 14:28); he lifts his eyes to him (Jn 17:1); he calls him his God and our God (Jn 20:17).

Certainly the Father himself also knows that he is God, and how and why he is God. But this knowledge would not interest him if it only stirred within himself. As knowledge it comes to life where there is a Thou, where the exchange of love takes place. Love is always an act of preferring the other. For love, any attempt at a comparison between I and Thou ("Which of us is the greater?") is ridiculous from the start. Even among men, no one would think of building love on the basis of measuring the worthiness or unworthiness, goodness or badness, of the partners. Love begins by preferring the Thou. And within this preference the qualities of the Thou become visible, but they are already colored by love. Between people who love each other there is no possibility of an "objective" evaluation of goods, such as might be valid outside love. And in God love is so absolute that it reveals God's real, objective goodness. His goodness consists in each Person, in love, seeing what is good in the others. It consists in the exchange which is thus brought about.

God recognizes God. All that the Father sees in the Son is

part of the Son's divine nature; it is totally, naturally and harmoniously his own. The Father knows that the Son as God is one in nature with him; but this knowledge, referring back to himself, is not the central issue for him. Rather, because he is God, he perceives, with every mode of knowledge and feeling and of his divine capacity for perception, God everywhere in the Son; the Father "sees, hears, smells, tastes" God in the Son. All his "senses" react to the manifestation of the Son's divinity. And this impression both results from and extends uniformly to all particulars in such a unity that the whole divine perception, in every respect and direction, is absorbed in discovering and worshipping love. The discovery of the full nature of God in the beloved is the highest experience possible; therefore it continually calls forth worship. Worship is the loving recognition of God. Its love and recognition are such that it cannot but lay its whole unique self at the other's feet in endless love. Worship contains much astonishment and gratitude: astonishment that God is so great and gratitude that he allows himself to be contemplated. Then it is as if, in contemplating the Son, the Father always sees more and more what he, the Father, is; yet it is as if the only significance that this sight and experience have for the Father is that he sees thereby how the Son uninterruptedly accepts the gift of divinity, gratefully accepts everything from the Father, and in gratitude has become what the Father expected of him.

This first worship is like a great silence between Father and Son. At first they have no other wish than to contemplate and know each other in worship. But this is no mere intellectual activity: From the first it is the expression of love, given and returned. Hence in worship, prior to its differentiation, action and contemplation consist in nothing other than the love of the Three, actively loving and passively being loved, where the core of every action and every contemplation is always love.

This love is a constantly increasing knowledge, a knowledge that in turn causes an increase of love, so that in God knowledge and love are not side by side but generate one another and are living and active through each other.

If a lover says, "This is my favorite book", and the beloved reads it and also finds it superlative, it is doubtful whether he would have come to this conclusion if the lover had not first announced it. The beloved may have adopted it as his favorite book out of love to the other. Or it may in fact have objectively pleased the beloved—perhaps because, through love, the two possess or have acquired a similar taste. In God all these possibilities coincide. There is nothing objective in him outside love, and love itself is the most objective thing because it is absolute. Certainly, in him love is reciprocally contemplating and influencing, giving and taking, but despite its personal qualities it is a perfectly factual and objective love. Provided that the two people who share a favorite book both have absolutely good taste, they will also agree in their judgment of details of the book, although each observes them with his own eyes and expresses them in words of his own. And since in spite of their agreement there is this personal angle of approach, there can be a fruitful conversation about the thing they both love. But this is only possible in love. If their love were not quite perfect, it would be in great danger of becoming indiscreet. One of them might try to "get inside" the other as deeply as possible, but in reality he would be seeking himself in his partner, scouring the other self, straining to listen to every sound, endeavoring to build the other's uniqueness into his own self, acting as if, through love, he were no longer himself but had actually become the other. And if he were even to try to spy out the prayer of the person he imagined he loved so much, trying to discover the place in the other's soul where he meets God—for instance, kneeling next to him at prayer and thinking, "Now he is experiencing this or that, as I know from its reflection in my own soul"—this would be the very height of indiscretion. In true love there is no substitution. There is no such thing because there is no such thing in God. In God there is no dominance of knowledge over love, no possibility of increasing insight to a point where it no longer corresponds to love, no possibility of the Father seeing no longer the Son but himself when he looks at the Son. To try to substitute persons in this way is an abuse of love. For this is where worship has its place. An essential feature of worship is reverence. In worship love invents and creates distance. Each partner in reverence truly desires the other, and not himself in the other. Love consists, not in comparing Thou and I, but in eternally contemplating the Thou. The I has become instrumental, serving to enable knowledge and love of the Thou. It is almost only the means to an end, an end which resides in the other. The Thou is loved for his own sake, not for the sake of individual attributes; as such these could be possessed by the I as well, but in love they are seen, loved and admired only for the sake of the Thou. If love were to be built only on admiration for the other's individual attributes and advantages, it would be simply the sum of one's own defects. Love would say, "You are greater and cleverer than I", but the point of reference would be the I which lacked these qualities. It would be only a step away from a love which loves the Thou because he has the power or the means which one lacks oneself. Love of this kind would degrade the Thou into an improved, heightened, rounded I. If this were love, a fundamental self-contemplation and self-knowledge would have to precede and accompany love; the more one knew of oneself, the more one could project into the Thou. This spells the end of worship, or rather totally inhibits it. Worship will not let love lean on what is its own: It goes directly to the Thou and wants nothing but the Thou.

As we know it, worship is being seized by the totality of God. It concentrates and unites; it is the opposite of that analysis into details which is demanded by examination of conscience and confession. It is the response to the weight which lies in every revelation, every self-unveiling of God. That is why it does not delay over God's individual attributes but sees the whole in each one. The worshipper is so over-powered by this totality that whether he is active or passive in worship is almost immaterial. Only one thing counts: that God *is*. Consequently, worship requires no preparation, no getting in tune, no development. It is all of a piece. It is the form given to us by God when we are really in his presence. But all this is only because worship as we know it is a grace which comes from the triune worship. Nothing is more rooted in God than worship. It is something so eternal in origin and destination that the way we are seized by God is only a faint echo of the way God is eternally seized by God.

Our worship is not empty; God's fullness is revealed in it, quite differently than in contemplation. Each detail can be contemplated in the spirit of the whole, yet in such a way that one remains with the detail. In worship each part immediately falls back into place in the whole. It is God's fullness, God's divinity, that occupies the foreground and dominates every-thing. At whatever point he begins, the worshipper is flung back to the center. So too it is what is perfect, whole and one in God that is always causing God himself to worship God. In contemplation the person at prayer may occasionally refer to himself and insert himself into the mystery. The worshipper cannot. God too can include himself in his contemplation: the Son, for example, when he attunes himself to the Father's will and thereby compares it, in some measure, to his own will. In worship every glance at the I is subsumed in the pure sight of the Thou.

Petition

Face to face with God, God sees that God has a will, that purposes lie hidden in the repose of God and that God's action becomes visible in and through God's contemplation. The first in God to have carried out a purpose is the Father, and the realization of his purpose is the Son. The begetting of the Son is rooted in a purpose of the Father, who loves the Son. If one looks only at the Father, his purpose resides totally in himself, in a necessity of his knowing and willing which always appears as deed. In the same power of a purpose residing in their nature, Father and Son together cause the Spirit to proceed. The Father's primal, original purpose has been found in the Son as well, so that the Spirit proceeds according to the purpose of both. And now, as the Three face each other, their will seems to have acquired a new color. What up to now was bound in the nature of God is now, through the process of generation and spiration, in a certain sense free: It receives a form which is no longer bound to any necessity of essence. Each one sees this divine will in the other. But whereas, in the context of the necessity of the processions, the will was of necessity bound as it passed from Father to Son and from both to the Spirit, in a sequence determined as of nature, now, in the context of the mutual relations of the Persons, the will demonstrates, in its freedom and unity, a hierarchy established by the processions. Freedom in God knows about the priority of the necessary processions, and they determine a hierarchical priority within freedom.

This is freedom's primal shape. In order for a will to be

free, it must be part of a hierarchy. Even the freest freedom must manifest something of the precedence of the Father over the Son and of Father and Son over the Spirit; man must remember that the preeminent will resides in the Father. Thus Christian obedience is an act of a free will. The Son and Spirit must recognize the Father's precedence, and the Father must be aware of them. Only in this way can he permit the Son to say: "Not my will but thine be done."

The Father's first, primal purpose is not free. Or rather, in its absolute sovereignty it is beyond necessity and freedom. Once the Son is begotten, however, he adopts the Father's will by freely desiring to be what the Father's purpose has determined. And now, from the vantage point of this free will, it is as if even the Father's begetting and the Son's being begotten acquire characteristics of freedom, as if in their freedom Father and Son recapitulate their natural relationship, in order freely to be what they are of necessity. In fact, this is the opposite of what takes place in the human relationship, where the man freely decides on the act of generation which, however, once begun, takes a necessary and natural course. But in God necessity is not a blind necessity of nature, preliminary to his qualities of mind and personhood. It is a divine necessity which expresses his spiritual nature. It has no parallel among us creatures; we can only describe it as lying beyond all creaturely freedom and necessity.

Each of the three divine Persons is free. But the Father's will takes precedence over the Son's, and the Father's and Son's over the Spirit's: The Son can send forth the Spirit. But one cannot say that, because the Spirit is dependent on two Persons, he is more bound than the Son. It is a different mode of subordination. If the Son wishes to move the Spirit's will, he cannot do so without considering the fact that the Spirit is equally subordinate to the Father as he is to the Son.

Thus in order to move the Spirit's will he must be certain that the Spirit apprehends the Son's will as matching that of the Father.

The Father has given the Son everything, and the Son can dispose over all things. In addition, the Father has put his will at the Son's disposal, so that whenever he makes a decision he can be certain of acting according to the Father's will and to his utmost satisfaction. But the Father has not imposed his will on the Son: In a kind of divine discretion he has impressed on his will the stamp of his paternal precedence. The Son remains free to do his own perfect will, but the mark of precedence on the Father's will means that, in spite of the perfection of his filial will, it seems to the Son preferable, a more perfect and a better expression of his filial love, to carry out the will of his Father.

In the act of begetting, the Son is occupied with experiencing the Father who begets him. His contemplation is not directed to the goal of the begetting, i.e., himself. He lives in admiration of the Father's act which expresses his divine omnipotence. On the other hand the Father sees that the Son lets himself be begotten, admitting the fullness of the Father's necessary will and in no way intervening with the free will with which he was begotten, as if to contribute toward his own fashioning. Rather, the Son is totally absorbed in being begotten just as the Father desires; he uses the first act of his freedom to retract his own will in favor of the Father's will which is growing within him, so that he can be more freely in the service of the Father's purposes which lie beyond his begetting. This is not yet the adopting of the Father's will which is expressed in "Not my will but thine be done." It is the original encounter between the Father's necessary will and the Son's free will and thus a kind of rehearsal for the subordination of the Son's will to the Father's. It takes place even before the Son has used his free will, before he has seen that the Father has a free will. It takes place in a pristine state where the Son possesses his will, and yet, unaware that the Father has one too, sees in the Father nothing other than *the* will manifested in the act of begetting. (An earthly analogy would be the religious who initially approaches his superior's request as a free man but suddenly becomes aware of the precedence of rank and observes how his act of free obedience fits into the rule of obedience. Or even clearer: where two friends find themselves suddenly placed in a relationship of superior and subordinate.) And if the Son wields his free will so discreetly that, as it were, he does not draw the Father's attention to it, it means that for the moment he takes no account of it, consults only the Father's intention, the expression of his necessary will, without regard to himself. Genuine free will presupposes a certain knowledge of itself: It is not something instinctual but springs from a spiritual purpose and consideration. But at his origin the Son is so taken up with contemplating the begetting Father that he avoids everything which might divert his attention from this worshipful vision. In beholding the Father's perpetual act of begetting, he discovers that the Father as God is much more, containing all eternity and infinity; that hidden and veiled within the Father's own necessary will there lies a unique, more personal and active free will which he can use as he sees fit. Contemplating the Father, the Son discovers the former's active possibilities and possible intentions, seeing that these intentions also concern him and that he must therefore be at the Father's disposal. In order to do that, he must come to see himself in a new way, be aware of who he is and whom he must commission to carry out the Father's plans which concern him. Consequently his self-knowledge becomes a necessity within his relationship to the Father's will. And now he sees that as he unveils his purposes the Father counts on the

Son's collaboration and on the influence of a third, the Spirit. From this it follows that, in the knowledge that the Father needs him, the Son makes himself available to him for the generation of the Spirit. The Son's making himself available, however, corresponds both to his necessary will and to the free will of which he is aware. It is as if he uses his free will to offer his bound will to the Father for the generation of the Spirit, as if two decisions meet in him: a free decision and one determined by his nature.

So the Spirit proceeds, seeming on the one hand to be the most bound of the Persons, and on the other to possess free will in a perfect measure. Will is his essential character: He blows where he will. He is bound to the necessary will of the Father and to that of the Son, and also to the Son's free will. And as he sees how the Son restrains his free will in favor of the Father and is obedient to him, the Spirit wishes to exercise the same obedience toward both Father and Son. Now it is as though Father and Son observe this restraint, this reserve, this kind of self-abnegation on the part of the Spirit, and immediately cry "No!", definitively bestowing on him complete divine freedom. The Spirit is no late arrival in God, the last of a series originating in the Father, in which the Son imitates the Father and the Spirit imitates the Son. Rather, his relationship to Father and Son is totally new and original, determined by his twofold bond; yet it immediately bursts this bond with the demand that he be *will*. It demands that he manifest something of the Father's paramount will and something of the Son's subordinate will in an original and unified way, in which the relationship of superordination and subordination is no longer completely visible; instead something arises that is most intimately connected with the way he was brought forth, revealing him vis-à-vis the Father and Son as the possessor of a complete freedom. He exercises this freedom but always between Father and Son; it always fulfills the purposes of Father and Son, yet does so in a free manner. Hence it belongs to him particularly to choose. Freedom of choice is not only a precondition for his operations; it is an inner quality of them. It is visible in God's "election of grace" in the world, his favoring of this person rather than that one, the fact that, out of all the apparently identical seeds, he causes this one to sprout rather than that one. The Spirit manifests himself in this elective quality in his continual blowing between Father and Son. And one can no more ask why there is a Holy Spirit than why he chooses this person and not that one, irrespective of any response or merit on man's part. This freedom of the Spirit is rooted in his position between Father and Son; it is something internal to God, not dependent on creation.

The Spirit is like someone who may do whatever he will. But he can only do what is between Father and Son, from whom he proceeds. In his freedom he is always being adopted into the divine conformity between Father and Son, although everything is given to him, everything is permitted. So too the Christian is bound precisely because he is free in the deepest sense; he believes freely, yet he is held firm by the law of his free faith. For him, every step outside the freedom of his faith would be a falling into slavery; therefore he will only operate within the conformity of his faith. The Spirit is free in his divinity (he cannot be other than he is) and hence free in his standing and his moving between Father and Son, in the eternal worship and contemplation of Father and Son, in their purposes and the implementing of them in the Spirit. The Christian puts his will into his faith, summons his will to realize itself within his faith and sets faith before his will as its law. The law for the Spirit's will is his relationship to Father and Son. But in this he need not imitate the Son. He must be himself, the free Spirit of Father and Son. That is why he can be a "Rule" for the incarnate Son, for he is free and yet sums up in himself the essence of the intentions of Father and Son. They are not imposed on him, but out of love he gives them whatever corresponds with the love of the Father and of the Son and will help realize them. The distance between the Persons becomes important again here: The Spirit is not stifled between Father and Son but has more and more room for his freedom. He can freely do whatever he can devise to promote the love of Father and Son.

Having said all this, we have exposed the roots of petitionary prayer in God. When the Father sees the Son before him and sees how spontaneously love answers him in the Son, how the Son both worships him and accepts his worship, contemplates him and accepts his contemplation, the Father introduces petition. He asks the Son to help promote the fatherly purposes he has revealed in contemplation. Everything which has the nature of purpose in him he hands over to the Son, showing him possibilities of action which are not already contained in his fatherly nature. The Father's intentions, now committed to the Son, are like preludes, beginnings taken up by the Son to be realized. Here we have a parallel to the Son's words, "Into your hands, Father, I commend my spirit." For here the Father gives his spirit (his purposes, his work, his creation) into the Son's hands. The Father has begotten the Son, but now it is the Son who brings certain of the Father's acts to full maturity: He becomes the carrier and fulfiller of the Father's plans. In the Father's original plans his fatherly will reveals itself. The Son takes them up, in order to proclaim his filial will by carrying them out. The Father realizes his purposes primarily by begetting the Son who will realize them; and therefore the Father realizes the Old Covenant, preparing in love for the Son who he knows will realize the Father's plans in the New Covenant. And then each one who is asked finds joy in granting the request. Thus the Father is the first to ask, and he asks the Son, in order to give him the joy of granting his request. One could even say that the Father's necessary will in begetting the Son expresses the granting of a request, as if the Father, through his necessary will, had granted the request of his free will, as if he had fulfilled a request of his own by begetting the Son. In men and women, too, there can be a tension in the will: between a more spiritual and a more natural will. When a man is tired and ought to keep on working, he can "permit himself" a rest. Similarly, in the Father, his necessary will grants the request of his free will to beget the Son. The Father desires this Son; and this very Son is the one he *must* have. But one cannot say that the Father delights in granting his own request; rather, he delights in the Son. The joy of granting the request is at most an anticipatory joy, inseparable from its fulfillment in the Son, just as all expectations are already fulfilled in God from all time. The Father eternally looks forward to the Son; but the Son who eternally stands before him is infinitely more than what the almighty and all-knowing Father expects, and his delight is infinitely more than his anticipatory joy. His begetting has resulted in more splendid fruit. And so he knows that his granting of the Son's request will also contain a divine "more-than"; that this heightening, this surprise, this superabundance is a divine aspect reappearing everywhere, so that God's joy can never be exhausted. This is the experience he wishes to give the Son immediately: Even before the Son asks him, the Father wants to make his request, as if to give the Son precedence in the delight of granting. Ultimately it is only on the basis of the divine joy in granting requests that the Spirit can be understood as having perfect freedom. Father and Son together create a mode of granting requests which lies behind the Spirit's freedom. They ask the Spirit, as it were, to dispose freely over their plans.

Thus the begetting itself seems to contain a kind of petition, but one which is already granted: Even as the Father begets, the Son has always been. As the Father is about to give the kiss of love, the Son has already offered his cheek. So the Son takes from the Father the intention which is just developing and carries it out—as the Father's deed and plan—by making himself ready for it. In God everything is full of these loving details which contribute essentially to understanding the Trinity, full of these prior ententes built into and fulfilled in reality. The Son even cooperates in his begetting by *letting* himself be begotten, by holding himself in readiness to be begotten. And within the relationship based on nature, everything is repeated on the level of freedom. When little St. Thérèse says, "God always makes me yearn for what he wants to give me", she reveals a deep insight into the essence of triune love. The purest love is a continual weaving and flux of concessions and fulfillments. Wishes and requests are not the sign of an impure or selfish love. Some women start an argument with their husbands simply in order to ask for something upon reconciliation: That is a misuse of the petition of love. Love has selfless wishes and is glad to know what the situation is, glad to know of preferences. It gives love an opportunity of adapting itself to the other. And the border is dissolved between what a person would do if left to himself and what he does to give joy to the other. Love does not fulfill the beloved's wishes by snatching them from his lips, so that the beloved falls into the tedium of having nothing to wish. In wishing and fulfillment, love preserves that distance which reverence demands, that area of freedom which is necessary for keeping the relationship alive. Among human beings this means that the one must leave the other alone so that love has room to develop in solitude as well. The one must have time to think of the other, to devise new plans of love, to prepare new surprises or simply to be himself, lest he fall into a slavery to love. In God no spatial separation is possible or necessary. It is replaced by the hierarchical distance of the processions. There is a primal beginning in which the Father is "alone", even if he was never without the Son, for ultimately it is he, unique and alone, who begets the Son. And the Son sees this in the Father. But since the Father gives the Son everything, he gives him this too. It is as though the Son permits the Father to be alone, but instantaneously the Father offers the same thing to the Son; and to him everything the Father desires is desirable. Some things can be said better near at hand, others at a distance; lovers can put into letters things that have occurred to them in the quiet contemplation of their mutual love, things which did not come out while they were together. In this way the recipient of the letter sees how beneficial to the other this solitude has been and how their love has been promoted by it.

Leaving the other free is something which goes back to the distance which is established in the begetting. The Father does not beget within himself but out of himself. In true love the lovers do not cling to each other: They have the distance which is essential if they are to see and encounter each other completely. In God the gift is always just what he wanted, yet a certain "time" and opportunity is left to desire it and a certain "time" for the gift to be got ready. The Son gives the Father the opportunity of making his will known so that he can accept it. Similarly, in marriage, the husband must let his wife have time to be a woman, and vice versa. And perhaps there are certain wishes of the Father which the Son does not carry out, so that the Spirit may do so. Perhaps at some point the husband needs to have a talk with a colleague in which his wife cannot participate; she will not try to change her feminine qualities and adopt masculine ones but will perhaps do everything to encourage this meeting and not be present herself. In God, of course, the Third Person is never excluded, but he is able to be present and to make his contribution in different ways, perhaps simply by making room for the others to act. Definite forms are exhibited by the will, by love, by wishes. Results do not flow automatically from a characterless amalgam. The same result can be achieved by the most diverse constellations of causes. One cannot deduce from equal total sums that their component numbers are the same.

The Son prefers nothing to doing the Father's will, for even in being begotten he carries it out. The creature has no opportunity to consent to its birth. The Son has. He immediately responds to the Father's act of begetting with an obedience which consents to be begotten. His whole freedom seems to him to have no other purpose than to consent to the begetting. On the other hand the Father also gives him the distance inherent in his independence. Yet the Son acts independently within the Father's permission and invitation to be free and independent. For himself, the Son would never tire of doing the Father's will. But the Father wishes the Son to do his own will, and the Son will not refuse this wish. If the Spirit is the Son's "Rule" on earth, the Father is the Son's "office" in heaven. In the context of the Incarnation this relationship becomes clearer to us. In order to reveal the Father's will to the world, the Son must know this will as no one else does. He must himself have rendered the utmost obedience if he is to require something like obedience from the believers. But his practice of this knowing and obeying does not begin with the Incarnation: As man he only does what, as God, he has done from eternity. In order, as God, to be man, he must also know all the aspects of his relationship, as God, with the Father; he must have lived in eternity in free subordination to the Father, although this subordination already had its basis within the divine necessity. Only thus can he represent the divine on earth. On earth it is the reverse of heaven: Here the believer first freely consents, then God takes him at his word and perhaps introduces him to a suffering repugnant to his nature. But the voluntariness of his consent embraces the suffering which is against his will. On the contrary, the divine Son first assents within the divine nature in order subsequently to assent in free will. In divine necessity, he affirms in heaven whatever the Father wills. And since this assent does not contain the least resistance but expresses the Son's whole nature, he puts all his freedom into it. And as man the Son receives a new, human free will, but he employs this too in a manner completely subordinate to the Father's will. When he prays on the Mount of Olives, "Not my will but thine be done", he is repeating in a new way the request already uttered in his eternal origin. But human nature and his office of representing sinners give it new aspects of obedience and submission.

If a novice were perfectly obedient to his superior in every action and with every breath, and for some reason the superior decided to release him from his obedience for an hour or two, he would nevertheless do nothing but what he imagined to be according to the superior's will. He would do nothing of such an independent character that the superior, if he wanted to, could not command him to do it. And if, instead of releasing him from his obedience, the superior were to reverse the relationship and take on the obedience of the novice for an hour, the latter would not command anything which would conflict with his former obedience: He would either request the original relationship to be restored or else order things according to the superior's mind. He would not refuse to command, but he would do so as the one now obeying him would have commanded. The spirit engendered by the superior in commanding is the spirit which the novice recognizes as true, which lives in him and according to which he now commands. In God, too, the Son could be independent and free—to choose obedience again and again. And since he has the Father's spirit, he knows no better way of loving him than to obey him. Even in heaven, the Father's will seems to him so excellent that he does not have to learn how to be obedient when he becomes man. For his human obedience can consist in nothing other than seeing the Father's will as exemplary in all matters. And this is something he does from eternity in heaven. All the actions he will perform on earth in freedom and sovereignty will be nothing other than an expression of his obedience, for this is the freedom which the Father has granted him and desires of him.

At the point where the triune God decides upon the creation of the world, where there is no talk yet of future sin, where the Son affirms the Father's plan in everything, at that point he puts himself at the disposal of creation, to take up his dwelling there. It is like an intimation of the Eucharist, not yet in sacramental form and with no reference to suffering or even to a body. Rather, the Son sees initially the great similarity between his eternal begetting and the procession from God of a creation imbued with grace; he imagines all the Father's joy at encountering his Son in the world. To delight the Father he wants this encounter to take place in every human being. And as if to clothe the Son's wish with a concrete form, to create a central point from which the Son's Eucharist can flow and spread forth, Father, Son and Spirit together choose one human being for the Son to dwell in: a woman. This one woman will receive the Son and be his mother. In this sense, Eve is already a woman in God's foreknowledge before Adam becomes a man. For, mysteriously, Christ and Mary are the first couple but are held as it were in reserve like a hidden basis. The ultimate, normative distance from God is determined by Christ and Mary, and not by Adam and Eve, who are drawn from the first separation from God in which they existed into the final distance determined by Christ and Mary. The Son's plan of glorification, prior to and more final than that of redemption, has always continually involved Mary and, through her, all creatures who join in the Father's praise. Just as the Father has his plan in creation which is particular to his fatherly point of view, so the Son has his according to his filial point of view; and the Spirit has his plan as well, since he carries out the plan of Father and Son in the freest possible manner. He brings about the Immaculate Conception; he overshadows the Mother; he works the miracle of the Virgin Birth. Thus all three Persons are involved in the origin of this first couple, who embody the epitome of creation. But the functions exercised by each Person in the work of creation are ultimately determined in the context of the divine petitionary prayer, not only in the contemplation from which action issues as its fruit. Certainly these functions are outlined here, but they only become concrete when Son and Spirit offer themselves for the sake of the Father's work, when they ask to be allowed to cooperate in it and when the Father asks for their collaboration. They want to explore and experience in eternity what mankind will do and experience later in petitionary prayer. The Lord's word, "All that you ask the Father in my name will be done for you", is to have its basis in God himself. And just as all three Persons petition each other together, they also grant fulfillment to one another. The whole work of creation lies in this divine granting. Each one gladly does the will of the other because in love he wants to delight him, because it is something which corresponds to his own will, and finally because his own will is completely shaped by the will and the judgment of the other. But this loving game of asking and granting in creation is seen most clearly at its highest point, in God's primal creation: Mary.

Decision

In all human prayer there are decisions. In fact, as a totality it is the result and expression of a decision for God. The praying person has decided to stand by God, to live in his presence, to contemplate him, to open himself up to him and to request something of him. But this human decision is always the answer to a decision of God's: to let himself be worshipped and contemplated, to reveal himself to man, to be available to him and to fulfill his requests. This divine decision, which includes and is presupposed by the human decision to pray, contains the particular decision whereby God lets himself be moved to decisions by our prayers. God's answer to our prayer lies not only in the fact that he shows himself and allows us to enter into dialogue with him but also in the fact that he himself shapes this dialogue, in a genuine reciprocity in which he always remains free to respond to man's invocation in whatever way he may decide. Thus his decision may seem to match our requests, but it may also be an answer that, from a purely human point of view, seems scarcely to have any connection with our prayer.

And when God speaks with God, all possible forms of decision are present in this conversation. The mutual worship and contemplation of the divine Persons is the fruit of a decision in love. But decisions must continually be made in petition and fulfillment as well. For instance, the Son decides to make a request of the Father; the Father decides to answer it in a particular way, and so on. Divine prayer has the character of decision, a character that expresses a trait of the divine nature: In God nothing is undecided. It is the nature of God that he is differentiated as Father, Son and Spirit, and that in this threefold being he is perpetually deciding. He decides both to give and to receive. God's conversation is not formless, his contemplation is not without direction: Everything is differentiated and decided to the highest degree. But for that very reason everything is continually pressing back into unity. God differentiates in order continually to reunite; but he unites in order continually to make new decisions.

An analogy for this is the Son's Eucharist, in which he is always sharing himself out; yet the more he is shared out, the more he strives to recapture unity. The Son's integrity is heightened by every Communion. In a similar way there is a communion in God, an exchange of the divine nature in which differentiation and unification are one. And this exchange in God is something quite concrete. Love's concrete gift is encompassed with love and illuminates and demonstrates it. Between human beings the exchange is limited; no one can impart his memory or spirit to the other. He can only express it. In God there is nothing that cannot be given; every gift is the thing itself, not a representation of it. One man can tell another of his childhood memories, but he cannot give him his childhood itself (it is not rare for hypnosis, analysis and such things to approach blasphemy by trying to enter an area which God has reserved for himself). The Lord on earth, however, is not a memory but a living, real presence, the concrete offering of himself; the triune life is the basis for this. Whoever rejects the Lord's real eucharistic Presence, therefore, is without access to the trinitarian fellowship. People very often speak of "mere symbols" when they can go no further, when they can no longer rise to the significance of what, for God, is a pure reality. With its realism, the Eucharist is a bridge to heaven for believers. It shows that in heaven there are decisions and concretizations, decisions which are as concrete in God as the Lord is for the believer when he has the Host on his tongue. In God, wishes and acts of the will are realized. God the Father can wish the Son to wish something; he can impart this wish to the Son so that the Son wishes it most concretely, yet without interfering with the Son's personality. It is the opposite of a hypnosis in which the hypnotist's will overpowers and suppresses that of the subject, leaving him to wake from the hypnosis with a reduced will of his own. For the lover to ask the beloved to become like him would be an abuse of love; it would be self-love, narcissism. In the Son, God the Father sees the Son, not himself. And in the Spirit he sees the Spirit and not Son or Father. There is no confusion in God. The Father does not want the Son to act as if he were Father; in the Son's work he wishes to see the Son's glory, not his own fatherly glory. In God each is to be himself, not a copy of the other. And each shares himself with the other in such a way that he is not thereby compelled to be any less himself. This is part of God's firmness of decision.

The more Father, Son and Spirit contemplate, worship and converse with each other, the more they become themselves, so to speak, at the other's request. The more the Son is uttered by the begetting Father, the more paternal, as it were, the Father becomes. The Father in no way thinks of becoming the Son, nor the Son of becoming the Father. The "many mansions" of which the Lord speaks and which he is keeping ready in his Father's house are differentiated in God himself. In human love the man does not desire to be the woman, nor the woman the man. The more they are united, the more the other is a Thou, not an I. And the more different the other is, the more worthy of love he appears. There may come a point of interpenetration in their union where neither is aware any longer of where one begins and the other ends; but in this very unity the Thou is even more exalted. And in love each has the right to determine the union. Even the woman, who is at the man's disposal, within this condition has power to dispose over him. So it pleases the Father that the Son should make his own decisions. It is the Son's glory which the Father wants to see when the Son glorifies him. And the Spirit wants to see the glory of both, paying no attention to the fact that he himself completes their glorification.

Everything we can say about divine prayer is only an intimation. Outside of love, people can reduce everything to certain concepts and say it is "nothing but. . . ." In love we know that everything is much richer and more colorful than we can express. And if what we are trying to describe is the love of God, it can only find expression in itself. But the more a person loves, the nearer he is to the love of God and the more he understands how much God loves and how the triune life is the living wellspring of all love.

2. PRAYER IN CREATION

The eternal Son uses every form of prayer as he prays to the Father. The Spirit inspires this prayer and is thus the Spirit of prayer. And the vision of himself which the Father gives to the Son and the Spirit is from eternity part of his form of prayer. This does not only mean that the Father manifests himself, thereby stimulating prayer and providing its content: In revealing himself he also reveals his own prayer. Nor is God's nature changed when the Father becomes the Creator of the world: His act of creation, in which he reveals himself externally, takes place within his prayer. The actions of believers only count as Christian actions when they arise out of Christian prayer; similarly, God's actions spring not only from his divine

74

nature but also from the fact that he is prayer, from his praying. God does nothing without giving himself an account of his action. When he looks back on the evening of each day of creation at what he has done and judges it to be good, this opinion is addressed to Son and Spirit; it is an invitation to them both to share in and approve of the Father's work and is thus also an acknowledgment that the Son and the Spirit are with him and are collaborating, revealing and praying together with him.

Prior to creating, God lived from eternity in the unity of giving, participating and sharing which exists between the divine Persons. And we must not imagine this threefold unity to be an inert state. It is motion, charged energy, stimulus, event, exchange, creation mounting from one degree to another. It is the highest form of life, eternal life. In becoming Creator, the Father places himself before the Son and Spirit, in this new action and new self-revelation, to some extent in a new light; but in acknowledging that his work is very good he returns to the Son and the Spirit and gives them a share in it. Certainly Son and Spirit participated in creation, for God said, "Let *us* make man in our own image". But their cooperation was veiled within the Father's creating activity, and this veiling will find a parallel in the veiling of Father and Spirit in the incarnate God who is the Son. During creation it is only the one face of God, the Father's, which is seen. But speaking of and evaluating it on the seventh day, in the face of the completed creation, he addresses Son and Spirit. And so the statement, "It is good", is a prayer because it is spoken from God to God. One might think it superfluous, for even during creation the Father begets the Son and the Spirit proceeds, and all is created in the Son, and the Spirit moves over the face of the waters. They participate from the outset. But it is not superfluous because prayer is a conversation and uses words, since it has a shape, and because, when God the Creator subsequently gives mankind the opportunity of fellowship with him, of prayer and of answers to prayer, he will be giving something of his own divine treasure, something eternal and deeply rooted in him. In praying, man will not be calling something new into being. His prayer will be a participation in the eternal conversation between Father, Son and Spirit. This conversation is the most profound and sublime possible, and God creates the world "very good" for man's sake, so that he too can take part in the conversation. Everything in the world must be very good so that man, likewise created good, can be stimulated by his own being and by his environment to share in the eternal conversation.

God's Sabbath comes at the end of the whole work of creation, giving us a glimpse of the eternity prior to creation. It is a holy day because God takes his rest in it, because it is the day of him who now rests from creation; the work of his hands and his pronouncement of its goodness are now behind him, and he returns to the holiness of his triune life. He retires from prominence into a certain distance; he retires to the repose of the sanctuary which he shares with the Son and the Spirit. In doing so, he also gives his creation the opportunity of rest and contemplative prayer. What he does now is no longer "good" but holy. It is no longer action but contemplation. It is no longer a working but a letting happen. It is holy because it is his day of rest, the day on which he has nothing else to do but to receive worship: worship from Son and Spirit but also from what he has created. Man, acquainted with the course of the days, now receives a day in which nothing is to take place but the vision of God in heaven who rejoices over his work, glad to have pronounced it good in his prayer with the Son and the Spirit. This pronouncement makes possible the Sabbath thanksgiving: not only by his action, then, but also by his pronouncement. Hence the thanksgiving is not arbitrary, the result of a merely human evaluation; it is not subject to man's disposal. It is something holy, belonging by right to God, bestowed by him and therefore a participation in his holiness.

Christians must take to themselves this rule of the Sabbath, pronounced holy by God. It must be a day of real prayer, of cessation of the work of creation, and thus a participation in the whole of creation, not by action, but by a rejoicing which is not of our own choosing but which is guaranteed by God's holiness. Grace invites us to do this: grace not only in the form of the enablement to and the fulfillment of prayer but also in the form of the sacraments and of God's omnipresence, which reveals and offers itself. There is a kind of accommodation in our being permitted to share in God's activity: We have eyes to see, ears to hear, senses to perceive. But now we are invited to join in the day of holiness without being accommodated with any faculty for it, and this lack of accommodation is bridged by grace. There is something much stronger and more substantial than our faculties: the supernatural. It has pity on our nature, placing us before God and enabling us to receive what God wishes to give us from his holy sanctuary, coming to us in a visibility and reality which is beyond the created world and arises from the holy world of God. On the one hand it is not to be found in the created world, and yet it is perfectly related and connected to it because the seventh day follows the first six in which God worked. God provides the framework of this seventh day: It is the day of his rest, the holy day. He proclaims it with a loud voice. But he also provides its content, namely himself, with his holiness and repose, and that content is not of this world. The framework of the other days lies in the differentiating of what was undifferentiated, the creating of what was not; their content was God's action. The Sabbath's content is no longer God's action but God himself. Man is raised to be able to enter into dialogue with God the Invisible, God at rest, allowed to enter his holiest of holies where God floods him with his grace. Sunday is the day of supernature, which builds on nature.

3. THE PRAYER OF CHRIST

The Prayer of Incarnation

When the incarnate Son stands as a man among human beings, his prayer must be of such a kind that he can communicate it to his brothers. His prayer in heaven was one of pure vision. He must now experience a prayer which can become a prayer of faith in his brothers. In his human nature he must experience how man comes to terms with God. He still possesses the vision of the Father, but now he must veil it, put it into shadow, leave it in abeyance, refrain from using it. He must put it into his Father's hands as he will do with his spirit on the Cross. His prayer in heaven sprang from a unity comprising his being begotten by the Father and his vision of the Father. Now his prayer is to arise from his being incarnate as a human being and from the faith which men are to have, the faith which the New Covenant brings.

We are purely creatures, brought into being from nothing. The Son became man out of his own eternal being. In the difference between our being created and his becoming in-carnate (by raising human nature up to himself and taking it on) lies something that he adopts, in order to be able to give us faith out of this possession. A human being might have been given the grace of vision, and he might have been enabled to see into the mystery of a certain feast each year; but one time God might deprive him of this vision. Then he would have to learn to manage without it or to connect the previous vision with the present nonvision and experience the feast in just as Catholic a manner and celebrate it just as joyfully as in the earlier years. In a similar way the incarnate Son carries in himself the difference between the heavenly vision and the possibility of faith given to created man, in order to prepare from it the Christian faith that he intends to give to those who are his. As *the* Son of Man he possesses the vision of the Father. But if he had not also reached down to our mode of fellowship with God, the gift of faith would not really have come from him. He would not really have been in our place and represented us. The difference between his vision and our faith does not consist in the dissolution of one by the other but in the simultaneity of the two. He must live in such a way that he is in contact with both poles, especially the human pole. Obedience to the Father requires that he be a genuine human being. And he can only transmit to man this obedience to the Father if he has completely experienced and suffered it as man. So he must leave behind with the Father whatever would make human obedience impossible. If an experienced doctor wishes to instruct nurses, he will have to learn to treat the patient in quite a different way than he does as a physician. He himself will have to learn the skills the nurses will need. Mere theoretical knowledge is not enough. But it is clear that the doctor has not lost his higher and more complete knowledge, and equally that, in his own profession, he does not need the new knowledge he has had to acquire.

Every form of trinitarian prayer has its origin in vision. It is this vision which opens God to God, causing worship, contemplation and petition to arise as one. Now, on earth, the Son must find the formula that he can give to mankind. According to the Father's wish, he must and will learn how to live in his sight as the first Christian. For himself, he could pray just as he did in heaven, but that would not help mankind. He must be for them the way to the Father not merely in a general sense: Specifically, he must be the way to Christian prayer. Now he prays for two reasons. First, he prays from a divine necessity, from his nature and need as the Son of God, which includes the freewill aspect of divine prayer. At the same time, he prays as man in a creaturely spontaneity and freedom of will, and this form of free will entails a consequent necessity. This second fount of prayer is again twofold: He wants to show the Father that his creation is good and what a man is like who is committed to God; and from his attitude of prayer he wants to show mankind what genuine prayer is.

While he was in heaven with the Father and beheld him, he also saw and experienced the Old Covenant. He knew how the Father and the Father's voice were represented to men and how the Father revealed himself to Adam, to the prophets and to all the believers of pre-Christian times. Thus he knew the given basis of man's faith. He knew the law. But he knew all this as God in heaven. His knowledge of man was God's knowledge in heaven. Now he is man, and he intends to be man in such a way that he experiences how a man knows God. The second experience is contained in the first like a small dish lying in a bigger dish, and yet the second experience must be gone through independently. And the experience of the Old Covenant cannot be taken in isolation, for his purpose is to bring the faith of the New Covenant. So he must take his Incarnation into account; he must include his own intimate relationship with the Father and equally the Father's relationship with him, and he must also include the Spirit. In the Old Covenant the Trinity was hidden behind the Father. Now, as the exponent of the revealed triune God, the Son must be man, but in such a way as to manifest the trinitarian existence even of the God of the Old Testament.

Consequently he must learn to fashion his trinitarian experience of prayer so as to make it serviceable for men who do not share his gift of vision. He must communicate his knowledge of the Old Covenant and of his coming New Covenant in such a way that they can find in it the basis and enablement of a living Christian faith. They must not get the impression that he is bringing them something "cut down to size", all that is left when the Son of God has become a mere man. They must sense that what he gives is a plenitude leading to an even greater plenitude. By restricting his own vision as God, he expands us men in our faith. On the other hand, he cannot appear before the Father and say, "Father, you see how much I have renounced in order to give something to men!" He must be able to say to the Father, "You have given me such fullness as man that I cannot take it all in: It fills me to overflowing, and I must give it to others!" He must not feel that what the one praying receives as man is a miserable fragment of what he, as God, has always known and possessed. On the contrary, he must become man so seriously that he experiences God's gift to the creature as something overwhelming. He experiences the plenitude which the Father had originally planned for men, which they lost through sin, and which he is now winning back for them. For it is for their sake that he experiences this plenitude, and he is grateful to them for it. The Christian faith is by no means an impoverished vision, a mere "not-yet", the negative of vision. It is a unique intercourse with God with its own laws, lying at a different level than vision. The two do not coincide, but both must be fulfilled, and both must fulfill man completely. Love has the most diverse ways of expressing itself: a present, a kiss, an embrace or a spiritual support; and it cannot be said that one is better or richer or more complete than another.

The Father does not want the Son to feel that human life is a poor thing. Nor does the Son want to give his

Father this impression. They are not engaging in make-believe. It is less a case of setting aside divine possibilities than of bringing human possibilities into prominence and drawing the maximum from them. It would be too small a thing for the Son, coming from his heavenly worship, simply to continue it on earth. People would say, "It is easy for him to worship out of the fullness of his divine life, having spent an eternity with the Father. But what are *we* to do?" Consequently, he must draw his life and his prayer from the Old Covenant and from that part of himself which he will give to men; and from his present life and prayer, in turn, he must draw that which he gives to men: faith. For this purpose, however, his human nature is not adequate: He needs to draw on his divine substance, on that which he as God can bestow, to fashion the gift of faith. As man he must attain to, press forward to, the awareness of his divinity. Thus, from his human nature, he can make a path for mankind to his divinity, to the whole triune divinity; he can also reveal and communicate his divinity in such a way that men will be able to grasp something of it.

When he includes the Old Covenant and cites its prophecies in order to fulfill them, he must also build a bridge at this point between the human word and the real, inner, triune relationships as God sees them. And he must make these relationships visible in his word, yet at the same time he must hold them as if in the background, lest mankind should be overwhelmed by too much fullness, by things which can really only be comprehended in vision. (This is often the case with the experiences of the Christian mystics: They experience things that they may not communicate, but they are to draw from them what definitely must be communicated. Thus they experience the incommunicable, not for themselves, but for the sake of others, who are to learn something through them.) If believers had to understand everything, they would need to be

God, or at least to see everything from his vantage point. Instead, they are to remain men who have their own vantage point, and therefore the Son must show them what he has seen in such a way that their faith can grasp it, albeit in a way which leaves the divine vision all the room that is its due: in such a way that faith understands that God sees things in a larger compass than we, human beings and Christians, can experience them.

Adoration

The Son's adoration on earth is markedly conditioned by the Old Covenant: It was his wish to build up his adoration from the point at which the chosen people stood, or rather where they should have stood if their continuing sin had not hindered them from true adoration. He takes up adoration at the point where it has gone through the whole development of the Old Covenant. He does not begin with Adam, nor Abraham, nor Solomon, but with adoration as it stands in his own period. It embraces knowledge of all that has taken place in the course of the Old Covenant: the revelations and promises of the Father and the fulfillment which he, the Son, may bring. His adoration is the adoration due to God at the moment when the Old Covenant is to be burst asunder by the New. It is adoration in the distance which man senses between himself and God, and this distance is filled up entirely by God's divinity. Hence it is not a distance which separates but sight: sight, that is, not as direct vision, but as experiential knowledge of the living God. And the Son must learn to stand where, in the Old Covenant, man stood in adoration before God; he must translate the divine distance between Father and Son into the Christian distance between God and man. Conversely, in spite of the distance between God and man he must attain, through prayer and adoration, to the intimacy of the distance between Father and Son. At the same time he must not experience the intimacy between Father and Son in such a way that he forgets the distance between God and man, into which he must enter by prayer. On the one hand he must learn this distance, and on the other hand it is so much part of him that, in order to learn it, he has ultimately to *draw it out of himself*: For all his "learning" is contained in his mission, a mission he took upon himself as all-knowing and all-powerful God. He knows what he is doing in becoming man, and he also knows what it means to learn as a man.

It can be taken as a first premise that the Son adores the Father as the Father expects from a perfect believer unsullied by sin. On the basis of this purity, his adoration, corresponding to its own nature, calls for ever more and higher adoration. The Son is so overwhelmed by the Father's being which confronts him that wherever he encounters him in adoration he is filled with joy, and he needs that joy to live. There is nothing selfish in this need: He experiences it as a pure human being does, and it is part of his vocation. He must be so filled with adoration that he can bestow it on others from the fullness of his whole being, so that simply by seeing him people are seized by an urge to adore. In adoring, the Son fulfills the promises of the Old Covenant, not so much by looking back to it as by taking into his adoration all the promises with their whole atmosphere, their proclamation and reception and the expectation of fulfillment, and bringing them to maturity. If two friends promise to go on a journey and look forward to it, their very expectation contains a certain fulfillment that is part of the journey; but the actual fulfillment of what they have promised envelops this anticipatory fulfillment in order to bring it to complete fulfillment. Thus in himself the Son fulfills everything which had already begun to be fulfilled with a view to his coming, and in doing this he almost forgets that he is himself the content and fulfillment of the promise: Everywhere he sees the glory of the Father's plans, he understands everything in its true sense and its full context, and thus in everything he adores the Father. (It is like a doctor who is treated by another doctor and cannot sufficiently admire the latter's skill, although his own is no less.) In all this, the Son's adoration is human. It is not simply the corollary and the continuation of his divine vision. In his adoration on earth, rather, the reasons behind all that the Father has so far given and revealed to men come into prominence and are separately visible. The principal reason is the Son; but he does not see himself. In the whole unfolding of salvation up to and including him, he sees only the glory of the Father who is manifesting himself.

Thus the point of departure is supplied: The Son adores the Father as man, and he does so on the basis of the Old Covenant which he is fulfilling and of the New which he is bringing and proclaiming to mankind. But here the point of departure is far exceeded, for to bring the New Covenant is part of his divine mission. When the Father sends his own Son to bring the adoration of the New Covenant, it is clear that this task needs a God to carry it out: not only the work of redemption but also that of leading faith and adoration, as they were heretofore, into the new faith and adoration. Thus it is expressly and necessarily as *God*-Man that the Son on earth adores the Father. The first part of this task is that he must translate the vision which he possessed in heaven as God and which remains natural to him on earth as the God-Man. But, secondly, this vision becomes in him an imparted vision, which must be in him the origin and harbinger of the vision of many who are to come after him. As such it is closely connected with faith: It is based almost more on faith than on the heavenly vision.

85

Thirdly, however, it is a vision of "recall", that is, one that maintains its influence in temporality and sequence, whereas in the eternal vision everything is present at once, outside time, and can be looked at either as a coincident unity or in detail. (So, for instance, in the eternal vision, the actuality of the Incarnation is included in the Son's promise to become man.) While dwelling on earth, the Son experiences even in his vision the noncoincidence of times. This "recall" keeps the reality of his heavenly promise living and awake in him. He does not have to make an effort to be aware of the vitality of his decision; but he must continually return to the thought of it in order to match, with his human life, the eternal plenitude of its origin. He must conform his whole humanity to the heavenly vision. He is like a woman who bears the pains of childbirth by recalling her betrothal, her wedding and the joy of the moment when the child comes into existence.

This adoration on the part of the God-Man, however differentiated it may appear, is all of a piece, like himself. It can be compared to a finding that wants to seek, that begins to seek through having found; it is like a fulfillment that yearns for the promise. It is as if the Son, who possesses adoration fully—and adoration effects his nearness to the Father and contains his perfect, insatiable love which does everything for love's sake and lives and exists only for love—tries to guide this love along human paths so that the Father shall receive the homage of loving adoration not only from the Son but equally from mankind, from those who love him, believe in him and are willing to be sent out by him. And in fact it is in the mission itself, in grasping it and keeping it alive, that the unity of the Son's adoration is shown and fulfilled, a unity which strives increasingly to become a unity of the adoring believer—fully and visibly achieving this in the Cross. It is as if in his divine-human adoration the Son wants to make his divinity more and more invisible, so that the Father shall see the human being in him more and more. In adoration God is so great that the adorer disappears and ceases to count. The Son who adores confirms this, for in his adoration he is almost *indifferent* about whether he is God or man but prefers, since he has a mission from his Father to carry out on earth, to be one of us in adoring the Father, so that the Father can see how he can be adored on earth. It is adoration which *forms* the Son's whole life, to such an extent that, in adoration, each day of his life seems like the first. It is almost like a process of growth that makes him more and more a human being, until he is on the Cross with no strength left for adoration and can do nothing more than *be* the evidence of his own adoring, laying aside the form of God in order to be nothing more than naked man. This laying aside of his divine form in favor of his human form is already reflected during his life in his adoration. But what was here the finding which searches, on the Cross becomes the seeking which tries to find. Divinity must decrease so that the humanity may increase.

Petition

The more the Son worships, the more clearly he sees the concerns of men. This is the origin of his petitionary prayer. He sees their needs; he sees that they stand in great need of living in union with God and that they need to have this union made tangible for them. And petitionary prayer as such, in its presentation and in the granting of it, can make God tangible for men. Here men can lay before God all that concerns them, material things and spiritual things, private and public matters, family issues and those of all human communities; and they may also expect an answer from God. In worship, which is a *state*, it was less a matter of men than of God, his

87

greatness and his love, and of the reverence due to him. In petitionary prayer God's *relationships* with men come into prominence. The whole of human daily life can be included. And in this world man cannot live by worship alone. He lives in particular conditions and has a particular destiny and is bound to other human beings who have destinies of their own. Thus his petition becomes a bridge between his world and God's.

The Son is already acquainted with petitionary prayer from heaven, where each divine Person asks the others to let him carry out the others' wishes in order to experience the joy of asking and of granting and to intensify those joys infinitely. But since the Son has come into the sinful world, petition has acquired a different aspect for him. His mission as a whole has the appearance of granting a request of the Father's: The Father was about to lose his world in the alienation of sin, and the Son brings it back by responding to a request, a wish of the Father. And now this mission is translated into everyday human terms and made concrete; now it is the Son who must plead for the world so that the Father may grant him grace to do his will and redeem the world. He translates his whole mission into prayers of petition and lets it come to life in these prayers, which are so numerous that his whole mission can be read in them, taken together. He points to all that is lacking in the world and to men, and, in doing so, he also initiates them into petitionary prayer: He shows them what they lack and where God in his grace can and will redeem them, and how. He petitions for them, but *as* man, for an anonymous world to which he belongs; he petitions, therefore, as every Christian could. Of course the task of redemption is one and indivisible. But from the acceptance of the task to its accomplishment on the Cross, what an infinite number of detailed labors it involves! That is why the prayer of petition is so manifold and encompasses so much. Often one takes on some responsibility and only later comes to see how many separate operations it involves. The Son cannot envisage them all: First there is each individual human being with his particular sins and estrangements, then there are the destinies of nations throughout all time, and again there is a particular individual who needs to have God's word made plain to him, and then the question of whether to speak or remain silent, to work a miracle or not. . . . Redemption is like the building of a house; the finished house is the Cross. But the building of it demands an immense number of concerns and consultations and considerations. They fill the Lord's life. In petitionary prayer there are two movements: The one pursues the particular into the smallest details, and the other collects and gathers together, culminating in the prayer for the Church and the world. In his prayer the Lord is acquainted with both movements.

He knows that the Father hears all his requests. But he also leaves him free to fulfill them as the Father wishes: "Thy will be done." It is true that the Son carries out the plan of redemption and that the Father has approved it. But it is as if the Son immediately recalls that it is the Father's creation, and he continually has recourse to the Father so that all shall be done according to his mind. In turn the Father grants the Son everything so that his mission within the Father's work shall be fulfilled. First and foremost he grants him the mission itself. He does not make it easier for him by taking the world's sin away first so that the Son will not need to go to the Cross. That would render the mission null and void. Mission and Cross are fulfilled petition. And petition is also the way in which the Son includes the Father in the work of redemption: as if the Son were to prefer one request, granted by the Father, to anything he might devise himself. He never treats his mission as if it concerned him alone. He continually keeps it in contact with

89

the Father, seeks the Father's will, endeavors, through petitionary prayer, to fit in perfectly with the Father's intentions. Through the content of his petitions he is always showing the Father how the world is and what opportunities there are for the Father to take action in it, showing him how he, the Son, is now *obliged* as man to see things. By his choice of petitions he shows the Father where he stands as man, what he thinks important, how he distinguishes what is present from what is to come.

He asks in humility: bringing things to light, but protectively. His petitions are protective in that he always endeavors to present man to the Father as he created him, and man's concerns as arising to a large extent from human nature. He takes on and into himself that which constitutes the distance of sin to such an extent that the Father's attention is more drawn toward the needs of good people trying to reach the New Covenant, while the Son bears the alienation of sin. His petitions bring things to light by revealing the whole multiplicity of needs, laying before the Father all that makes up human life: night and day, dawn and dusk, every burden, every difficulty. In himself he represents the whole world and the vast numbers of individuals whose condition seems so hopeless that they are not able of themselves to grasp the truth of love in the New Covenant, to believe in it and live according to it. Unceasingly he prays for all whom he meets, and also for all whom *he* needs to realize his mission, for all whom the Father needs in order to have a redeemed world, for the removal of obstacles affecting whole groups of people; he prays about mistakes, virtues, weaknesses, strengths, for communities and individuals, for families, historical movements, nations, for everything which makes up the world, for everything which is given to or withheld from anyone.

And he asks so that the Father can grant the petition, so that the Father can come into an ever closer relationship with the world, can see in the fulfillment of the Son's mission the accomplishment of his own will and can share in everything that constitutes the Son's life, so that the Father never feels alone for an instant. He asks in humility: not attaching any importance to his own activity, letting the Father choose, letting him decide everything. He lays everything before him in a preliminary form, as befits the Son, not binding the Father to a particular course. The Son will not let himself be bound by the conditions of his life: He will only be bound by the Father.

Contemplation

The same law recurs in his *contemplation* as the Incarnate One. On the one hand the Lord invents contemplation for men by translating the heavenly into the earthly for them; on the other he perfects it by linking up with what he finds in the Old Covenant, right up to his Mother's assent. In the Old Covenant there was more of a contemplative *attitude* than an actual, developed contemplation. The substance of contemplation was restricted; it was chiefly a matter of attitude and chiefly concerned the promises. Contemplation required a state of expectation and hope; one might never lose faith in the fulfillment, yet one never experienced it oneself. The man of the Old Testament kept the commandments; they bound him, took root in his life, drew him closer to God and at the same time enabled him to live more in the spirit of the promises. By not sinning, he tried to be open to the promises. The basis was a kind of limited righteousness: Man did more or less what was expected of him, and hence he could expect God eventually to do more. So keeping the commandments was the starting point for contemplation. But the hope to which it was directed was only contained in the words of promise; it was hard to clothe these words with a real objectivity, and equally hard to arrive at a personal standpoint in this contemplation. God's mighty acts in the history of the people could also be material for contemplation, and they were like the beginning of a fulfillment of the promises. Primarily, they inspired worship; secondarily, they could be used in contemplation.

Thus things stood with the best of the people at the time the Son came. He has seen the Father and knows that he himself is God. And in addition to worship and petition he would like to give mankind a share in his contemplation. To do this he must have recourse to himself, in two ways. He must *represent* what he is, the Son of God: not only in a general way, by dwelling among men, but in such a way that they can see heaven, the kingdom of the Father, in all his words, and can be led through his concrete life to the unknown God, the God hidden behind the Son. On the other hand, he must embody all that he is continually receiving from eternity so as to make it accessible to man. The first is a kind of extension of his humanity away from man and toward the Father and the Spirit; the second is a kind of restriction of his nature to what human beings can understand and grasp to some extent. It is as if the beholder must become a believer for their sake; he who possesses the power of God must become him who possesses the power of faith (exercised according to the Father's mind), the one who will lead the way back to the Father, who as a sign of this return already—or still—possesses the eternal vision.

To begin contemplation he uses the word of God which since the Old Covenant is available to the world. He himself is this Word, and each word he speaks is also addressed to the Father; consequently his character as Word receives his divinity as its core. Its covering and goal is his being heard by the Father. And since he initiates the New Covenant as the continuation and completion of the Old, his teaching on contemplation draws on the Old Covenant. Often he bases himself on what "is written". Often what he says is quite simply the word of the law, but in being adopted by him it is broadened into what is new. He continues and extends the word of the law until it becomes the Word which he is: He makes it an introduction to himself. At other times he cites a prophetic word and announces that it is fulfilled by his coming. And when his hearers contemplate the word announced by him, they must follow the same path: Setting out from a familiar word which for them meant a hope, since it contained the Father's promise and as such had a place in their faith, they must learn to find its unfolding, fulfillment and application in the Son who stands before them. In this way his revelation is a contemplation that is strictly guided by himself. He leads his hearers from what, by the Father's grace, they already have, to what he, as the Father's Word and Son, wishes to give them, what he wishes to reveal of his nature at this particular moment. And when later they recall his word, they cannot isolate it from the whole situation, theirs and his, nor from the interpretation which became evident to them in that situation. They link this word to others he spoke to them and are drawn deeper and deeper into a contemplation whose center is the Lord, yet which leaves this center in its context of the Old Covenant, using it to reflect the mysteries of the Father, to reveal and interpret the truths of heaven and of creation. For instance, when the Son says, "I have come to glorify the Father", one sees the Father as he was in the Old Covenant. The concept "Father" has a meaning for his hearers. Similarly it means something to them when he says, "I", and they learn that this "I" has come to glorify the Father. Then they see his life and work and learn to interpret it as glorification. And they begin to have intimations of the Father's greatness and his goodness because he has given them this Son

93

and has become for them the Father of the New Covenant. Their contemplation must lead them to work out how they too, in their life and activity, can glorify this Father more.

But they also come to understand more and more deeply that his whole dwelling among them is a reflection of his eternal vision. And the word he speaks to them, the Word he is for them in his whole being and which they can contemplate in faith, is for them like a substitute for his eternal vision. They can forever behold him who beholds the Father, and they know that everything they do in discipleship is connected with his vision of the Father and that the gaze which they direct to him does not find its end in him but is taken up by him into his vision of the Father. He bears within himself as it were the prolongation of their contemplative perceptions. When someone says, "Pray for me", he is putting an obligation on the other's prayer, and the one receiving the request takes up the concern of him who asks into his own relationship with God. It is similar with the Son: Anyone who contemplates him puts him under an obligation, and the Son takes up such contemplation into his vision of the Father.

Now, however, the Son himself has become man to such an extent that in his prayer he uses the human contemplation in its tension between Old and New Covenant. He tests it in order to give it to mankind as a Christian possibility. But in doing so he must go in the opposite direction from man, who begins his contemplation with the word of promise and moves toward its fulfillment in the Son. The Son must direct his contemplation away from himself toward mankind. He must contemplate the divine matter he brings from heaven in terms of its goal, which is man. He must see how man can receive it; he must also see what it means to be man and have a human nature, so that here, at the goal of his Incarnation, he can experience God afresh. In the Old Covenant it was said, "Love your neighbor as yourself." In the New Covenant it is, "Love one another as I have loved you." The Son's contemplation operates in the space between these two commands. He does not have to learn to see God in his neighbor. He has to do almost the opposite of what we must do: to learn to love himself as if he were the neighbor, or—what comes to the same thing—so to adopt the neighbor into himself that he understands him like himself; to lay aside what he possesses as God and manage only with the human powers such as are given to his neighbors; to accept in a human way what he wishes to communicate to men; to regard what he says to them as being addressed to himself, in order on the basis of this contemplation to be able to replace the Old Testament command of love by that of the New.

If one wants to give a friend an especially personal gift, one takes account in the most sensitive way of his needs and tastes. One tries to enter into his mind, to see how he will regard it and how he will feel, and one must ignore one's own habits and customs. In this way the Son now restricts himself to his humanity, turning away from his vision and the advantages if offers; he "neglects" his divinity in favor of taking seriously, of exalting, creaturely existence. Above all he now wants to see the Father in his works so that he can glorify him, not now in heaven, but on earth and in every detail. He strives and extends himself toward the level of the creature. Consequently, for him, contemplation now occupies the place formerly held by vision: Contemplation is now to be the most important. To do this is the greatest proof of his love, his love that renounces and bends down to us. It yields the following insight which is important for instruction in prayer: *From now on, contemplation can never be regarded as a preliminary stage of mystical vision.* Both vision and contemplation have their origin in the Son's eternal vision. But man has no right to strive to rise from contem-

95

plation to vision if the Son of God has descended from vision to contemplation for love of us. He can give us a share in both, and both are signs of his love. And the Son intends his contemplation equally for the Father and for mankind. In his human contemplation he shows the Father how truly he has created man in his own image, how man is even able to contemplate him, the Father, using the Son so that the latter leads man to contemplate eternity and the triune being. Man uses the Son to come to the Father, and now the Son too uses himself—in a unique way. As a man contemplating he remains the Son, but his filial nature is entirely veiled within the contemplating subject. "*A* sower went out to sow." The sower is the Son. But the Son is absorbed by the process: He disappears in the objective word he speaks and in the work he does. Consider as an analogy a religious founder drawing up the rule of his order. No doubt he tests this rule on himself most intimately. Yet he disappears in the objective word of the text; he lets his spirit become the objective spirit of his order; his personal spirit has become the instrument of the order's spirit to such a degree that the seam is invisible. Thus the Son contemplates as a man among men. And since contemplation causes the divine will to listen and summons an answer from God which is then expressed in further contemplation or action, the Son is glad if the Father accepts his contemplation as that of any believer and answers him as such in contemplation. In this way his contemplation is directed to God. It is also directed to men insofar as when he contemplates he wishes to embody his anonymous neighbor—anyone, everyone—and so introduce him to contemplation. To love himself as his neighbor here means that he lets himself become any neighbor. But he does this in order to become, for each and all, a way to the Father.

So we must not say that he makes his vision to be contemplation for us so that, through contemplation, we may arrive at vision. In heaven this statement will be true, but it must be treated with caution on earth. On earth vision is not a more highly developed form of contemplation. Anyone on earth who is granted vision knows no higher obligation than to *transpose* it immediately into contemplation. If vision were the higher, man would have to do everything possible to arrive at it and, once there, to stay in it. The Son's contemplation, however, shows that this is not so. Vision is something borrowed from heaven and must be treated with the greatest discretion. It is like a spice which makes a meal tasty. But the meal is contemplation; it is what nourishes the soul. Perhaps one can say that vision has the effect of promoting better and longer contemplation. And that, even for the one to whom vision is granted, is its best effect.

4. MARY'S PRAYER

The Child

In her youth, Mary's prayer has two forms. First she is endowed with an attitude of prayer which is so much a part of her nature and an expression of her orientation to God that it is hers long before she can speak, long before she knows God. It is the attitude of the immaculate child, open to everything which presents itself to her and, since she is not touched by original sin, apprehending things with a great seriousness and an unclouded mind. And when for the first time she learns about God and hears his name, when she is shown how to pray and is taken to religious ceremonies, it all corresponds to what she already knows without words. As yet there is no complete integration; only as she gets older and learns more about God does she try to bring her attitude and practice of prayer into her whole approach to life, striving and making attempts which cost her a certain effort. In this she has no subjective feeling of success; she does not suspect that, in her, God is encountering God, that the attitude to life with which, in God's grace, she has been endowed is a part of the new prayer which can be fixed in words. She likes to pray and prays ardently, but because she is perfectly pure she is also happy to be without an expressly formulated prayer. Whatever she does leaves a door open to God. So she does not need to exert herself specially in prayer, nor to act with unusual ardor. Everything is natural, both her attitude in vocal prayer and her attitude outside of it. But as she prays and endeavors to root her prayer in her life, it is like a discovery of her true home: She enters an expansive sphere which suits her and which is her own. In bringing her personal world into the world of God she feels how well her own world fits in with God's—not in reflection, but in a natural, childlike trust.

And then she loves God and she loves the men and women she meets, and all that goes to make up her life belongs to this love. And love causes her to grow into an obedience which, for her, is nothing other than an expanded form of love. The obedience which she feels and practices toward God is for her an expression of her love. For Mary the child it is perhaps a matter of not wanting to hurt the person she loves, and hence obedience. Later, in a love that is more aware, it is an obedience that wants to show God that he can count on her.

Nothing she learns of prayers and religious exercises is alien and unintelligible to her or incapable of being harmonized with her life. In prayer God's sphere unfolds and opens out before her, and she is always aware that it is God's world. But she moves unconstrainedly within it. And whatever new thing she experiences complements what she already knows, expands it and makes it more beautiful.

The Growing Girl

As she grows up she begins to face her challenge. In some ways it is like a convert's struggle: He loves God and wants to serve him, and yet he knows that the present framework is insufficient, not ultimate. In no way can one say that Mary feels called to do something special or to be the "founder" of something. But she does know two things: first, that she must acquire as quickly as possible whatever can be "attained" by her own efforts, less through learning than through understanding; next, that she must be ready and that her readiness and understanding are two things which must go hand in hand. Her understanding is not so much the dogmatic kind as that which springs from the heart. It is made easier by the mystery which is in her life and which she senses will one day be a demand. As far as possible she does everything in the presence of God, openly. She permits nothing to find a niche in her that could create the least obstacle between herself and God. In this period, her prayer is above all worship, but a worship which delights in the theme of the promises to Israel, not because she wishes it so, but because that is what is presented to her. And in prayer she surrenders herself, dedicates herself to God: not with impressive promises, but by making sure that her open readiness matches God's expectation. And then she begins to make discoveries, everyday things like words she happens to hear, people she meets and her own signs of love toward others; and all these seem to her to be parts of a divine mystery that belong in prayer. She sees them less as fruits of her prayer than as things which must become part of prayer. She brings to God the little things she experiences, so that he may bless them. Perhaps she even offers them to him as tiny building blocks, as if she were aware that God has something in view and needs something like readiness. She brings it to him in complete naturalness and naiveté, yet knowing all the time that it is precisely what God asks of her and that what she is doing is not importunity but response.

Prior to the Angel's Appearance

Directly before the appearance of the angel Mary's prayer undergoes a kind of expansion. It is not in her but around her. She has the feeling that now she must pray with a greater sense of responsibility, for the world around her, if not more comprehensible, is more real, more challenging, making greater demands of her readiness for sacrifice. She shares in a prayer of the angels. No doubt she had it before, but now it has come closer. And now she knows something of how prayer is handed on and taken up. When her thoughts have to be completely occupied by some task which is not explicitly prayer, she feels that the real world takes up the prayer. God takes it up, but between God and her there are other beings to continue the prayer. She is also aware that everything is difficult and yet very good, that times for decision come and yet that the decisions have already been made. In all this she has no concrete intimation of what is to come. Nor can it be said that she changes. Only her capacity for understanding is enlarged. She is already burdened with something of the seriousness of the coming responsibility, but she is also given something of love's unbelievable confidence: She feels vulnerable and protected at the same time. Her prayer is like a risk, as if the more she feels secure, the more she must expose herself and ask God to do everything in her according to his will. It is not the "night" of the later mystics, and yet this risk, this uncertainty, is related to that night. She knows that assurances, security and protection must come to an end in favor of something else which will be safety in its turn, and must take her through the narrow valley of some event. It is as if the joy she experienced heretofore, mixed with a faint anxiety, must now be reversed, as if what was most her own has suddenly become unusable, as if God is no longer willing to give her in the future what he had given her up to now. In every respect she must keep herself ready for some new thing, feeling at the end of something which has by no means come to an end. Her life so far has been shaped like a funnel; now everything has narrowed in on her as it presses toward an event which will open up new vistas.

The Angel

The angel appears quite suddenly. She did not expect him, nor did she expect that she could become the Mother of the Messiah. But once he has appeared, it is clear that the time is fulfilled. Everything up to now has been a preparation for this. It is as if a vessel were full to overflowing, as if there were no room left in her for her to use. God requisitions the room, and the angel brings the fullness of God into it. As she has learned, as a growing woman, to look after her future household, so now she is taken over, in her spiritual and prayer life, for a new task. Those who observe her can see that she has all that is necessary for the new task, for everything in her has been oriented to this goal.

At the angel's appearance one can see that her attitude and her prayer are on the same level, totally interwoven with one another. She says Yes out of the fullness of divine graces, but she also asks, "How can this be, since I do not know man?"

Here she shows herself to be clear-headed, normal, knowledgeable and intelligent, as well as perfectly dedicated. She calculates in human terms but also throws everything into the divine balance: "Let it be done to me according to thy word." Natural and supernatural are here in equilibrium. Sobriety and rapture, the everyday world and the world of God, all have a place in her. The one does not exclude the other: It complements it. Her natural response that she must make and the supernatural one she is privileged to make are both part of that which God has placed in her and now requires of her. Both her natural and her supernatural life are now mature. And her response is the response of this maturity. Her supernature is not astonished to see an angel. This sight too is mature, and to her supernature it is natural to see the angel. But her normal reason does not place any restrictions on the supernatural: She is not a problem to herself.

Faith, love and hope have also ripened in her. The encounter with the angel is the fulfillment of her hope for the Messiah. This hope, however, was so entwined with faith and love that it did not obtrude itself; only at the moment of its fulfillment does it reveal itself as hope, hope for the Redeemer and hence the hope of every believer, and suddenly, too, this remarkable hope that it is she who is the chosen one. But precisely because she is chosen, this hope has an unpremeditated quality; in her humility it has never attained an objective form. Faith and love have grown up together and grown into her prayer. And now the Son will be the unity of her divine and her human love. She loves God and her neighbor. But up to now she has had no opportunity to love God in her neighbor and in her neighbor to love God. The Son will bring this about. And her faith has always been as ready as her love to undergo this expansion. Nothing in her is forced. Everything is part of a development in God's hands: He controls it, and she responds to it in a loving, childlike manner. At a certain level her assent corresponds to the surrender of a bride to her bridegroom. All that came before was attuned to this act. And here it is God himself who has brought the bride to her bridal maturity, jealously guarding and nourishing her faith and love.

Pregnancy

Just as the Spirit's overshadowing was above all an experience within prayer, so at the beginning of her pregnancy her prayer is particularly addressed to the Holy Spirit. Her natural faculties would never have sufficed to understand what was happening to her. But in prayer she experiences an infinite reassurance and receives a strength enabling her to bear both the natural and the supernatural. It is no longer the case that she first has to translate the natural experience into prayer: Now she must transpose her prayer into the natural order, to maintain a growing relationship to her pregnancy, which would be incomprehensible without prayer and which can only be accepted peacefully in the context of prayer. And out of her prayer to the Holy Spirit is born her new prayer to the Son. In the prayer to the Holy Spirit she experiences the reality of her condition, the reality of the Son's growing within her. This reality is both a reassurance and an expansion, and in her prayerful experience she steps into Christianity. At this period the Spirit looks after her like a bridegroom, finding and providing everything she needs in her condition. He is solicitous about her, and in prayer she feels this solicitude, not referring it to herself but to the Child in the certainty that the Father's Spirit will live in the Child, that God will do everything for the Child and that wherever her human powers are not enough, the Spirit himself will step in. But even where she herself has to be the Mother looking after her Child, she need not be

103

overanxious because the Spirit will inspire her and show her what to do; he will protect her for the Son's sake. And as for herself, whenever the Spirit requires it, she will be able to cope with the Child, not because she feels equal to the task but rather because she has a prayerful awareness of corresponding to grace. It is grace which, for her, is predominant over everything she is able to do.

She knows that the Son of God becomes man and is coming into the world through her, and in her prayer, both to the Spirit and to the Son himself, she participates not only in his external coming-to-be but in everything which she feels concerns him. She does not know his precise plan. But she knows that he is the Messiah, and she applies much prayer to him and his work. Even now she prays to the Father and the Spirit for him, so that when he stands beside her as a man he will have a treasury of prayer at his disposal through her; so that he will not feel so alone; so that, as a result of this amassed prayer, the distance between his being God and being man will be easier for him to bear; so that he will not always be meeting obstacles; so that, in her and Saint Joseph, he will not only have human beings with whom he can find peace and who are there for him, but through both of them will receive a bond of prayer with the Father, which is different from his vision of the Father and which is quite simply a prayer that understands in faith, a prayer of availability.

She also worships the Son. She accustoms herself even now to a kind of dialogue in prayer with him, a dialogue which in no way refers to herself but which contains something of the commandment of love which he will bring. And through him, through prayer with him, she learns to love people in a different way: in the way she imagines the Son will love them, as he would have them love one another. She allows this prayer too—and, through it, the Son—to change her, even if this change can never become concrete because she is already, through her preredemption and the grace of the Lord, a transformed person.

There is also a development in her pregnancy, since the Son's growth enables her to become more and more along with him. She *becomes* the mediatrix, which she was not really before. The very character of her prayer shows this. Moreover, the Son lives with her and is always revealing new things to her. She is exposed to fellowship with him. And since she is human and not divine she naturally experiences a kind of progress. However perfect may be the love which joins two human beings, its fruitfulness is always shown in the way each influences and changes the other, not merely because each endeavors to carry out the other's wishes, but also because each wants to be transformed by the other. Mary is a woman, and it is part of her feminine nature to want this particularly. And finally there is the expansion involved in the inclusion of the triune God, whom she knew formerly only as God the Father. All these new areas are opened up and pour into her prayer.

Birth

The prayer of birth is one of the most mysterious things because, in the case of the Lord's Mother, the experience that woman generally goes through at a purely physical level takes place within prayer. This experience of being burst and torn asunder, of being no longer mistress of her own body, of being surrendered to the power of parturition, which is more urgent, active and compelling than anything a woman has imagined—Mary experiences all this primarily as a form of prayer. God takes her word of prayer and in a way bursts it with his divine Word. She shares in something happening within her that is prayer and the birth of the Word, and she is born again into this newborn Word. If, prior to this, she always had an intimation of the distance between man and God, of the towering greatness of God and his infinity, now she is as if carried through this distance and placed in God's infinity: not she as a person, but the Word in her which is God's Word and yet hers. In prayer she experiences that moment when the promise becomes fulfillment. It is a stupendous vision of what is happening and what is communicated to her in prayer. She is thrust into God's absoluteness. So her prayer is like a woman's birth pangs, and in order to bring about this birth God needs his handmaid's word: her word of prayer, her attitude of prayer, her consenting passivity. Certainly all this takes place spiritually but in such a way that it is reflected in her body. In prayer she undergoes the delivery— her virginal body becomes the counterpart of her virginal spirit—and prayer and body are a unity belonging to God. She no longer needs to offer: He is in control.

But his control does not simply go over her head. He wants to involve all her powers. She is wrenched beyond herself, yet she experiences that it is still she. And the prayer which begins in anxiety, in the fear that she is perhaps not equal to it, is carried, as it were, through the phases of a normal birth, to emerge into a prayer of jubilation, overflowing joy and thankfulness, but also of amazed beholding. This, then, is her Child! She first experiences her Child in prayer. From out of her prayer he is placed in her arms, a fruit of grace, a divine fruit of her prayer. The more the Child is hers, the more he is taken from her because God has so taken over her prayer that it has become his Word. And now, without any mixed feelings or difficulty, in amazement, she can see in her Child the full reality of what she has carried in grace these nine months and also what God has done in her following the appearance of the angel: in the inseparable oneness of God's will and her surrender, of the fruit of her prayer and the fruit of her body. She will never try to distinguish between what is her Child and what is God under her roof.

She prays with the same words she is accustomed to use in prayer; but she prays with all her senses, and now she does so in the strength given her by the Child, in the power of supernature newly imparted to her by the Child, and with the first words which she will teach to the Child. And when she gives thanks, she does so in her own name but also in the name of all the generations before her and of those yet to come. The Child is God on earth. But she, at the moment of birth, is every human being on earth. And yet she is this particular one, the Mother.

Flight into Egypt

There are different layers in her prayer at this time. There is the family prayer that Mary and Joseph say together, vocally but also in their inner attitude to the Child. It is a prayer arising from their state of life, the state formed by the three of them, foster father, Mother and Child. In the Mother's case this prayer is influenced by her trust in Saint Joseph. It is a prayer for their life together, in which she asks God to bless all three of them so that the Child will really be in the right place and in the right hands and, as man and as God, will experience what he is expecting in Joseph and herself. This new prayer, newborn through the birth of the Child after it was already newborn through her life with Joseph, that apparently should have unfolded so peacefully, is now in great agitation because of the flight. Mary is both reassured and anxious. She is not anxious about herself but because of the threat to the Child and because she now must leave to Joseph what has so far been her concern.

She said Yes to the angel and thus took on a responsibility. But now the journey with all its suddenness and unexpectedness is entrusted to Saint Joseph. And she must learn once more to entrust herself to a human being, after having entrusted herself to the angel, the Spirit, the Father and the Child. It is as if she can never belong to herself but in her obedience must always be free to take on new commitments, commitments which appear suddenly and change just as suddenly, although God remains the Lord; although the Father watches over everything; although she must remain true to the Spirit. All this is the expansion of her prayer, since she disappears more and more into it. It also seems to be a restriction, since it takes her destiny, the amazing things she has gone through in pregnancy and birth and during the flight to Egypt, which in human terms is an act of daring, puts this destiny once more into everyday terms: the destiny of a woman who does what her husband commands. She must lay aside a certain sensitivity in prayer which she knew at the vision of the angel, in order to be ready to be guided by Joseph, following the dispensation he has been given.

And then there is a remarkable third layer, extending from the purely maternal, as found in every believing woman who has a child, to the completely supernatural. Praying all the time, she must take the Child with her as they flee, for he has been entrusted to her and she loves him as a mother loves her child. She takes him with her into the region of uncertainty and must ask Father and Spirit to look after him. But she herself must also summon all her human care and ask the Child himself, as God, to be content. Even as she looks after the Child, she must worship him. The Child in her arms, whom she is taking with her, is her God whom she must follow, to whom she has dedicated herself. She must somehow explain to him about Saint Joseph's intention of fleeing. But Joseph's intention is itself a divine intention, so that the Child disposes of this intention and Mary is at the disposal of both Joseph and the Child—yet she can still dispose. She must look after the whole human side; but it is so enveloped and encompassed by the divine, the impenetrable, that she could never describe its nature. So all she can do is to surrender herself again, even more, once more. And every thought that occurs to her while she prays, every vision she receives in prayer, every contemplation she makes, all move between the danger of the earthly path and the infinite security in God, between the uncoordinated Child in her care and the Messiah's guidance of all men. The field of prayer has become so wide that she seems to have been set down somewhere or other and prays there almost at random, the Father having given her the matter and manner of her prayer in the Spirit through the Child. And then she sees the dangers that threaten the Child as completely human dangers against which her anxiety and her woman's nature have no weapons; at the same time they are dangers that threaten faith, for the Messiah embodies the new teaching. But then she knows that God the Father will protect them, even if the God of eternity has chosen her to help in this task which she cannot envisage, for which she can take every possible measure, and yet none. So she is both the naked creature before her Creator and also the wise virgin in the service of the Son's mission. She has been fashioned and must help to fashion. In prayer she feels that God is waiting for her prayer, that he needs it, that she may call nothing her own because everything must go into this prayer and because she who loves the Son must surrender him. Her renunciation must now be performed not only in her own sphere and her own personality; even more is required: For the sake of the mission she must renounce maternal possession of her Son. The more complete this renunciation is, the greater is her opportunity of doing

God's will in truth. Only in this way can she grow into her mission, which she must be ready to relinquish in that of her Son so that not even her mission is her own.

The Childhood of Jesus

She is a young mother with her Child. Her motherhood and the Son's childhood and all their life with Joseph form a happy unity. Certainly it is overshadowed from time to time by images of the future, by what she knows and suspects of it; but it is not really clouded by this, for she also knows that she is to address the present because God the Father wants a prayer in this present time. She worships the triune God and the incarnate Son; she must continually take her motherhood seriously, acting toward the Child as a mother does, and yet she must take his godhead seriously. In prayer she knows very well that she is introducing something new: Christian prayer in the family. It has been entrusted to her, and it is a gift from God and hence a joy for her, well qualified to join her other joys of being the Mother of God and having the divine Child with her. But it is also a responsibility, for she knows that her whole attitude of prayer must be of service and that God will use her person and her attitude, communicating them to other mothers in order to shape a Christian attitude in the family and also a Christian attitude toward the Son for everyone who follows him, inside or outside the family. But now, in these childhood years, the family plays a special role. And Mary must ask God the Father to give her the Spirit so that she may treat the Son humanly as he wishes and initiate him into his human life as a good mother can, and also so that the Spirit may give her an openness to the Son's concerns so that she can respond to all of them. She knows that God will supply this giving and taking. Her prayer is marked by much joy and natural lightness, and even in the Son's presence she is completely spontaneous. It comes naturally to her to worship the Son; it is not difficult or problematical. Nor does she think that every mother somehow has the right to make a god of her child. Both joys, the maternal joy with her Child and the Christian joy with her God, unite naturally in her life and prayer. And when she thinks of the future and understands that the two of them will not be spared the hours of pain, she knows all the same that the present is a source of joy and that it would be ungrateful not to want to stay there awhile and enjoy it as God gives it. There is much thanksgiving in her prayer: for the privilege of motherhood, that things are as they are, but also for all those who have not yet experienced it. She includes them too, making room for them in her prayer, not only interceding for them but as it were praying with them in advance. She prays for what those concerned cannot yet pray for themselves, though it is due to them. She also knows that there lies in her motherhood a task for all mothers, and moreover that all generations will call her blessed, that now and henceforth she will appear to them as she is through God's grace. She lives hidden, yet in the openness of her virginal soul. Her prayer, transparent to God as she offers and communicates it to him, is at the same time offered and communicated to all Christian people, smoothing the path for the Son, an example which she simply and freely gives so that others will gain something from it.

In prayer she continually gives God control over her soul. She holds fast her happiness since God wishes it, but her holding fast is wholly in his hands, done in obedience and surrender. She holds fast in obedience, not in herself. And through her renunciation and the Son's activity she is always receiving new stimuli for her prayer. It never dries up. She lives from a spring that is fed, she knows, by her Son. She accepts it as naturally as her Son accepted her milk and accepts her care. It is a human exchange but takes place in God. And she takes what is human and divine in the Son to give it, in her prayer, both to God and to mankind.

The Search for the Twelve-Year-Old

It was a deep shock in her life when she and Joseph lost the Son, to find him again only after three days. It was much more traumatic than the angel's visitation. And although the Mother knew that she would find the Son again, she was given in this loss an anticipation of the Cross which was strangely reflected in her prayer. On the one hand it was a prayer of confidence: He is God and so he has gone on some divine errand. But it was also an anxious prayer: He has been put into her care and she does not know where he is. And this human anxiety is invaded by the much greater fear of the coming suffering: an anxiety about the Son and his Passion, a feeling that he has already started out on the path which ultimately leads to the Cross. This fear rears its head right in the midst of her everyday life and her God-given joy. She cannot regard it as something merely temporary—there will still be many long years of silence—but she must accept it as God gives it: a great anxiety, powerful, dark and certain to come. Suddenly, humanly speaking, she can scarcely bear any longer, even in prayer, to be the Mother of God, to have God for a Son, to be drawn through her assent into circumstances which are obscure, difficult and totally in God's hands. She becomes acquainted with sin, not as those do who commit it, but as it will come to light in the Son's bearing of it on the Cross: something strange, incomprehensible, gnawing at her internally so that it is too much, so that now she cannot finish even the most determined prayer. For prayer's task now is to lead her more and more into night, into what is simply unintelligible. It will carry her beyond her limits, taking her where something of God's eternity is, something which presents no countenance to her except that of nameless anguish and torment.

And when the experience is behind her and God once more requires her to take up her daily life, her everyday prayer begins again, secure in God. But her worship of the Son has changed. He is God who disposes, one who is all-knowing, who must go his own way in such a fashion that no man can understand it, who must be so faithful to his mission that it almost seems to his Mother that her own mission is shattered on the threshold of her Son's. Their pleasant, ordered life together has come to an end. It will resume, but in the lacuna she experiences the loss of him, the surprise of the Temple scene, the evidence of omniscient wisdom before the teachers and of his relationship with the Father, a relationship which, in spite of her knowledge of Father and Son, the Mother had not known existed in this fashion. Now she cannot forget it; she must take it into her prayer, which henceforth has become less sweet. God has treated her harshly. Perhaps one of the most difficult things is having to grow into a totally new trust which God gives her but which is not her original womanly trust. On God's initiative a new trust grows in her; *he* gives it, but, even more, it is asked of him. She stands apart a little from this trust, and her prayer is not entirely her own anymore. No longer is it the perfect refuge. Now, at least at first, it is an area in which she has yet to get her bearings, in order to be shaped anew and also in order to know that peace is not to be hers, that she is put into the hand of a God who ruthlessly makes use of everything that has been entrusted to him and who continually renews this trust so that he may demand it in a better, stronger, deeper, more radical way. A rent has been torn in her everyday prayer. It remains everyday prayer, but now it is expressly bracketed between the Temple and the Cross. Worship must remain as the worship of a God whose divinity is now better comprehended and who consequently has become more in-comprehensible. It is the worship of a God, too, of whom the Father requires hard things, worship which must also be a support, a support through the trials which Mary sees that the Father has prepared for the Son and through which she learns to reverence the Father and his will. She is to recognize that the Son does the Father's will and see what a severe burden it will prove to be. And in spite of this burden she is to give thanks, on behalf of the Son, of herself and of mankind. It is the prayer of an adult led by the Spirit, but also the prayer of the Spirit in her, of her spirit, molded by the Holy Spirit; the prayer of the woman fashioned by God in this way, who cannot be otherwise; the prayer of an I and a Thou at the same time. It is a supportive prayer, a prayer which is both longed for and yet a little feared, a prayer that contains so much of the divine—all the elements of trust, of gratitude, of necessary searching, of fearing, of obeying—that sometimes it seems utterly foreign. But the more foreign it is, the more the Mother knows that it is her prayer. This is how God wants it. It is right.

Alone in Nazareth

In the years she spent with the Son she had him so close to her that her prayer was visibly—visibly for her—supported by his presence. She had a share in his prayer and he in hers. This prayer was something self-evident, to which she had become accustomed. And praying was as much part of her life as any necessity; she never felt it to be an obligation or a compulsion. To her, prayer was as natural as talking to the Son. Now that he has gone away, her prayer has become an office, with the burden and the tangible demands that such an office brings with it. The immediacy of prayer with the Son no longer arises out of their shared relationships. She knows little about him. She seldom sees him and has little news of him. She cannot clearly envisage what kind of work he is doing and what his active life is like. The unfamiliar, unknown side of his life has gained the upper hand; no longer, as at home, is it regulated and punctuated by an accustomed order. She hardly knows anything of his surroundings; most of the people he meets are unknown to her; she does not know whether he is among friends or enemies, how he is proclaiming the Father's message to the people, whether he is attracting them, has disciples or is getting the help he needs. She only sees the huge burden he has taken on his shoulders; she feels lonely and knows that the help she can give him now can only be prayer. And so now her prayer must acquire more the character of regularity, of the fulfilling of an obligation. She must accompany the hours of the Son, with which she is no longer familiar. Now the daily routine and schedule which they once shared somehow enter into her prayer life. And all the unknown things find their place there, all the Son's anguish which she no doubt can see and imagine as the coming suffering approaches, although the details are hidden from her. Whatever she finds hard in her loneliness, forsakenness and insecurity has its place in her prayer. She does not ask for her own load to be lightened: She asks God to send her everything in such a way that it can serve a purpose. He is to accept her anxiety so that others may be helped, but also that God the Son, who is her Son as well, may be helped.

The Lord's divinity and the divinity of his undertaking have become more central to her. That which is of the Father, the Spirit and the Son, the impenetrable area to which she has no human access, which moves in her premonitions and hopes, which she has taken over intact and sealed, as it were, from the

Son—for no one can understand God in more than a tentative way, except for God himself—all this is utterly mysterious to her. The first mystery from God which she personally experienced took place in her body. Now the core of the mystery is transferred more and more into the life of the Son which is far removed from her, into his flesh and his spirit. A transposition has occurred. And she prays her way into this transposition, a prayer of love to God, a prayer of discipleship, a prayer which is also shaped by the far-off Son. Often it is pure worship, sometimes only anguish or pain. It is a prayer that is given to her but that she experiences, that takes place in her life: It arises out of her life and also imparts a new quality to it. In her prayer she is made clearly aware that she has given up living for herself, for she is often led where she does not want to go and cannot go. And in prayer she must continually come up against the boundaries of what is human and inadequate. In part this is so that, in her, the Son may experience human limitation, so that he may find in her the consolation he needs if he is to go on living among sinners, and so that in her, the redeemed one, he may see what the redemption of his Cross can achieve. All this goes on in her prayer and her life, but her life has become more and more prayer, and her prayer has become more and more the form of life given to her by the Son. She is totally transformed by this attitude of prayer, this obedience to the triune God, this renunciation.

And all things have undergone a revaluation through the Son's being away. In one sense they have been confirmed in their value since the Son's mission has come visibly into prominence, but in another way they have lost it because now they have no importance in themselves. And the Mother cannot herself decide what is important and what is not; she has to accept both as they are given her. Once she had the Son at home with her; now there is no Eucharist for her. He is alive somewhere or other, and in spite of everything she learns to live in his presence but in a new and different way: in that presence which, before he came, she knew as promise and which now, during his active life, she must learn to recognize as fulfillment, through and in prayer.

At the Cross

Now the prayer is wordless, all anguish. That is its starting point: It terminates in the Son. The Father and the Holy Spirit have been withdrawn from her. She sees her Son hanging before her, and as mother she is at the end of her strength as she shares his suffering, oblivious of everything that has gone before. Everything maternal in her is held together by the Son. She contemplates him and experiences his death. And she sees in it at the same time the death of her God. And yet it is as if, for her, the continuity between the Son of Man and the Son in heaven is broken. The connections fall apart. She sees the dying of her beloved Son and of the God she worships. She experiences the end of every world. She cannot connect what she is going through with any thoughts which might save or console her or indicate a new way through and beyond these days toward Easter; she has so been appropriated and drawn into the Cross that she simply suffers with the Son, nothing else. And her prayer is the prayer of shared suffering, nothing else. This does not happen in such a way that she plunges headlong into suffering, deliberately acquiring a collection of sorrows; rather, she is placed into suffering so that she may experience what no human being has ever experienced. Everything takes place in an acceptance of night. It is night, the night of her divine Son; she shares in his night, not in her own. She sees no fruit. She does not see, while he is dying, that he is redeeming mankind. She does not see this end as finite and limited but as something eternal: an endless end, an end which devours everything that is before her, including the past and the promises and the fulfillment and the meaning of her assent and everything contained in her life with the Son. Once she said Yes to an angel who asked her to be the Mother of the Messiah and to accompany him to the last. She has said Yes to what is now happening: Yes to all this horror and Yes, evidently, to this dying too. Her Yes seems incomprehensible to her, like a wall hemming her in with no exit, a wall which she knew about and which did not hold her back. She did not first make sure of a way out, so now the wall has the mastery and imprisons her on every side. She does not understand that she said Yes precisely to this. It is not asked of her anymore. From somewhere or other she hears the echo of her Yes. She knows it, but she does not know it. It is her Yes, but she never thought it could take on this shape. And yet now, at the Cross, it is as if she never knew anything else but that this would be the result of her Yes.

She sees, without understanding it, that the sin of the whole world presses on the Son. She is not aware in the same sense that this sin weighs on her at the same time. She is only aware that she is being obliged to carry something that she cannot carry. She is at breaking point because something has grown too big. She is powerless because something has sapped her strength. The disciples see their Master's end. They see it in a human way: The Lord himself called and invited them to go his way, and that is why they are now involved; now they stand in the presence of what is incomprehensible in their Lord and the incomparable course of their destiny. Their faith no longer sees; but their suffering is not primarily in the area of faith. And they were not able to stop what is now happening; it was stronger than they. But the Mother, by her assent, initiated and set loose the whole process. Her pregnancy, her giving birth, her fruitfulness have led up to it. She is weighed down by her responsibility; not as if she might say now, "I should not have said Yes", but in that she sees the inevitability leading from her assent up to the Cross. She sees it somehow hidden and yet revealed in the Son, in him alone and then again completely in herself. She sees it as a manly and divine destiny, and yet as her womanly consent. It hovers between the Son and her as if now he, now she had said the Yes. And everywhere there is anguish and obscurity and meaninglessness. Her prayer is like a violent opening of her whole being, like an assent which is no longer freely given but is imposed on her, taking total possession of her, body and soul. It tears her as no birth ever tore a woman. It requites her harshly as no mission ever requited its messenger. It stops her being what she was at the very point where she thought that there was something that she must—and might—accomplish.

And this prayer, this attitude, this anguish, find no answer. She feels neither protected nor taken into consideration nor in any way required to do anything. And when she looks at the Son it is as if she does not see him, for he cannot fulfill her gaze. She sees death. And when she hears him cry out, his cry has perhaps nothing to do with her soul any longer. She cries out too, but their cries pass each other by. There is no attunement, no reply. There is on neither side a "Look, I am with you", "Look, I am suffering with you." This is a togetherness as a heightened form of forsakenness.

And when the Son finally dies, he takes this anguish with him; but she is not aware of it. She sees only that he has now emptied his cup of suffering and that an end has been appointed for her somewhere in this anguish, an end which, for the time being, remains just that: an end.

It is as if the Mother not only joins in celebrating the Resurrection but also experiences something of it: Suddenly, out of the world of Holy Saturday which she has seen in a privileged way, she enters a world that is eternal life and perfect earthly joy at the same time. She is still taken up with all she has gone through and is completely exhausted physically, but all this changes so dramatically that she almost reels into the new world in a delirium of joy and thankfulness and bewilderment. Her bewilderment now is like her bewilderment at the Cross, but with its minus sign changed into a plus. In order to experience a joy of this kind in her prayer she must surrender herself, her prayer, the Son, her fellow human beings and everything she has gone through, in a great confusion of thanksgiving to God the Father, spreading it out before him and breaking out into new thanks, new joy over everything that bears features which she can in some way grasp. People and things have acquired a completely different aspect and are newly incorporated into her life.

Her joy is so great that it does not remain with her for an instant but rather communicates itself. She gives it to the Son, to the Apostles, very specially to John, to everyone she meets, even people she does not know. She gives it to God. She gives it to the Spirit. And with all its breathlessness, confusion and unexpectedness, this joy has the character of peace because in all events and experiences the Mother always receives something of the joy of eternity, the joy of the Father, and passes it on.

Her prayer is vocal and contemplative. Words pass her lips and are immediately taken up by God and refashioned, to be given a new timbre and combined into new harmonies: harmonies of eternity, which are fulfilled in the Father. And she who was otherwise so reserved and shy and never wished for prominence is now compelled by her own joy to go and be everywhere in order to share in the heavenly joy because she knows, without being able to explain it to herself, that she is everywhere a part of this joy. There would be something missing if she herself did not decide to go out and take a place of honor everywhere, with her prayer, her attitude, her vision and her words. If she held herself back at this point it would be like a withdrawal of responsibility, a refusal which would have diminished the heavenly joy. Now her joy is so much a part of the heavenly joy that it takes the initiative in supplying any lack, finding the missing words and completing the fullness. It is a prayer in heaven but also a prayer on earth: a new conjoining of heaven and earth, of God and men, of the mission and its fruit. Now her assent resounds everywhere, echoing like bells from place to place, coming true, realizing itself, spreading abroad, carrying the message. Her act of assent is fulfilled; the fruit is perfect. Once again she and the angel are in conversation; the Holy Spirit inspires it and the Son listens, and, listening, he once more finds the path to the Father, the path to his mission, to the saving of mankind. The Mother is the link in the chain which was reliable, which proved itself. And now, in God's answer to her prayer, everything depends only on this link, which is important because it is part of the divine chain. Often the necessity of this position almost escaped her, but now it is full of utter joy, a joy which joins that of Father and Son. Thus Easter becomes her feast.

After the Ascension

Her prayer at the Ascension is fundamental to all that follows; from it develops all her succeeding prayer. At the Ascension there is a kind of split in the Mother's prayer. On the one hand she sees the event with her physical eyes. But, seeing what human eyes can discern, she must renounce this kind of sight so that she sees only what the divine vision presents to her. She sees God going into heaven. She sees this infinite, radiant presence, come from out of eternity to live as a man among us, now, for her, taken back again into the light of eternity. What she sees can be called Christian doctrine: the Word, spoken in and to the world and heard by it; love, that was lived and gave itself; and daily life, in which a plenitude of the divine will always remained living. Now she sees it all transfigured, rising, ascending, transfigured in a light which is there to be received by her. She sees it bathed in a light of eternity that streams into today; clothed in a call to love which merges into love itself; in love's demand which is itself a response. In this moment she knows that it is all true, true in a way that belongs only to God. Every sense is fulfilled by a meaning which she cannot totally comprehend but which God supplies. And she has a share in this truth and this plenitude of meaning, not only because now it has all come true for her, but because she is the Mother of God and it is through her cooperation that everything has come true: because she has given herself, surrendered herself into this truth. And as in a rapid survey of the past, in which the details stand out as silhouettes that one can and perhaps even must now recall, so now all the various episodes are parts of a complete, perfect whole, microcosms with a vast content only now becoming visible, parts of that infinite truth which is love. And the Passion too and the Cross, and her own forsakenness and inability to understand, and her great anguish and her little anxieties—now all this shares in the truth of the Ascension. It has been put in a new light and has a fresh meaning. Everywhere everything is like a seed which overnight has become tree and fruit. Easter was the promise of a rich crop. Now, in the Ascension, the fruit is there, radiant and abundant.

Then, with John, she returns to everyday life. Once again she experiences the little things which are often questionable and uncertain; perhaps news comes from the communities that sounds alarming but also joyful messages of the spread of the teaching and the growing influence of the revelation. Whatever it is, for the Mother it is part of the Ascension, the fulfillment. Now her prayer manifests a luminosity which spreads to everything and irradiates all that is developing and not yet mature, not least so that she can see how it will look when it is complete and all fruits are ripe, so that she can delight in it already and regard her daily cares and joys in the context of the joy of the Ascension. She is not removed from participation; she is in a new condition in which she experiences less agitation and less fluctuation between joy and sorrow. God takes her prayer to a region where it lives from the Son's Resurrection. Values have shifted again, and the center of gravity lies in the Son who is in heaven. Her own destiny, the destinies of men, her love for them and for God—all is held fast where God wishes it to be, pre-illumined by the eternity for which it is bound. Now her prayer operates between the eternal vision of heaven and prayer on earth, in a place which God created specially for her in the Resurrection. She mediates graces and prayer and nearness to God. But she experiences these too; and what she mediates clings to her prayer, her thoughts and her understanding and is communicated to the person she touches in these various ways. For now she has the ability not only to see things as they are seen from eternity through the Son's Resurrection but also to impart something of this radiance to them, in order to mediate to men that faith which they are to have through the Resurrection, even if at present they cannot experience it as radiantly as the Mother does. But this is how that faith is in reality. Her truth has now become a Resurrection truth, her body has moved close to being assumed into heaven, and from now on until she too enters eternity, her prayer lives from the truth of the Resurrection.

When she prays to God the Father or the Son or the Holy Spirit, she worships in the truth of the Resurrection. Or when God requires or asks something of her, he always does so in the light of this truth which has been given to her. No longer does she need to stumble over her own lack of understanding. It has been taken away. In her prayer she is in the condition which corresponds exactly to God's intentions, which he makes known in causing her to appear as the Immaculate Conception.

Death

Her death is the shedding of even this final condition. The truth of the Resurrection remains the same. But it is no longer a truth which confronts us; now it is the truth in which we live, the truth which is so true that it includes us. It is not that heaven opens to receive Mary; it is open together with her. She is part of heaven's opening, she passes over, she is transposed; the divine presence of the Father, the Son and the Spirit is now the medium in which she lives. There is no point of transition, no coming to an end, no breaking off. Where previously there was multiplicity, suddenly there is the All, and there is no longer any need for a curtain to be drawn away. She lives in the unveiled truth of eternity. What she leaves behind is not really left behind her because it was never separated from the Son and because she sees and recognizes all her previous experience now in the Son, as his experience, as necessary components of his own life, as his truth and his glory. Just as the Son on earth does the Father's will, so she recognizes in the Son her own performance of his filial will. And men and their prayer find her afresh at the point where her assent is so expanded that what she once said to the angel is now said for the blessedness of all and for the salvation of all in the Son.

III

THE GROWTH OF PRAYER

1. THE CHILD'S PRAYER

A mother kneels by the bedside and prays with her child. He is so little that he does not yet understand anything. He only knows that mother takes him in her arms every day, puts his little hands together and then says something in a particular tone of voice. This has been repeated so often that it is now part of daily life. And if, once the child is bigger and has a better memory, she were to leave something out or change it, the child would be aware of something missing in this rite. The child has been initiated into prayer without knowing what prayer is; he only senses that something different happens here and that, since it is done in his mother's love, it is part of her love. It is a way in which the child experiences the love of the mother who is present and looks after him.

Very soon, however, the child's imagination expands so that the mother does not always need to be visible. He comes to understand that, even when she leaves the room or the house, the mother is still concerned with her child. She goes to prepare or buy him something and returns with something good for the child. Using this idea that invisibility can be something good, the mother can begin to explain to the child something about God. Here two things come together: the words of prayer and their explanation. And no one can tell which of the two first makes an impression on the child. Perhaps the mother tells him about the heavenly Mother, and gradually the child understands that this invisible Mother has qualities similar to the mother he can see. He grasps something of the heavenly Mother's love and concern for him and learns to associate these thoughts with his own mother's attitude of prayer and with the words she uses. The world of prayer is an invisible world, but it acquires a reality in the arms of the visible mother and in her words. Once he has opened his eyes to it, the child knows that this world has always existed, for his mother has always prayed; he grows into it as a matter of course. It is something right in itself, even if it is only partially understood. Then, for the first time, the child learns to pray with his mother. A few words are formulated, "Come Lord Jesus", or "Hail Mary"; and perhaps more through the request itself than through an immediate concern with the persons themselves, a contact is created: The child awaits a person who is coming, he greets someone, and these things take place before the child actually knows who is expected or who he is greeting.

Two new ideas then crystallize. The first is that there is a time for prayer. The mother determines and initiates it. This fixed point is part of the normal course of the day. The second is that he must put his hands together and do nothing else during this time. This can make a big impression on the child: At other times he uses his hands for all kinds of things, but when speaking to God it is not allowed. The child perceives that praying really is business.

And the mother prays. She knows how it is done, whereas the child does not yet know. So in her prayer she takes up the child's prayer. And she keeps on praying; she leads in prayer. She is able to pray and does so for the child as well. Yet her praying on his behalf does not dispense him from the obligation of being involved, of paying attention and following. Soon he will have to join in with the words. It will not be enough to say, "Hail Mary", and let his mother continue the prayer on her own. And even when he cannot remember any more he

127

must stay until all is finished. In this way he learns that within prayer there is a kind of distribution of roles in which each person must play his part from beginning to end. He understands this much at least: that they are praying. He may not understand what they are praying. But for the moment, understanding is not as important as being there and wanting to follow. Mother too folds her hands; she too does nothing else and must not be disturbed during this time, not only because the child is there, but because she must do so herself.

My mother tells me, the child, that other mothers pray with their children, too: children I know and those I meet on the street. She tells me that when we pray together she asks God to look after me and that God hears what she says, and not only what she says but what I say, too. He hears both things together at the same time. But he also hears all the words that all the mothers and all the children say. And all these mothers and all these children, who do not know each other at all, are still one big family because together they all belong to God and are heard by him. And the Mother in heaven looks after all mothers and children just as an earthly mother looks after her children. Perhaps I am struck by this especially and ask my mother how it can be: You have so much to do with your two or three children, and the heavenly Mother is supposed to care for everyone! This practical question which arises out of the child's experience can be an opportunity for him to understand the difference between earth and heaven, between the inhabitants of the visible and those of the invisible world. All these praying mothers and children can lead him to an understanding of the Church. Perhaps he asks his mother: Does it matter if I cannot say the difficult words and you say them for me? And mother replies: No, it doesn't matter; I pray for you, and you pray together with me; but you can also pray for me and for all children, for the children who have no mother to pray for them and show them how to pray. And you can also pray for all the children who forget to pray or for those who pray by themselves, for if you pray for them God will hear their voices a bit better. And of course the others pray for you too.

And since mother has told me that others pray too and that I must not disturb them while they pray, now I can see how they pray and how not to disturb them. And so she shows me that there are houses where people pray that are always open, where everyone who wants to pray may go in and be quiet. They must not be disturbed, but I can watch them praying, and I can pray there too if I am good and very quiet. It is not allowed to pray out loud there, as we do at home. But when we pray together with the others, the prayer is gathered up together, and there is more of it, like coins in a purse. And now I understand that it unifies things for God when many people pray together. Now I see that my mother was right when she said that many other people pray, children and grown-ups. And I know practically none of the ones who are praying here. But because of what my mother said, I know that they all still belong together and that God knows them all.

And then I am allowed to go to Mass or to some devotion that includes community prayer. Now the priest is there in the church, praying in the name of everyone. I do not understand his words, and everything is different from what we do at home. But I know that this is prayer too; I only have to be quiet and leave the prayer to him, just as, at home, I left it to my mother when I could not follow anymore.

Mother also tells me that I was baptized. She says that I was very little at the time and did not notice anything. But together they promised God that they would give me to him. And they made the sign of the Cross on me with water as a sign that I belong to God. And from then on, my parents and godparents

129

had to make sure that I really was completely his. It was as if God had said: When you are bigger you will live for me; until then the grown-ups must pray for you and look after you, so that the gate of heaven which was opened at baptism will never shut. Through baptism, my mother says, a person begins to rejoice in God, and we must always keep thinking of him because we belong to him already. And together with all the baptized we make up the great family of God. At baptism I was so small that I did not understand anything; the others understood in my place. But even they did not understand it all, for only God understands everything. And now when my mother takes me to church with her and shows me other children being baptized or tells me when the Savior comes down onto the altar at the Consecration, it is true that I grasp very little of it, but then even the grown-ups are like children before God when it comes to understanding. And everyone ought to pray a great deal, my mother says, and think a great deal about God—and this "a great deal" does not exclude a "more": In fact it calls for more. She says that the sacraments are part of prayer; they call forth from us a particular form of worship that reaches beyond our understanding.

Sometimes, if I have done something I ought not, mother says that God too is displeased, for God sees everything and is sad when we are not obedient and do wrong. We must say that we are sorry not only to our parents but to him too. She says that I must put things right again before I pray, when I begin to pray. And I realize that being bad is the only thing that can disturb the relationship with God; otherwise I can be happy and play as much as I like, and everything is all right. Play does not take me far from God. The way back to God is no longer than it was before. I am with him right away. There is no distance between daily life and God, only between sin and God.

When I ask God's forgiveness for something and promise not to do it again, then perhaps I understand better how important it is to cooperate. If I do it again, I cannot say: Why didn't God stop me? It is my own fault. And it is up to me to keep in mind that I asked for forgiveness, especially if I have the desire and the occasion to do wrong again. I must be steadfast so that God can better keep me away from it. Furthermore, I become acquainted with punishment and penance. On the one hand, I have deserved punishment not only from my parents but also from God, and mother can punish me in God's name. On the other hand, in order to do penance, I must learn to do without certain things. I must do penance for my own fault, then on another occasion perhaps for some other child who did not ask pardon of God, and now it is as if the dear Lord has a punishment or a penance which no one wants to accept. I could offer myself and spare the guilty person. One often knows on whose behalf one has taken on prayer and penance, but often not. Perhaps the child knows which other child it is who does not pray or is naughty and can thus take something upon himself. Or perhaps only the mother knows. Or no one knows. In this way the child experiences something of the invisible Church and the communion of saints.

And then there are the things we can do that make others happy, like putting flowers in front of a statue of the Mother of God or decorating an altar with them. All I know is that God lives here: Mother explains how he comes although he cannot be seen. And he is glad to see his home made beautiful. He is glad when people let him share in their own joys. So, whenever I have a lot of flowers, I will give some of them to him; then he will share in my happiness about the flowers I have picked. There are other things that I cannot give him: my chocolate, for instance. In that case he is glad if I make another child happy by sharing it with him. But the people who come to church are glad too; they are glad because the Lord is glad and also because they are experiencing something beautiful. Or perhaps they have come to church sad, and when they see the flowers it cheers and uplifts them, and they are better able to talk to God.

Through all this the child learns how all the day's events, pleasant and unpleasant, can be linked with the thought of God. Furthermore he learns that he does not need a special occasion for praying and thinking about God. He can pray not only in words that he has learned, not only in moods of repentance and of joy, but as it were for no reason at all, simply to be with God and to become better acquainted with him, dwelling perhaps on the thought that he too was once a child with his mother, that he picked flowers and liked to go for walks, that he was delighted with some beautiful thing and sad when children were unkind to one another, that he participated in the whole world of a child. And at the same time this Child was God himself, and so he understood everything much better and loved much more. In everything a child does he must always reflect on how Jesus did it. Often the child does not know how he ought to do something, but he only need look at the Child Jesus and immediately it will be clear. Jesus too, for instance, would not have continued playing but would have gone to help his mother. In this way the Child Jesus becomes the child's playmate and life companion.

2. THE DECISION TO PRAY

For a time the child lives in a prayer that is handed down and learned, that was given to him by his mother and that later, while he is still under the care of his parents, will be taken up by the Church through catechism and the classroom. A slight tension can arise here between the long-familiar prayer at home, supervised by his mother, and the new instructions on prayer which the child receives from the Church's representative. Part of his school work is to learn this or that prayer, and not only to learn it but actually to pray it. The child obeys and does both. Almost always the two coincide: The priest admonishes the children not to go to sleep without commending themselves to God and their guardian angel, and that is precisely what the mother has done with her child. He learns to build a bridge between the family and the Church.

Eventually a time comes when the child wants to appear before God not only through the guidance of others but by his own decision, not distancing himself from his mother or the Church, but sensing that now he is bigger and must gradually assume certain responsibilities before God. He will naturally start with what he has learned and develop it. But he will also add something of his own. At this point the child's first confession can play an important part. The child prepares for it together with his mother, and she knows all or most of what he has done. And yet he begins to understand that he is accountable above all to God. From now on it will not be so essential to tell his mother everything, for now the most important thing is that the confessor knows it all. This gives him a sense of independence, of distinct personal identity before God. Perhaps it is in preparing for confession that he will say prayers which have not been given to him; he will say his penance and will be asked to do something voluntarily over and above it. He may speak to his mother or the priest about it, but he has acquired a new awareness of what is required and what is possible in terms of prayer. From reading or talking to others, he also learns of vocal prayers which are new to him, which appeal to him and which he takes up for his own use.

He will have concerns of his own and will pray about them.

Perhaps they are numerous, giving rise to a whole chain of prayers. Children's prayer can often be very long and complex because they go through each individual point separately and are inclined to make a fixed and unalterable rule out of the task before them. There is a danger in that. But if all goes well the child will learn from it that merely to recite vocal prayers is not enough. One is not supposed to start a kind of prayer collection—for children do like collecting things—and there should be no room for the feeling that a predetermined list must be completed, as if anything missed out must be made up again. One must not allow prayer to be clouded over by worries about correctness or completeness, as if form and numbers were suddenly more important than content. The value even of vocal prayer lies in its content. It is enough to dwell upon the word, letting it have its full meaning, trying to put one's whole soul into it. Another danger would be, instead of counting prayers, simply spending a fixed amount of time in prayer. This would lead to a scrupulous distinction between hours of prayer and hours of non-prayer and the fear of excluding something from the allotted time. If in prayer a person dwells totally upon the content, something of the content and the attitude of prayer will necessarily stay alive in his daily occupation. Of course it is a good custom to have a definite time for prayer. But its fruitfulness is not dependent upon its length. Even though a great variety of prayers may seem worth praying and attractive in their formulation, there is still a danger in collecting them. And the Our Father should never be displaced by any such wealth of material, for that is the prayer the Son has recommended to us. Remembering this, one begins to enter into the Son's attitude of prayer, to perceive something of his intention in praying and to understand his state of mind at the time when he taught this prayer to the Apostles. Then our prayer becomes as though enveloped

134

in his vision; the simplest prayer, to which we believe we have added nothing of our own, acquires a contemplative side originating in the Son's prayer. It is as if the Lord had given his prayer an advance out of the treasures of his contemplation. From the very first word, he beholds the Father, and each subsequent word unfolds out of a perfect plenitude which in his case comes from vision and in our case is to come from faith, from a faith which lives and is continually nourished by him and his vision and which has the power to fill our prayer with something of his vision. In faith a conversation with God is initiated in which God replies in a way that is similar to the way he reveals himself to the praying Son. The words we use in prayer are not merely profane, everyday sounds addressed to a God who remains concealed in his heaven but words which have mysteriously participated in God's Incarnation: words of heaven which are given to us, which live from the Son's substance, which have received something of him that remains in them, filling them with life above and beyond their earthly capacity and temporality. Their limitations are suspended because each word is freighted with a heavenly content which, from the outset, directs it toward God.

Now the person at prayer can accept in its totality, as it were, this element of vision which resides in the words; he can plunge his whole prayer into it and let his attitude of prayer be governed by this contemplative aspect. He can also go from one word to another, dwelling on each one which unveils something of this vision to him; beholding the vision, he can utter the words and sentences in a reverence which comes not only from the thought of standing in the presence of God but essentially from knowing that the Son has spoken these words in his vision of the Father and that they are infused with his love, his worship and his obedience to the Father. One can use this thought as a starting point, a prelude, a way of attuning one's own prayer; or one can include it in one's prayer, praying everything in its light. Thus one can pray as one reads the printed page. One can attend to the black print, only indirectly noticing the white interstices and broad white margins; here the black represents the vocal word, the white, contemplation. Or one can attend to the white itself and contemplate it expressly; then the letters appear more separate, each in its own setting, and one can look now at this one, now at that. In this way vocal prayer becomes a constituent of contemplation.

When the Christian discovers, as he matures, that vision and word can be united in this way, he is immediately faced with the question of the relationship between these elements. One cannot dwell forever upon the contemplative aspect during vocal prayer; its very nature requires that one make progress. And yet each individual sentence provides enough material to fill the entire time of prayer; and at the end one would still be at the first word. A glance at the Son will help us out of this dilemma. His prayer is vocal and his spoken prayer is accompanied by a vision which does not disturb the progress of his vocal praying. But in his nocturnal prayer he reserves a special time for contemplation in which he is not restricted by the rule of the succession of words. The Christian will act accordingly. He will cultivate both forms. His delight in the newfound contemplation will not lead him to give up vocal prayer, nor will his joy in vocal prayer cause him to relegate contemplation to exceptional times such as major feast days. Everyone who decides to lead a life of prayer will have to attain a particular rhythm and balance. In religious life it is prescribed by the rule; in secular life it must be sought and fashioned by each individual personally.

Many people never arrive at this decision because they have never recognized the beauty of prayer. Therefore young people who become aware of the possibility of independent, personal prayer should seize this moment of their lives and consider very seriously the significance of what is revealed to them here. They have been addressed by God, and they have personal access to God; they can speak to him face to face, see their lives and the whole of creation with his eyes and immerse themselves continually in his light. A door has been opened to them, and for the rest of their lives they are free to enter. Many decide not to, and so the life of prayer in its fullness and depth remains closed to them. They do not get beyond the child's stage of reciting vocal prayers. Consequently, their prayer life lacks the power to penetrate the rest of their existence with the truth of faith. At this point it is almost essential for them to talk with a spiritual advisor about their prayer. Like everything else, the life of prayer has its own rules which are known to the Church through experience and which cannot be disregarded. These include the relationship just mentioned between vocal and contemplative prayer. Humility belongs here too, lest one should be guided in prayer solely by one's own enthusiasm or by a dry self-righteousness; this humility must acknowledge that the Church is the mistress of prayer, that she can show her children how to pray properly, and that anyone who declines her teaching in order to build his prayer with his own re-sources is in the greatest danger of going astray. In any case the Christian does not pray as an individual but within the Church, within the praying community of saints, participating in their treasury of prayer. And just as this treasury is not a kind of emergency reserve in case one's own private store gives out, but rather a seed which is to germinate in each praying soul, so too the Church's experience of prayer is the earth in which the Christian plants his personal experience so that it may strike root there and draw strength from it.

If he has faith, the person who decides to pray already knows that he is not entering a purely private relationship with

God; he knows about prayer's fruitfulness and that praying itself serves to increase that fruitfulness. Like everything else about him, his prayer must be Catholic, especially what is most personal in his relationship to God in prayer. This most personal aspect, in its fruit, is to be at the disposal of the Church, of all believers and all who do not yet believe. For that reason, he who prays should let himself be directed toward the greatest possible fruitfulness. He should be willing to be shown how to pray better. Of course, guidance should never force him; to a large extent the correct nature and proportion of his prayer will become evident in prayer itself. But if he were to be comfortable and satisfied with his own insight, it would be a sign that he did not possess the true openness of contemplation. For the Christian, openness and humility before God are always openness and humility before the Church too. Christian contemplation lives not only by the power which comes from the Father and is at work in the Son but also by the vision of all contemplatives, all believers, by the contemplation of the whole Church, which has a common fruit and to a certain extent a common experience. Thus a physician can specialize in one organ, but unless he also has a comprehensive knowledge of medicine, or if he is so convinced of his own competence as a specialist that he no longer keeps up with contemporary research, he will cease to be a good doctor.

The Christian knows that he can never be an isolated individual before God. He must share in the fellowship of the Holy Mass, and he must let himself be nourished by the grace of the sacraments which provides both sustenance and direction for his prayer. At the outset he is drawn away from every kind of solitariness and every sectarian tendency into the center of the ecclesial community. Thus, in adulthood and in the approach to it, the Church is more and more the place where what is personal and understood in prayer is further opened up to the contemplation of what is greater because the community understands and receives more than the individual and, as the Church, preserves the gift of contemplation for each individual. Outside the Catholic Church, prayer is more exclusively personal and is hence much more exposed to human limitations. Since it lacks the ecclesial dimension it also lacks the fullness that is attained through contemplation. The Protestant cannot be acquainted with contemplation in the same sense as the Catholic because he is without the Mass, the sacraments, the priesthood, the whole tradition of prayer. If someone outside the Church were to try to penetrate into contemplation, he would not get very far because he lacks the Church's treasury of prayer, which is filled with the Son's vision and the prayer experience of all the saints and the faithful.

3. THE PATH TO THE LIFE DECISION

When the Christian avails himself of the Lord's words in his prayer, he understands that he is being drawn into the Son's dialogue with the Father; consequently, it is not enough to repeat the words outwardly. Instead, his whole attitude toward life, like the Son's, must grow into harmony with the words. To use the Son's words and then to turn around and do things which are totally incompatible with them would be a contradiction which would tear his life apart. He knows that when the Son speaks with the Father he abides in union with him, even when his words have died away. The dialogue is not broken off; he is always in the Father's presence, and all that he does is accomplished in that presence. When a person concludes his prayer with an "Amen", he does not return to the isolation of a private existence.

Of course, as a beginner in prayer he cannot enter at one stroke into the full, all-embracing attitude of prayer. The young person in particular, if he takes it seriously, will suffer from a certain discrepancy between prayer and life. He feels distracted in his life; he thinks he is going away from God, and he does not find the harmony between the two worlds. Perhaps he endeavors to bridge the hours between his times of prayer with little islands of prayer. Quick reflections upon God, brief thoughts of him, a few words addressed to him, a glance upward from the daily round to the world of God—all these are designed to link together the longer times of prayer. On the whole this bridge consists perhaps less of words than of intentions, of the desire to do everything in God's presence and to let him share in everything. Increasingly this desire becomes the expression of a more settled attitude which seeks more single-mindedly for God, determined to do nothing except in his sight and under his guidance. Sooner or later the believer will notice that this attitude, this longing for God, becomes less and less distinguishable from his attitude during the actual time of prayer. The longing arises out of prayer and leads back to it; thus it is doubly dependent on it and can neither be evaluated nor attained except as the effect of prayer.

When prayer bears this fruit and leads to increased prayer, the person knows that God is blessing his endeavors. The earlier danger of taking too much time for prayer out of his day and of taking such boundless delight in prayer that it comes into conflict with his other obligations has been overcome through obedience. Now he might encounter another danger: The ongoing relation with God in his work which he has experienced as a fruit of his prayer could seem sufficient in itself and lead him to shorten or even omit his time of explicit prayer. But this same experience will prevent that from happening. He remains close to God in his daily round only so long as he keeps to his times of prayer. The fruit of his prayer, the character of prayer that his work possesses, is vouchsafed to him only if he continues to cultivate prayer. It is by virtue of this prayer that his attitude in routine matters acquires an aspect which makes them seem like a continuation in God's presence, and his daily work is blessed so as to afford completely adequate transitions between prayer times so that he need not tear himself from activity in order to pray, nor from prayer in order to pursue his activity. The two are so integrated that he both prays and works in a unity of being and spirit. The one flows into the other without interruption or contradiction. And yet externally the times remain separate. The effortlessness which has been achieved does not imply a loss of all distinction, as if prayer were simply dissolved in life and replaced by work.

Then the young person comes to see that in deciding to pray he has already made a prior decision. Because of his prayer at particular times, all his times have undergone a change. His prayer accompanies them all; without really noticing it he has decided to live as a Christian all day long, not to withdraw from the Lord anything of his daily occupation. All the day's activities are under God's influence and lived in God's light, those of today and of every day on which he prays. And since God has given him his life as a totality, he looks on it as such and expects of it a total result which ought to depend on a total decision. Now his previous prayer seems to have been provisional. He chose and fashioned his prayer; prayer followed spontaneously on prayer, and everything was right and good. But through prayer he has changed. Until now he has, as it were, given his time of prayer to God and received the

141

intervening time from God as a gift. Now he knows that this gift includes a demand. He must unite his life, also, to his gift of prayer, extending that same decision to his life. He must gather up his whole life and spread it out before God, offering it to God whole and receiving it back from God whole, imbued with a new meaning. His prayer was training, and now the question is: for what? For a life, certainly, which is to belong more and more to God. Although he cannot demand that God reveal his will to him at every moment in every detail, he does know that if he offers his life wholly to God, he can be entrusted with a mission from him which will be the core and content of his life and which will provide the orientation for his activity.

In this stage the young person is very much alone with God. The watchword is, "God and the soul". It is a wrestling with God for the meaning of his own life before God. It is the path leading up to his "life decision". Now a deepened contemplation is required, a contemplation above all of the life of Christ. This contemplation must exclude the danger of subjectivity—even where well meant and pious—in making the choice. It must be undertaken in response to the challenge of the gospel and in its light. And in contemplation the person must at least attempt to envisage the various paths of Christian life. The will of God which determines and unifies a Christian's life cannot be discovered in the light of personal whim, nor even in the light of one's subjective relationship with God, but only in the light of the gospel which contains the objective standards of the Christian life.

The young person inclines in general to a subjective religion. Once he has passed the stage of merely vocal prayer, he may draw his whole personal life into his prayer in an emotionally charged form. He would thus be in danger of falling into a one-sided religious personalism. Then he sees the danger—or he must be made aware of it—that everything will become narrow unless he has recourse to examples set forth in the gospel. Only the gospel is able to mediate to him the true content of Christ's words to the Father and to indicate, by reference to his commandment of love, the true place of the neighbor in his prayer. There is personal prayer, but everyone prays within the chorus of the community. There is a unique relationship with the Lord, but it must always take its measure from the relation of all men to the Lord, particularly that of the Apostles as the Gospels record it. And on the other hand Scripture provides a total picture of the Lord: It shows the person who prays to whom he is really turning, how the Lord wants to be addressed and how he likes to reply. If a person thinks he can pray without the Spirit and the inspiration of Scripture, his image of God will contract and will be in danger of becoming very one-sided and incomplete. Prayer does not necessarily have to bear a directly scriptural stamp, but, whether imperceptibly or evidently, prayer is broadened by reading Scripture, and it cannot help being more in touch with the Church's tradition as a result. In a living manner, tradition fills the gap between the Lord's time and the present. And the Christian, as a man of today, is bound up with the gospel, not in a timeless manner, but through a living chronological order. This order does not interpose itself between the Lord and him; it does not separate them but connects them. It incorporates him into the chorus of all those who have come close to the Lord in the gospel. It forms a bridge of people at prayer, conveying the person who is at prayer today into the Lord's presence. Much of what he prays would be unthinkable, except that countless people have prayed before him and a whole development of prayer has taken place in the Church. The spirit in which a person today reads and contemplates the gospel is partly a product of his own time and partly a product

143

of tradition, and part of it comes directly from the gospel and, through the reader, shapes new tradition. He receives much of what tradition communicates through the Church's Magisterium, which presents Scripture and tradition to the Christian of today in a living form, and he will be attentive to it in seeking for the objective norms of Christian life.

In contact with the gospel, the person who prays discovers that the Apostles whom he reveres and the disciples and believers whom he encounters also made a life decision in faith. Mary Magdalene, for instance, sins no more, and later she is to be found among the women at the Cross. In encountering the Lord, all of them have been given a new meaning for their lives, and far from returning with it to their own concerns and putting it to use as seemed best to them, they fulfilled this new purpose by following the Lord. The encounter with the Lord— which for the Christian takes place primarily in prayer—had for them a meaning which changed their whole lives, not only in a hidden, interior way, but so that all the external things too were newly ordered. It was a transformation, a breakthrough, a cutoff. So he who prays knows that his discipleship cannot be purely spiritual but must refashion his whole being; he must not live aimlessly and randomly from one prayer to another, but all his prayers must be rolled up into *one* sense of life and placed in the hand of the Lord for him to judge and dispense at will. The moment comes when, instead of making countless small decisions arising from prayer or reading, he must gather up everything into one decision. And he perceives that, to do this, he shares in all the graces which the Lord gives to his own: that baptism and the Eucharist and the outpouring of the Spirit have lost nothing of their power, that everything is as full of life as in the Lord's time, and that Christendom has not been exhausted by being sent out into all the world.

Up to now the person praying has thought primarily of his

own concerns and brought them to the Lord. Now he sees that the Lord comes to him with his divine concerns and wants to appropriate his life for those purposes. He has experienced the Lord's blessing upon his personal life. Now he must allow the Lord enough room that the Lord will bestow on him his mission as well.

4. PRAYER AND THE CHOICE OF VOCATION

The encounters between believers and the Lord reported in the Gospels always led to a kind of choice. This is least explicit where he spoke to the crowd or where he met people to whom he gave no instructions and no recommendation to change their state of life; what choice means here is that the Lord gave to the person concerned a new fullness of faith without giving him a different direction in life. The believer was infinitely enriched after this encounter, which was comparable to a prayer capable of having an ongoing, incalculable effect on him. The memory of this meeting kept leading him back to prayer; that, for him, was the decision.

In rare cases the Lord turned someone away who wanted to follow him more closely, and outlined his place in his previous state of life in the world. This happened to one man for whom the Lord had performed a miracle and who had suddenly acquired faith. This man's task was to stay in his accustomed sphere and to let his allotted portion of the word come to fruition there.

But there are others whom the Lord invites to follow him outright. They are to leave everything, and the Lord takes all responsibility for them, in every respect looking after the life entrusted to him. He molds this life as he sees fit. Here it is much more evident how the encounter becomes prayer, for here the very state of life becomes a standing with the Lord, an abiding in the Lord which includes countless new and fruitful meetings with him. And if he thus accepts someone, it is forever, not on probation or until some future dismissal. A person invited in this way has, as far as the Lord is concerned, an irrevocable state of life.

Whereas all the Apostles were called by the Lord without having offered themselves, the rich young man introduces himself. He offers himself. The others are enabled to accept the Lord's conditions, even if they are unspoken, on the basis of his call. This young man, however, comes on his own initiative, and only then does the Lord stipulate conditions. He comes unbidden, and hence the call and conditions do not include each other. And yet this unity must be achieved if discipleship is to become a reality. The invitation to create this unity lies in the command, "Go and sell all that you have", so that he will be on equal footing with those who heard the call, "Follow me." When the bridegroom calls the bride, knowing that she loves him, then in his "Come to me", he counts on her love; he bears her love within him, and he takes responsibility for all that will happen through her coming to him. But if he is not sure whether she loves him, and she wants to come on her own account, he must first show her what his life is like and see whether she is happy with it. She must not come with her own notions and stay with him while abiding within her own ideas; she must be divested of everything in order to take on what is his. Whether the new house be rich or poor, the things that she has been accustomed to will no longer apply. By his call to the Apostles the Lord becomes the guarantor of their love which is to come. He sees them as he saw Nathanael under the fig tree: without guile. He sees them as they truly are, that is, as they can become in him. In the case of the rich young man, however, he sees him in his entanglement, his wealth, his habit

146

of owning things. But since the young man asks, he explains to him, and within that explanation he makes the demand. And since the explanation is not clear to the young man, he also refuses the demand. It is all a question of prayer. The rich young man did not pray in complete nakedness of soul. His prayer was in keeping with his accustomed background; interiorly he had never parted from it. When the call came to him it came up against this unity of man and thing, of goodwill and worldly habit. The prayer of the choice of vocation presupposes complete nakedness: "Just as I am, Lord, and as I can become through you, I wish to serve you. But what I can become through you lies in your hand alone, so much so that nothing of what I was formerly matters to me anymore; all that I am and have is at your disposal." In the prayer of vocational choice more than anywhere else, the maxim applies: "No man can serve two masters." No one can decide for God and for himself at the same time, offering himself and yet holding something back. The rich young man wants both the Lord with what the Lord can offer and himself with what he possesses.

The prayer of the choice of vocation is the prayer of complete readiness and nakedness. Nothing may come between the soul and the Lord; everything belonging to the soul is as though loosed from it, in a suspension that leaves all decision to the Lord. Things are so far removed that one can either leave them completely or take them up again with the Lord's blessing; one waits for a sign from the Lord which will determine what kind of renunciation or relationship to things is called for. Certainly, the purer the inner renunciation in one's heart and the more absolute one's indifference to all prior material or spiritual wealth and to all that one is used to, the more surely will the ground be prepared for the Lord's call and assent. And if the inner renunciation is perfect, the Lord will recognize his work in it and call the person who is practicing renunciation. If he is really in earnest in his indifference it will be a sign that the grace of the Lord has brought it about in him. Consequently, indifference can only be achieved in contact with the Lord, that is, only in prayer. A mere superiority over the things of this world would be insufficient for a Christian choice, since the Lord could not send out his call into such a context. The Lord's will can be comprehended only by the person who prays and who, at this stage of his life more than ever, can surrender himself totally to the Lord.

Even if the choice is for marriage, it must take place within prayer: all the more since, if it was a genuine choice of one's state of life, the religious state was not excluded at the start. The same prayer encompasses both states. Of course most people who choose marriage would be astonished to hear that they should have reached their decision based on a prayer of indifference. For them, most of the determining factors are natural motives; only subsequently, often as an afterthought, do they look for a blessing from God. Such a procedure may be common, but that does not mean that it is right. The value of an actual decision about one's state of life should be made evident to everyone, at least to Christians. If the choice of marriage was made in prayer, God's blessing is upon it right from the start, and there is a guarantee that something of the prayer which pervaded the time of choice will be carried over into marriage and remain living in it.

Of its nature the religious state is a constant encounter with the Lord; therefore it is essentially prayer, whether the form of life is more active or more contemplative. Hence the care with which those in religious life are introduced to and guided in the life of prayer. Whereas in the secular state of life the path on which a person meets God personally is left largely up to him, there has to be a certain method to it in the religious state.

But since a proper choice of one's state somehow potentially includes the possibility of religious life, or better, since it is essential in reaching a decision that the person experience that encounter with the Lord which is further developed in religious life, a certain introduction to and guidance in prayer is advisable here too. The young person must not think, "If I choose religious life, that will be time enough to seek guidance in prayer." He should possess a genuine knowledge of prayer even before making his choice of life. In his heightened subjectivity the young person in particular, in attempting to make his decision in prayer without supervision, has no guarantee that he will choose objectively. He needs the advice and direction of an experienced priest or a retreat given by an experienced vocation director. These are ways in which he can proceed safely and avoid the danger of acting upon a short-lived enthusiasm, or of thinking that the unusual amount of prayer and the feelings which characterize the period of choice are proof of being called, or the danger of confusing God's supernatural and perhaps tangible nearness with a particular vocation.

At this time of decision a person should withdraw from the world interiorly and, better still, exteriorly as well. He should try to gain a certain distance from things, to cast off the husks of everyday which have enveloped him until now. And this distance must be prayerful. Here his own life seems somehow foreign to him; the essential separates from the inessential, and the eternal perspective becomes clearer. A feeling that was previously experienced perhaps during a vacation grows stronger. But this sensation is not a sign of a calling, even if it occurs during prayer; nor is a certain pleasure in this new situation, released by prayer, by time spent with the gospel, by a feeling of lightness and elevation. Even this feeling is not to be confused with a genuine, supernatural inclination or suitability for a particular state. Very often a vocation retreat can elicit a powerful enthusiasm for all high ideals, which does not facilitate the clear view of things which the choice requires. Rather, in order to be objective in his choice, the retreatant should return to dry prayer and adopt a deliberate sobriety. The fluctuations in prayer prior to the choice can also provide clear indications to the counselling priest as to the kind of life for which the person is suited. Naturally the subsequent life of prayer in a religious order, embracing the whole man and his whole life, with all his different moods and states of health at every stage of life, provides many more opportunities for discernment than the short days of a retreat. But to a practiced director and confessor the very smallest signs of disgust are visible and he can evaluate them much better than the person who is inexperienced in prayer. The latter will draw conclusions from his consolations in prayer which are quite different from those drawn by the director, who, as well as his own personal experience, has at his disposal the vast experience of tradition. Just as the Church contains a treasury of prayer, she also contains the epitome of all forms and states of prayer, which is somehow revealed to the priest on account of his priestly office. If a sick person wanted to be his own doctor, he would treat himself quite differently than would the physician, for the subjective symptoms are almost always misleading as to the nature and extent of the actual trouble. It is true that the retreatant attains distance from his life, but not from his prayer. Only the priest, who stands outside the retreatant's life and prays with him, can do this. Of course it is necessary for him to pray too, for one cannot judge the prayer of a person under one's care except from within an accompanying fellowship of prayer. In return for his right to intervene creatively in others' prayer, the priest gives his own prayer and his Christian readiness to serve. Once this premise is accepted, the director can also pay attention to externals: whether the retreatant prays at length or briefly, willingly or reluctantly, in dryness or with fervor. He has the right to question the retreatant about his prayer, a right which arises from prayer itself. It is in fact his duty. He questions within the context of their common conversation with God. All the spiritual director's efforts are designed to bring about a complete openness to God in the retreatant's prayer—an attitude closely related to that in confession. Retreat prayer and retreat confession belong together. Of course there is a certain discretion in the retreat. But enough must be disclosed so that the following points may be guaranteed: The prayer is objective and receptive to the will of God; the praying person has surrendered control of his prayer; the retreat is a means of receiving instruction from God, not for the retreatant to instruct God.

Let us assume that, in his choice of vocation, someone wishes to discover whether he is suitable for religious life. In that case, surely, would he not welcome the retreat director's assuming the role of the superior for a short trial period? The retreat conference is like the examination of conscience in the presence of the superior. Through the same prayer by which the religious superior receives his office, the spiritual director has been put in the position of one whose business it is to know. If a religious order were not a place of prayer, the superior would have no right at all to command and to form the consciences of his subordinates. Religious life is essentially prayer, encounter with the Lord and life in his life, and the vows simply flow from this encounter by which the Lord incorporates followers into his life.

The most important thing in the entire prayer of choice is the encounter. The person praying must not inundate the Lord with words and protestations. He must allow the Lord to speak and answer. The priest's supervision is necessary so that this can happen; he removes all obstructions and masks so that the prayer can be a real encounter. And even if his intervention should prove unnecessary, one would at least have to ascertain that this were so.

All prayer during a retreat has the vocational choice as its objective, even at the beginning, when the choice itself is not yet of primary importance. Perhaps the retreatant wants to head for a decision right away in the first week. But he is given something else to do. He must learn to pray with objectivity and indifference. Through the prayer of indifference he is to be enabled to make the right choice later on, in an atmosphere of prayer which, right from the beginning, is really no longer his own. At the beginning the choice is as if sealed up in this prayer which he now chooses. He prays patiently in the manner shown to him, meditating on the points provided. He tries simply and straightforwardly to carry out all that he is asked to do—as far as both the attitude of prayer and the content of meditation are concerned—to see God as he is being presented now and not as he was accustomed to seeing him, calmly putting aside all that he wrongly thought to be so urgent, practicing a kind of renunciation even with regard to the reason for his being on retreat at all. This is itself a training in objectivity, an overcoming of one's own narrowness. I forget about the "I" that I felt had to be chosen. Only when the days of choice come is the ability to choose returned to me, fresh from the hand of the priest, from the Lord's hand, like an unsuspected gift of grace, which is all the more a surprise since, in the gift of objective obedience, I had practically forgotten it. And the gift should find me as I have now become: detached, trained in objectivity. All I need to do is remain within this impartiality, choose objectively and submit myself objectively to the necessity of a choice and to the laws which apply, as shown to me by the spiritual director; to a degree I can even leave the Yes or No to him, to the extent that he embodies the law of objectivity and I objectively lay before him the reasons for and against. The retreatant must have progressed so far in prayer that he no longer colors the things that he discloses. He must show them as they are, neutral and without judgment, leaving their evaluation entirely to the director in the same way that a physician's patient must refrain from secretly insinuating the diagnosis into his description of the symptoms. He must lay his cards on the table without selecting them and without even looking at them. It is for the director to indicate the pros and cons. The criteria by which he assesses the phenomena are not the same as the retreatant's. The latter, for instance, will imagine that his enthusiasm is an absolute proof of a vocation or that his feelings of aversion are clear enough evidence against it. The director sees differently and deeper.

The one purpose of this whole objectifying process through prayer is that God may act freely. He alone has the last word. The person's deliberate detachment from himself should show whether he is ready to give up controlling his own prayer, that is, whether he knows what prayer really is: doing the Father's will. The prayer of choice ultimately draws its life from the Son's prayer of mission in the Trinity. When he offers himself to the Father, ready to accept his mission to bring the world back to the Father, this offer is completely objective. He lets the Father's answer take its effect in him. He is only a vessel to receive it. He presents his proposal objectively and then is silent, as it were, until the Father replies. He does not insist, he does not presume; he has done his part by offering and continues to do it by waiting in full readiness for the Father's answer. And since the Father says Yes, this Yes becomes his own Yes. And when the retreatant says Yes, the Son imparts to him this form of his filial Yes; and if he accepts it, his Yes in the Lord becomes the Lord's Yes. If someone who prays has taken up the Lord's Yes, he is free to follow his path into discipleship in obedience, just as the Son was free to go along the way of his earthly mission in obedience to the Father. Certainly one can say that the Son, in his eternal deliberation, saw urgent reasons for offering himself to the Father, but it is also possible that, in considering the plan of redemption, he perceived reasons against it. After having weighed these arguments for and against and having decided in favor of the plan, he offers it all to the Father for him to choose.

All the ways of choice that are to be found in retreat exercises are already present in the Son. The first way, sudden certainty without reflection, lies in the eternal Now of the mutual assent between Father and Son. The second way, being drawn inwardly, is implied in the way the Son experiences in the Father both his consolation and his desolation, weighing the consolation which his redemption will bring to the Father against the desolation his suffering and Cross will bring. And the third way, the objective evaluation of reasons, is enfolded in the eternal Wisdom which can survey in absolute objectivity every argument for and against and can weigh them up.

Everything in the retreat that follows upon the decision is a matter of ratifying, strengthening and abiding by the decision. It is also a return to the subjectivity of personal life, equipped with the new objective meaning; it is the start of training for the chosen life, a preparation which equally can only be undertaken in prayer. In prayer the personal self is integrated into the objective self which God has revealed in the choice and given to the retreatant to be brought to reality.

As a whole, retreat exercises are a kind of summary, a concentration, a plan for life, which one can take back into daily life. Having gone through them, one knows this: I can pray. I can perceive the will of God. I possess this opening which leads beyond earth to a divine world. Later on, if days or years come when one cannot do this, one can return to the previous experience. This can be of importance in religious life, too. The person who does not set out on the path of religious life will take three things with him from his retreat: the certainty of having made a correct life decision, the memory of the graces of this time of prayer and a great understanding of the religious life. For some days he has lived as in the religious state. For him, too, it is important to have learned of prayer's objectivity, variety and consolation—and perhaps also its desolation. He has seen something of the battle which must be fought if one is to remain alive in prayer, and he has realized something of the beauty and difficulty of religious life, which will make him think and speak more reverently of it than most people do.

Anyone who has not attained any clarity through the retreat exercises has not penetrated to complete objectivity. He has the opportunity of a new decision later on. For some, the decision may simply be to have gone on a retreat; in this they think they have done so much that they will not initiate anything else in the foreseeable future. A few, perhaps, came prematurely. Some have shied away from the demands and have missed the offer. They will continue to live with their subjective selves. They have taken in the meditations like food without letting themselves be refashioned by them. Perhaps they did not even present themselves for a single private conference. They have made a retreat without wanting, deep down, to make a choice at all.

5. INDIVIDUAL AND COMMUNITY PRAYER

Through baptism, every Christian belongs to the communion of saints: to the Church, which is a praying community. He enters it before he can contribute anything to it himself. He lives by the prayer of those close to him and by the prayer of the Church long before he can participate consciously in it. In this way he shares in public prayer; it is given to him, it accompanies and watches over his Christian development, it entrusts him to God, and its effects are demonstrated in him. The sacrament of baptism entitles him to receive it, to count on it and to be nourished by it for as long as he cannot pray himself. He is a product of prayer until he is able to participate in its productivity.

When he begins to pray, his prayer certainly is initially private. He learns it from his mother, and at this period he has no idea that he exists in the Church. But when he begins to discover the Church he finds that he encounters, not something foreign, but something which he has always been a part of without knowing it. He discovers an extended homeland. He has not chosen it, for he has been a citizen there since his baptism. The sacrament has bound him but—such is the blessing of this bond—has bestowed on him the Church. Thus he was a beneficiary long before he was a contributor. Every child ought really to be introduced to the Church as to his true homeland, which is both familiar and unfamiliar to him and which he has been inhabiting without being aware of it; but now he will remember many things which will help him to get to know her properly. The Christian has received from the Church the privilege and the duty of praying. He has not thought about this before; prayer was something between himself, his mother and God. If the Church's role strikes him now as an interference, however, it should be explained to him that the Church initiated him into prayer even before his mother did. The little child who is baptized does not pray as a seeker but rather as one who is finding. Someone who begins to pray as an adult outside the Church must grope about, beset by a thousand questions and anxieties. The baptized child does not need to be anxious about anything. He has a right to pray; he is a citizen of the Church. Like the child nursing at his mother's breast, he drinks quite naturally; and when later he begins to take different kinds of food, it is all on the basis of this first, immediate and unconscious feeding. The process of achieving independence is a result of a prior dependence. The child lives in the Church's care before he can care about her at all. By the time the child begins to grow in ecclesial prayer, through religious instruction and the sacraments, he has already been surrounded by it. Here one can see that the Church's claims are far from being an "invasion of privacy", that she does not violate an individual's rights by making demands. The private sphere is not primary. When the Church requires prayer, she is only asking the individual to take up and continue what she has always done for him. The time comes, therefore, when the child knows and practices both private and public prayer, and in such a way that there is a unity between them from the very first.

For his private prayer the Christian can use any time at his disposal. He is free to determine the nature and content of his prayer. Its purpose is above all to open and develop his personal relationship with God. The Christian lives in the sight of God; and this standing before God is expressed outwardly in his attitude of prayer and inwardly in his involvement and his conversation with God, which should have its effect throughout his daily activity. In prayer he brings his concerns to God, everything that moves him inwardly; he shows him how things are, asks for help and commends to

157

God all that involves him personally, all that makes up his life, all that concerns those dear to him, all that pertains to his widest interests. These overlap, however, with the interests of God himself: his kingdom in the world, his redemption, the propagation of the faith, the Church. By its very content, private prayer immediately reaches beyond the personal sphere. Yet even the manner in which this duty is performed is not strictly personal: Many prayers, such as morning and night prayer, are said in solitude; others, like grace at meals, take place in the bosom of the family, and others in church. And even the most solitary prayer is not devoid of connections with ecclesial prayer, for all prayer, even in the secret of one's room, takes place in the communion of saints. All Christians who pray in solitude are bound together in the Church. Together they belong to God; together they live in the unity of faith and love which shows itself tangibly and visibly in their membership in the Church.

The Christian can pray privately anywhere, but he can also do so in church. If, while he is praying in church, a public liturgy is going on, this takes precedence over his private prayer. The Christian will not cut himself off and encapsulate himself in his own prayer but will try to pray together with the Church and in the Church's mind and spirit. The Lord's own words give this primacy to public prayer: "Where two or three are gathered in my name, there am I in the midst of them." Prayer in common creates that unity in the name of the Lord, who calls people together to pray and who also provides prayer's common subject matter. In the Mass, for instance, the complete attention of the worshippers is drawn to his sacrifice and his real Presence, to his coming, to his will to surrender himself and receive believers into himself. It would be quite wrong to participate in the Mass only from the Consecration on, so as to be free until then, or to act only as a spectator, or even to remain enclosed in one's prayer; for the Lord has entrusted his coming to the official Church. The priest performs the holy Consecration in an official capacity, in an action which is accompanied by prayers appointed by the Church, prayers which refer to the Lord's coming, his coming today. They are designed for this day's feast, and in their unity they express the unity of the Lord who comes and the Church which receives him. To withdraw into one's private prayer would be to take it more seriously than the prayer of the Church; it would be a transgression against the laws of the communion of saints, in whose midst the Lord forever comes and is to be found anew.

In personal prayer the keynote is freedom; in public prayer it is freedom and commitment. One is committed to times and forms which express one's incorporation into the community. The believer is committed to a minimum of public prayer, but he is free to go as far beyond this minimum as he likes and is able to: for instance, attending Mass and receiving Communion daily. Public prayer is the door to the sacraments and sacramentals, which the Church offers to those who pray as a kind of recompense for their participation in it. They are indeed inseparable from public prayer, but, again, the individual is left the greatest freedom in his use of them. Thus one may on occasion be kept from going to Mass during the week but can still go to Communion, borne up by the public prayer of the others who have followed the Mass. The community of prayer never supplants the importance of the individual: In every act of public prayer he is at once a free person and an obedient member. People rely on him, and he responds to this trust by taking his place in the anonymous multitude of all who pray. The Blessed Sacrament is exposed in a chapel; here the Church expresses her wish that the Lord should constantly be visited and adored. The idea is not that you or I should be there, but that someone should always be there in adoration. And as a Christian I feel called to do this. And when I make a visit, I do so freely, as someone who prays personally, and yet at the same time anonymously, interchangeably: I can make a visit for you, you for me. Or in a penitential service, something of the guilt of everyone is borne; in participating here one represents not so much oneself as any person at all among the many. There is a membership here that is a genuine expression of the whole communion of saints. That is perhaps what is most deeply characteristic of the Catholic Church: Within her there is the possibility of being anyone and everyone. The meaning and measure of this possibility, however, is service to God.

In private prayer, too, one tries to forget oneself in order to turn to God, to listen to him and follow him. In public prayer, on the other hand, one forgets this forgetting of self, so that in one's own sight and in God's one can be a person, among all the others, who is ready to serve him. The form of service is different in each case, but in both it can and should be perfect. Private prayer is mainly concerned with what God expects from the individual's mission. Public prayer focuses more on what God expects of his Church. Yet this distinction is not absolute, because even in personal prayer, God's demands upon the individual and the latter's mission are only possible within the Church and always involve the Church. Furthermore, what God requires of the believer is always a part of what he requires of the Church. Conversely, he who prays at a public liturgy is always included in the Church's prayer, along with his personal mission. Thus a reciprocal fertilization and intensification results: Public prayer lends to private prayer a potential which it would not have by itself, and private prayer gives public prayer its strength and scope. This reciprocal relationship is ultimately and mysteriously rooted in the Son, who is both Son of Man and Son of God. As Son of Man he is the Son of all; all share in his being, which has its meaning in the Cross, in the bearing of the burdens of all men. All who have brought him to the Cross have a share in his redemption, just as he has acquired a share in each of us through his Incarnation. And he is the Son of God, perfectly and totally divine, eternally in the Father, and his Incarnation is in no way opposed to his godhead: He is the unique, only-begotten Son of the Father and at the same time the Son of all men, of all sinners. The Father sees in him on the Cross his beloved Son and at the same time the guilt of us all, and he sees these, not in contradiction, but in a unity achieved by the Son by his being both Son of God and Son of Man. In thus being both one and all, unique and anonymous, he is the paradigm of both forms of prayer. Therefore we can also look at things from man's point of view: All of us together have brought him to the Cross, and yet each of us has done so on his own account. No one, therefore, can console himself with the thought that he is submerged in the mass of sinners. Similarly, in prayer, each person is always one—this particular one, and one member of the community.

The practical result of this is that, in the Church, the believer must not act solely as an individual. He may find himself in a liturgy which at the time means little to him: a Mass, a sermon, a funeral, a pilgrimage. In this liturgy he will recognize something of what animates the Church. And what the Church does, she never intends in a closed and restraining spirit: It is intended as an open and welcoming gesture. She expects the faithful to join in, to be docile and to support this present form of her prayer. When the Church celebrates Good Friday all her members celebrate too. The individual adapts himself, as if anonymously, to the celebration and then in turn takes the mystery of this holy day into the sphere of his private life and prayer. From her objective realm the Church brings power and vitality not only into the life of faith but also into the most secret and personal prayer life of her members. But she also takes the individual, just as he is, with his private prayer, into her great prayer. When he stands alone before God, speaks alone with him and receives his instructions alone, the Church is at his side and within him, praying and receiving with him. Everything he feels and receives and gives is also felt, received and given by the Church in unity with him. In this way a growing interaction arises between the individual and the community, an awakening from rest into a new vitality.

IV

PRAYER IN THE STATES OF LIFE

1. PRAYER IN RELIGIOUS LIFE

On entering a religious order, a novice will almost always
have to change his way of praying so as to adapt his personal
prayer to the prayer of the community; and the change will
affect not only his preference for certain kinds and times of
prayer but also the essence of prayer itself. In a certain respect
he will have to start again from scratch. The contrast may be so
great that his earlier prayer, which he considered upon his
entrance to be a serious preparation for prayer as a religious,
seems now to have no connection with the new form. He
resembles the piano student who, having learned many things
on his own, has to relearn everything from the start now
that he has a teacher. The novice is introduced into both
contemplative and liturgical prayer.

He has to attend the *liturgy* in the new community. There are
a great number of externals to which he must adapt himself so
that the community prayer will not suffer through his arrival.
In praying with others, he must immediately behave as they
do. And he must first of all attend to what seem the most
external and formal aspects. He may be so preoccupied by
observing and following that initially the content of the prayer
means little to him. In a rather drastic way he gets to know the
life of prayer from another aspect: Instead of being primarily a
personal conversation with God, it is now almost exclusively a
way of controlling himself, of joining in at the right moment,
of using his voice in the appropriate way, of taking a certain
bodily position and no other. This shift in the center of gravity

163

to the external can make prayer a self-conquest and a sacrifice. Only when the novice has learned all this does the content acquire a new meaning as well; only then has he the leisure to consider the words and gradually come to see the forms of prayer as simply an accompaniment. The more these forms recede into the background in community prayer because they are taken for granted, the more the content must come to the foreground: This must never be taken for granted and become mere habit. When the religious has overcome the initial difficulties in contemplative prayer as well, the result should be that his personal prayer in daily contemplation has an effect on his liturgical prayer; his spirit of faith must be so fructified by contemplation that, although the daily Hours may be identical or similar, he experiences them new and fresh each day.

If his contemplation is to be fertile in this way, it too must conform to the character of the religious order. Prior to entering, one had contemplated personally in a way that was perhaps completely adapted to one's state of life. Now a great change takes place: One learns to contemplate in the spirit of obedience; one is initiated step by step, perhaps having to start at some point which means little to one personally, and this initiation reveals and establishes from the outset the inner relationship between the gospel and the spirit of the order. The experienced novice master will have a precise idea of this spirit. He knows how it can be awakened in the novices and will school each one of them in it individually. But the personal appropriation of it, which would have been first and foremost in the life outside, here comes last. Contemplation must above all be formed in such a way that it is nourished wholly by the gospel, considering and learning to understand the life and disposition of the Lord in greatest detail. The introduction into this contemplative prayer will be neutral, objective and Christian, but it will offer many openings to interpretation and application, openings which are in accord with the spirit of the order and which reveal the rule of the order and its uniqueness in the very content of the gospel. The novice must get to know the tension and the harmony between them: He must know what is the breadth of the Lord's commandment of love and what is its reflection in this particular rule and this particular form of the apostolate. He must learn what points of the rule reflect general Christian principles and what aspects bear a particular stamp, and why.

The personal relation to God which is established in contemplation now appears as if bracketed between the general Christian relation to God and the order's relation to him. This bracketing gives prayer its character of obedience. What it seems to lose of its spontaneity, it gains in depth and richness. Several levels of prayer are differentiated, which illuminate and complement each other: the Christian and ecclesial level, the level of religious life in general, the level of the particular order and finally the level of the personal relationship with God. This richness is so great that it not only makes the time of contemplation full and fruitful but necessarily overflows beyond it. The matter that is proposed and embarked upon is by no means exhausted with the passing of the hour of contemplation. A wealth remains that can be carried over into daily work and liturgical prayer. Just as the husband remembers his wife's kiss when he leaves her to go to work and her love transforms his task, so the religious is accompanied by his contemplation as he goes to pray the Hours. The words of the liturgy are no longer monotonously strung together, each with its isolated meaning: They acquire a deeper, comprehensive meaning, and they fit together like the notes of a melody or instruments in a symphony because of the contemplation which resounds with them. It is like contemplation itself: However dry and sober it may be, everything shares in a common grace from the Lord and participates in an effectiveness and a fruitfulness which come from him. A single word from a psalm prayed in choir becomes a word from God in relation to the Scripture passage that came up during contemplation; the surrounding circle of words meets the circle of truths which were understood in contemplation. This is especially the case if the contemplation was carried out correctly and had been planned with a view to the gospel message in its entirety. In contemplation the order of importance was this: the gospel, the religious order, the individual person; indeed, this latter might occasionally be disregarded altogether. Yet precisely because the personal aspect was relegated to the background during contemplation so that one's entire spirit could be filled with the Spirit of God and the spirit of the order, contemplation has a personalizing effect during the liturgy, imparting to everything the color of experience. Someone who prays liturgically must be convinced that he, the person at prayer, matters. Liturgy is not an "impersonal" prayer with a vague "collective subject", the Church; everyone who participates must pray genuinely and personally. He must not recite the words mechanically, with a supposed "objectivity". Inwardly he must be genuinely and sincerely involved with them. Besides contemplation, vitality in liturgical prayer can have another source, namely, the sacrifice entailed in liturgy itself. Today perhaps I am not in the mood for it; and the conquest of self which I must achieve and which no one else can achieve for me is precisely what opens up a fresh approach to genuine prayer.

In liturgical prayer a whole development can take place. At the start of the training period its deeper meaning seems veiled: The main effort is to do things correctly. Once the outer form has become familiar, a great danger arises: One has had to neglect the content to some degree, and now one could continue to neglect it; since the outer form is a matter of course, the inner content may also seem self-evident. It is accepted as something given and constant, and one's capacity for attentiveness to it begins to diminish. This must be counteracted with unceasing effort, so that, just as at the beginning with the externals, so consequently for the inner content, all the soul's alertness is present and active. The conviction should grow that one is really speaking with God, that God is there and is listening, that he accepts the prayer directed to him and answers it, and that being recollected and avoiding distraction is therefore a serious task. Even where the text is difficult or less intelligible one must not give up but rather compel oneself to overlook one's own lack of understanding and to focus on God's understanding. If a pupil who has an inadequate command of a foreign language has to repeat a text to his teacher, he knows that the teacher hears him correctly and understands everything as it is intended. The person at prayer also knows that God understands the whole meaning of what he is praying, but that he too, like a good pupil, must try to understand as much of it as he can, putting into the words some of that fullness which they acquire in Christianity and in the religious life, so that they reach God, not empty, but full of meaning. Besides, the Christian knows in faith that every word of Scripture contains infinitely more than he can grasp. His task is to be so receptive that his narrow understanding of the word causes no distortion. He must pray in such a way that God is not disturbed, as it were, by his prayer but perceives in these words his love, obedience and striving. While he was being schooled in the formal elements, the novice was not to disturb the community. Now the task is not to disturb God. Earlier, his fellow religious needed to sense that he was praying with reverence, and it was like a preliminary test admitting him to prayer and preparing a place for interior

167

devotion. Naturally the externals such as the beauty of the chant and the harmony of movement are also to glorify God. But God is only pleased when the external is the expression of an inner reality and when the care that is taken with the form is aimed at guaranteeing and cultivating a solicitude for interior devotion.

On the other hand, what is superpersonal in liturgical prayer benefits contemplation. At the point where the person at prayer theoretically has total freedom, the regular scheme of liturgical prayer and the ecclesial form will have an effect on his contemplation, which in turn, as the contemplation of a religious, has its function and its goal within the Church. The beginner in contemplation is permitted to make things easier for himself in what concerns the choice of material, method or bodily position. Spiritually speaking he may make himself comfortable. But the contemplation of the mature religious has acquired something of the form of ecclesial prayer.

With regard to *contemplative prayer* itself, as a prayer of the religious state it has its own laws. In the world one was free in every respect to determine the time, place and matter of contemplation. In the novitiate, time and place are prescribed; personal preference and mood have to draw back. For a long time the matter of contemplation is also prescribed, and the novice must adhere to the points presented to him. In everything he has to leave behind the casualness allowed in the world and to begin a stricter regimen, which bears the order's particular stamp. Even though a wide scope still remains in contemplation for personal traits, its essential features are largely delineated by the given framework. The first result of this will be a certain dryness and a certain resistance on the part of the spirit. He has to use a foreign language. The pupil may be proud of every sentence he can put together correctly, yet he finds it an effort which he is not accustomed to making in his native language. Furthermore, his vocabulary for the present is limited; syntax is handled with care. Often great consolation occurs in prayer at the beginning of religious life, but this is not really the grace of contemplation but a grace of the novitiate, connected with the awareness of being on the right path and of having dared to take the great step. The pupil too is initially enthusiastic about the new language, but even more about learning and the privilege of learning itself; he is proud of being a "Latin scholar" more than he is inspired by the genius of the language, which is as yet beyond him. In the strict discipline, which can seem at first to be rather harsh, the experience and wisdom of tradition become visible. It is more important for the novice to be molded in a form that will last for a lifetime than for him to undertake pioneering adventures in the realm of prayer. God expects him now to be no longer a private person praying but a representative of his state of life, of his rule, of his order. His responsibility before God changes, too. This renunciation in an area which one had regarded as the most private between oneself and God can be the most difficult denial of self in religious life. Earlier the person praying strove to keep everything impersonal at a distance so that prayer could be as personal as possible. Now he has to grow beyond this personal element into an ecclesial form.

But once the initial difficulties are overcome and the form has been learned, the personal aspect gains a new validity. Time, place and process of contemplation are now matters of custom, and one is familiar with the order's particular character. One can now move quite naturally in what was at first like heavy armor. The time of supervised study is past; now comes the time of independent exploration. What seemed like compulsion proves now to be support. When the disciples first joined the Lord, perhaps they too thought that they could have done something quite different with their lives, or even that life with the Lord could have developed differently. Later they learn to understand that their path was by far the best and that the Lord did what was exactly right, bringing them along this path and through these particular demands to their freest and most personal development. But their freedom is an apostolic freedom, and the freedom of the religious is also in keeping with his state of life. It is a freedom which is no longer limited by an external framework but has taken the form into itself and transformed it into freedom. The form is now the active center, the core of the fruit.

In religious life the fruit of prayer is to benefit both the one who prays and the entire religious state. It benefits the one who prays so that he personally receives the strength to carry on (if he is a priest this fruit is mainly for the sake of his work, whereas with a religious it benefits more his own person); and it benefits the religious state in much the same way that the Church's treasury of prayer exists for the good of the whole communion of saints. Prayer and rule are to have a reciprocal influence. And ultimately the rule itself will have an effect on the rule through the contemplation of the order's members. It is the spirit which keeps the rule alive, preserving it in unwithered freshness through all the dust of time. Only the spirit can render the rule stronger than the law of time, so alive that it can adjust to every era. This spirit is as it were stored up and concentrated in the fruits of contemplation of all past and present members of the order, to the extent that they have brought forth fruit which is really alive. Nothing, perhaps, is more essential to the survival of an order than this fruit of prayer.

Often the believer can be struck almost sensibly by the "atmosphere of prayer" in a religious house. The faces he encounters bear the stamp of prayer. Perhaps he has come to talk with someone about a personal matter and is surprised at the understanding of worldly things that he finds in a person who has been enclosed for so long. He senses that this person is so detached from himself that a great power of understanding is released, enough for every concern brought to him. The answer is already there, hidden; all that is required is the question. This may come from outside, from people in the world, but also from within, from a member of the order. And the visitor begins to see that this grace is not the answer to one person's prayer but that in this house each supports the other and each represents every other; thus the spirit of the order becomes a living presence. This spirit arises out of contemplation: hence, too, the greater understanding of things. If a community such as this were told to change the text of its rule and adapt it to the present day, there would be no danger of harm being done to its content and spirit. This is true for every order acquainted with contemplation, not only the strictly contemplative. In the active orders a wealth of varied experience can come from activity, but it can never replace the experience which comes from contemplation.

Nowhere does the Christian receive a greater share in the Lord's superabundance than in contemplation in the religious life. He is privileged to live in an atmosphere which surpasses him on all sides because all paths lead to the Lord. The individual at prayer in the world, perhaps in a lonely church, can be overpowered by the Lord's superabundance. He becomes aware of the distance which separates him from the Lord; in his feeling of unworthiness he will humble himself more. The fruit of his prayer will be that, to him, God will have become greater. His new relation to God is such an experience that it almost seems that the former ties, all too routine and harmless, are broken off. The religious who prays and is overpowered by the Lord's greatness will sense, beyond this experience, a wonderfully unifying presence of this divine majesty in religious life itself. The form of life that he is allowed to live, his activity, his prayer—everything is bathed in and saturated with this superabundant greatness. No longer do the threads break off: On the contrary, they are strengthened. It is not primarily so that the individual can feel supported and developed by the religious form of life, as if he had been given the means of better penetrating the divine, but rather so that he yields himself more decisively to the unfathomable presence that sustains him and that is perceived as a treasury of prayer within the order. He can pay less attention to his unworthiness, his sin and his obstacles, because it is all subsumed into the grace of the form in which he shares. The person praying in the world goes to God like a sick man to the doctor; it is entirely an I–Thou relationship. When the patient goes to the hospital for a treatment, however, the nursing staff looks after him, and they are all trained to help the doctor, so that one cannot tell how much success is due to the doctor and how much to those who are his assistants, and how much to the achievements of research which are present in a totally impersonal way. It all goes to make the best possible environment for the patient. This is an image of the religious house. And just as the art of medicine can change the hospital environment fundamentally in fifty years without the personal dedication of the individual being altered, so the spirit of the order should remain alive and unchanged through the contemplation of its members, however much the order's work and manner of life may change. The relationship of individuals to the Lord is permanent throughout the centuries because new people are always coming into God's presence, but the spirit of a community, if it is to be constant, must resolutely renew itself from within.

2. THE PRIEST'S PRAYER

Through prayer the young man has arrived at the desire to become a priest. He knows from experience what he owes to prayer and so he wants to help keep the life of prayer alive in the Church. He also knows that, to do this, he himself will have to pray a great deal. Because of his office, however, he has many duties that leave him little time for prayer. Still he must find a way of lending sufficient strength to his prayer so that his ministry and all his actions are nourished by it. He will say his daily prayers, such as morning and evening prayers and grace at meals, like everyone else. Over and above this, his ministry obliges him to a great deal of vocal prayer: in the Holy Mass, the administration of the sacraments, the various devotional services, and not least the breviary. Furthermore, the Church desires him to cultivate contemplative prayer.

The first group of prayers will often have to be said quickly. He goes to bed late and gets up early, and is often interrupted: unexpectedly called to a dying person, for instance, perhaps even before saying Mass. As for his private vocal prayer, he must occasionally be content with a good intention. He has more time for the prayer which he can say during the day as he wishes. And he has plenty of time for the prayers he is to say officially in liturgical services. He does not pray these privately; they are heard by others, who join in and help to bring the prayers before God. As he says them he senses the community of prayer. It is a unity brought about by the Lord's presence: "Where two or three are gathered in my name, there am I in the midst of them." The priest does not need to feel that the whole burden rests on him: He can have confidence that God hears the congregation and that the Lord is present in it.

The priest's ecclesial prayer has a special relation to the Trinity. When he says the prayers of Holy Mass or of a sacrament, it is the Son who is the mediator and sends the Spirit who is contained in the sacraments, and this presence of Son and Spirit is hidden in the Father. In private prayer it is above all the incarnate Son who is present, and the Trinity is to a certain extent both represented and concealed in him; foremost is the nearness to us which God has attained on the basis of the Incarnation. In the official prayer, by contrast, the Son, who has given the office to his Church, grants it to her in the Father's name and mediates it through the sending of the Spirit: so much so that he remains concealed behind the Father and the Spirit, the Father who is addressed in prayer and the Spirit who fulfills it.

Both in private and official prayer the priest has a certain difficulty in introducing contemplation. But in prayer he has his parishioners in mind, for whom he is responsible; this is what makes his prayer fruitful. For instance, when the priest says the prayer of absolution or the prayer before distributing Communion, he experiences the administration of the sacrament together with the recipient, and its effect on the latter will impart a certain contemplative quality to his prayer. Thus his contemplation will discover its material not exclusively in the gospel or in the hereafter but in the Church and in those who, through the priest's mediation of grace, receive something of heaven and something of the real presence of God in Christ. Since this does not take place without the priest's mediating prayer, each time it is as if he has to put something of his own substance into this prayer of his, something that is seized so quickly by the recipient that the priest would never be able to replace it, were it not for God's providence. And what he has to give is not primarily his own but that which God has entrusted to him for distribution, so that ultimately he is only a vessel and a channel for grace. Just as he mediates God's graces and they pass through him in virtue of his ministry, he also mediates himself, for in his office he is nothing but a product of divine grace. There is an indissoluble bond between sacramental and sacerdotal grace. Connected with the grace of his priesthood there is his own renunciation that has made it possible for him to enter the priestly office, so that the fruitfulness of this renunciation enters each time into the administration of the sacrament and nourishes those who receive. It is not a renunciation which lies behind him as a finished thing, but one which he has to perform again each day of his life. He is continually being drained and plundered by his flock and filled and enriched by God. It is not as if he can carelessly let himself be plundered, taking God's replenishing for granted. For a moment he is in a state of suspension, giving with such complete surrender that he does not consider, does not calculate, does not notice whether he gets back what he has given away. And his enrichment consists above all in his sharing in the recipient's enrichment. He is like someone who brings good news, glad in anticipation of the joy it will give; and when he has told it he shares in the other's joy and is also glad that he was able to make someone happy. Thus, in hearing a confession, the priest shares in anticipation in the security and consolation to be imparted to the penitent whom he will absolve; and at the moment of absolution he again experiences this consolation.

The Church's prayer is part of the active side of the priest's life. But he also needs contemplation. The multiplicity of his ministerial activities is dependent upon the situations, states of life and characters with which he comes into contact. He has to find the appropriate word of support and strength for them all. He is ceaselessly having to give and to spend himself, and so he is in great danger of becoming lifeless and perfunctory. He will not be able to keep this danger at bay by remaining and appearing a "lively personality". The genuine solution lies in the objectivity of peaceful prayer, above all in contemplation and the breviary.

If, in the case of the religious, the framework of *contemplation* is primarily determined by the spirit of the order, in the priest's case it is formed more by the constant requirements of his flock. These requirements are already evident in the gospel, in the encounters of both believers and nonbelievers with the Lord, and they can be summed up in this phrase: reassurance in faith. This is what all who meet the priest are looking for, whether in the administration of the sacraments or in a personal discussion. The difficulties and concerns with which people come to the priest are the same as those which brought them to the Lord in the hope of being rescued and redeemed. Now the priest is in the Lord's place and shows the way to him. In order to do this he needs the objectivity of contemplation. He needs it to strengthen others, and he needs it equally for himself, in order to stay alive in faith. People's concerns are always unique to them; for him they become more and more the same, and it would seem natural to divide them into categories and have a handy prescription for each one. But that is precisely what he must not do. He must lead each one to the Lord personally. He may be inclined to go in for a "breezy" approach with his parishioners, entering into their lives in an all-too-human and unpriestly way. The only thing that can rescue him from this danger is the objectivity of his priesthood, which is ultimately rooted in contemplation: in an objective knowledge of revelation, of the Lord's situations in the gospel, his dealings with sinners, tax collectors, prostitutes, zealots and backsliders, the lukewarm and the skeptical, and the few who are faithful. Even before he learns of the pastoral situations which a priest can encounter, he must become acquainted with the Lord's approach and must contemplate it without having any particular application in mind. If he has this prior and general knowledge of Christ's care of souls, he will be able to solve the individual pastoral problem in its light. In his meditation he must not be selective and adapt the Lord's approach according to what he considers the strengths and weaknesses of his own personality. He must be filled with the Lord's attitude in all respects, even if at a particular time it does not seem applicable. First he contemplates the objectivity of the Lord's pastoral care; later, in his meetings with people, his personality will emerge. The objectivity achieved in this way will answer the genuine needs of his flock, which are not only the sum of the needs of individuals but also of the needs of a parish as such, which were the same in the Lord's time. In the parish, present events are subsumed into the past and into the supertemporal realm.

In general, the priest has less time for contemplation than the religious. For that very reason, he should proceed more slowly. He should take up and dwell on more definite, in-dividual points. Rather than seek wide perspectives, he should meditate verse by verse, word by word, taking only a little material for contemplation so as to introduce all the more fervor into his prayer. The faster he is obliged to pray his breviary and the rest of his vocal prayer, the more unhurried his contemplation should be. Otherwise his life would be swept up into a headlong tempo. In order to remain in the center, he must unite both poles. In both forms of prayer he is a representative of the Church before God, and so he should fulfill them and draw upon them both as thoroughly as he can.

The *breviary* must be prayed within a set period of time, at reading and reciting speed. It offers a wealth of material, part of which continually recurs. Here the very repetition promotes a proper comprehension of it. Each time the same psalm is prayed it can reveal a new aspect. And because it is the word of God, this renewal is inexhaustible. There will always be some greater or lesser opening. In the prescribed time, the person at prayer is introduced again and again to new aspects and possessions of God. Flashes of insight will occur now here, now there. He will not dwell on them. He keeps on praying, in company with all priests. Whenever the breviary is prayed there are these flashes of illumination; together they form the unity of the light. Whereas in contemplation the person sees something that no one else has noticed and his vision is more that of the individual who contemplates on behalf of others, with the breviary it is the reverse: The sum of the little illuminations of all those who pray the same psalm can result in an invisible unity in the presence of God. Here, then, by contrast, all are praying for one.

The breviary prayer is required of the priest as a time for worship, set apart from the rest of his daily work. He would do well to see that even its external features provide a contrast: If he has a busy life he will perhaps pray sitting quietly; if he is always travelling, then in his room; if he sits a great deal, he can pray walking about outside. He must take care, however, that the externals do not disturb his prayer. Walking up and down must not detract from his recollectedness; sitting must not be mere comfort, inhibiting his conversation with God. The externals ought to promote what is internal but should not be an end in themselves; the aim is to revive the spirit, not to give the body a "constitutional".

The daily prayers as prescribed are an expression of the will of the Church, who had her reasons for compiling the breviary in its present form. The individual might have made a different selection; he would have left out many a psalm, made the lives of the saints more interesting, chosen different passages from Scripture. But in all this he should be uplifted by the thought that in the breviary he is united with all priests, united above all in God. When it calls him to turn his mind to particular topics which necessitate a degree of self-conquest, he should recall that he is united with all who are doing the same, making a kind of sacrifice by going beyond their personal wishes. And whereas the liturgical prayers are heard by the congregation, God alone hears the prayer of the breviary. It is a conversation between the priest and God that receives its form through the Church, so that here the priest most clearly manifests his ecclesial disposition.

It is also a mode of contact with the words of revelation, carefully selected by the Church. It is advisable for a young priest to take his material for contemplation chiefly from the breviary. Thus his experience of contemplation will bear fruit in his breviary prayer, since the latter will be thrown into greater relief. Older priests might with greater advantage contemplate texts not contained in the breviary, so as to attain a more thorough knowledge of Scripture and to appropriate the word of God in all its fullness.

In the breviary the greatest danger is in the many repetitions of the most familiar prayers: the Our Father, Hail Mary, Creed, Glory Be to the Father, and so forth. Yet each repetition is like a return at a new level to gain deeper understanding and new strength. It is like breathing deeply or making a few relaxing movements after the more demanding gymnastic exercises. It is a pause which is so filled with the preceding contemplation or by one's personal experience of confession that, even if one is not aware of every word, the whole possesses a direction and a content. The atmosphere of prayer can bridge gaps in one's spiritual understanding and concentration.

Although the text is always the same, God hears the words anew each time. They are his Son's words, words of the Holy Spirit. And God can show the person who prays how the words can be said in a new and different way and with a particular quality each time. In praying the breviary, therefore, he should be in a kind of suspension and readiness, appropriate to the inexhaustible nature of the word and God's power to reveal something new here and now. One who claims to know in advance what a prayer contains closes himself off and receives nothing. A reader can return to a masterpiece of literature again and again, certain of discovering new facets and features; how much more, then, the masterpiece of the divine word! The priest with his breviary must await whatever God will grant him, and this attitude must be achieved in a forgetting of self. He must put away the everyday little anxieties and hurts; they too will be cleared up and healed by the breviary prayer, but not by his dwelling on them. Rather, he must hand them all over to God right at the start, with the first Our Father, so as to be completely free to converse with him. In contemplation, one is permitted to choose material which has a bearing on one's disposition at the time or on one's current problems, and thus to bathe them in the objective light of contemplation. With the breviary this should be avoided. It is a prescribed prayer, beyond personal matters. The latter can appear as prayer intentions, not as actual topics. When John Vianney, the parish priest worn out in his apostolate, prays his breviary, God does not want to see in him the man who is overburdened with a thousand worries but the soul that belongs to him, the soul he can refashion. When a sinner makes his confession, the priest's exhortation begins by addressing his subjective sinful condition and then moves on to the objectivity of the good Christian life. The breviary operates at this objective level from the start. Right at the beginning one shakes off everything concerning one's own sin and inadequacy, one's personal worries and apostolic interests. All that is left is the priest exercising his office before God, as if all his experiences and all the vicissitudes of his priestly existence had been for the moment phased out. The Church's words are prayed objectively—who prays them is almost incidental—words which proceed from the Church to God in such a way that, through the very objectivity of the prayer, God can work on the person praying in his most personal manner, which in the long run at least will have a visible effect on the priest's person.

In dealing with the priest thus, God starts with his priestly vocation, with his attempt to take it seriously and to be who he is meant to be. For this, God uses the matter of the breviary. When the young man resolved to dedicate himself to God, he thought he knew what it meant. Now he is a priest, and the reality only partly corresponds to those expectations. There is the objective tension between wanting to be a priest and being a priest; there is also the subjective difference in the way things seem, depending on one's mood at the time. Beyond all this, however, there is a correspondence: between what he knows of his own priesthood and what he really is. The breviary is concerned with this correspondence. It was present in its purity when he decided to be a priest, when the vocation was presented to the one choosing in all its objectivity. In the breviary God recalls this moment. He takes his priest as he was when he desired everything. The maturity of the later years was only the unfolding of that initial identity, the growth in understanding and putting into practice of what was implicit in the challenge of the priesthood. The breviary should be prayed in the calm of an immutability that corresponds to the immutability of God. It is no longer a matter of the person's vacillations and failures; it is a matter of the power he has received through his office and of the willingness which perseveres through everything and which must be brought, perhaps through much dross, to the purity of its first beginning. God wants the priest to have the childlikeness of his first days as a priest.

Readiness for contemplation and readiness for praying the

Divine Office are, at the outset, the same: The soul is naked before God. As contemplation progresses, it will acquire a much more subjective hue. The person who is totally attuned to God, letting God reveal himself as he wishes, will respond to him with his entire person, as he is by nature and as he has become through grace and his office in the Church. The area of contemplation is filled with the living process by which God's word is taken into the soul. The area of the breviary, on the other hand, is completely taken up by the Church's uniform prayer, and the person praying should adapt himself as perfectly as he can to this prayer of the Church. By introducing his own subjectivity he would only interfere with it.

Contemplation has an active quality, and the breviary has a static quality, but the same love unites everything. The priest's breviary, a strict requirement, is cradled in the free encounter of contemplation. The active love of God in contemplation has fixed him in the state of ecclesial prayer. But the latter deepens his knowledge of the will of God, of his purposes and of the state he requires at present; it teaches him that he must persevere and persist as long as God wishes, that God's words are beautiful because they come from him, that God accepts every word spoken to him and fashions it according to his good pleasure. All this further fructifies the priest's contemplation. All these unchangeable, prescribed elements enable him to expand his contemplation and to be available to God on a wider front.

And now it is the contemplation of the breviary which fructifies the action of contemplation; although contemplation is not evident in the succession of words from the breviary, it is nevertheless the core of the Divine Office. During the time for praying the breviary, contemplation is like a protective shell around it, whereas during contemplation the breviary becomes the latter's shell, but at a different level. The action of each on the other is not precisely reciprocal, nor can their joint effect be summed up; they enliven one another in a way beyond measure. What most opens up and stimulates contemplation is the objective attitude in praying the breviary. And the soul's openness in contemplation imparts the correct objectivity to breviary prayer. Ultimately it is *one* attitude manifesting and fructifying itself, just as love is one, both in the act of love and in the daily routine, and is continually unfolding in order to achieve a new unity.

The priest's *homily* is his interpretation of the word for the community. It too, like all proper dealings with God's word, is in an essential respect a prayer. But above all it is the effort to understand the word and to communicate this understanding to the congregation so that it comes nearer to God in an effective way. The homily should be for the congregation what contemplation is for the priest. If it were only a reading of the gospel or the repetition of some thoughts from a book, the effect would be at most an intellectual one. Only if it is derived from prayer and is a consequence of contemplation will it lead the hearers back to prayer. Nothing can fructify the homily more effectively than the priest's prayer and contemplation. Contemplation has a twofold effect on the homily. It so confirms the priest in his attitude of prayer that his attitude in the pulpit can only be a prayerful one: He stands in the presence of God and is attentive to him. Even when he himself speaks, the main thing will be to hear God's word and be guided by it. Thus contemplation is taken into the homily and is effective in it. But the priest should also take his homily into his contemplation. He must not confine himself to looking things up in books, dividing up the material and gathering examples; above all he must pray over the text. All the time he must remember that the congregation, not he, will be hearing his word. He will refrain from treating the congregation as a reflection of himself and his methods and habits of prayer, simply setting before them the fruits of his personal contemplation; rather, he will try even in his contemplation to hear the word of God together with the congregation, not explaining it in such a way that it becomes flat, but allowing it to become a word of prayer for the faithful. They must experience it as God's word intended for them. In order for this to happen, the priest, as a true hearer of the word, must previously have received it as a word meant for him, in his function as shepherd and in a unity of hearing with his flock. He needs this prior reception of the word, not to gain an advantage or to be able to prepare certain effects, but in order to prepare the soil, as it were, through his prayer and to lead those who hear him into an attitude of prayer before the word of God.

The word of the Gospels and of Scripture is a word given by God to man. It is powerful enough to interpret itself. Contemplation of the word and preaching of it should take place within the word itself. It would be presumptuous, under the pretext of having to be modern, to import all the current jargon into revelation in order to "help it along", as if for modern man it needed a new costume or some improvements. The Christian's life, as Scripture describes and demands, is his life in the presence of God, his earthly life in its relationship with God and in striving toward him. The Christian should learn to consider this life of his in God's light, that is, in the light of the word given to him by God. A congregation addressed in artificially modern terms, because the priest no longer finds the word's simple greatness powerful enough, would be led away from God instead of being drawn closer to him. In every development and every comparison the preacher uses, people must sense a reverence for the word, an inner relatedness to the scriptural way of thinking and a possibility of being used in prayer.

184

Few things foster the community of prayer between the priest and his flock so much as the homily. If the listener senses that the preacher is speaking in the spirit of prayer, if he himself is moved to prayer as a result of the priest's word because he wants to make this word valid in his own life, he will naturally pray more for his pastor too. The gift of prayer which the priest gives to the congregation through his contemplation of the word returns to him in their gratitude. It is this personal exchange of prayer that strengthens the sacerdotal office among the laity. They know very well that they must pray for this office, for they will benefit from it.

The pastor can no more share his whole prayer life with his hearers in his homily than he can introduce all his contemplation into his breviary prayer. With both the breviary and the homily there is a certain rhythm; he must move on, and hence he must select his material. This requires a particular clarity of thought so that what is said will be correctly understood. But it is no bad thing if the material is not too strictly marshalled but rather opens up vistas on all sides. This gives the listener food for thought and some unresolved matters to take home with him, much as the priest carries with him certain words from the breviary, pondering them or simply letting them take root in his soul.

It is not by chance that the homily comes in the middle of *Holy Mass*. This is the center of the Christian life for both the priest and the community. It is the highest expression of the power of prayer, the power that God himself imparted to it by allowing his Son, in response to the Church's word of prayer, to become embodied under the form of bread and wine, allowing his Son, who is the divine Word, to receive new life on earth. The praying Christian knows that God hears him and accepts his word of prayer. But God hears him in his Son, whom he gives anew to the world every day in transubstantiation, bodily in flesh and blood. It is here that God perpetually offers new access to himself; from this source every prayer is revitalized and made fruitful. All personal encounter with God draws its life from this sacramental encounter which he grants anew each time.

The priest at Mass knows that he stands before the Lord and that he may receive him in Communion and distribute him to the congregation. The Lord entrusts himself to the priest just as the priest has entrusted himself to the Lord. Perhaps a priest is always stumbling over his own weakness; perhaps he is plagued and tormented by thoughts of his unworthiness, which he sums up in the prayer, "*Domine, non sum dignus*". But immediately the Lord replies with his Presence and his full surrender. All failure and inability are taken over, forgotten and pardoned by the Lord at the moment when, in spite of everything, he appears in order to give the priest the reward of his Eucharist, trusting in him once more, indeed, entrusting himself to him, because beyond all failures he discerns signs of fidelity and love everywhere in him. The priest is like an artist who toils day and night over some recalcitrant work; but the moment he is convinced that he will never bring it off, it is suddenly given to him. The difference is that the Holy Mass is totally God's work. But it is God's work in the priest and for him. At every Mass the priest knows how much it is God's doing. In the Mass, furthermore, he has the guarantee that every prayer is heard and every one of God's words is alive— not with man's life but with the Lord's. All the rest of the priest's prayer is a sign of his sacrifice, of his life given to the Lord; and the Lord is there and accepts and listens and is available. And the sign that he is there and is listening is his Eucharist, his love expressed in the sacrifice of the altar. This expression is not independent of the priest's prayer, for it is precisely his prayer which calls it forth anew at the culmination, the Consecration. On the basis of this point, which for the priest contains the assurance that prayer is heard—since God obeys his word immediately—all prayer is seen to be answered. The priest's prayer is taken up into the Lord and with it the prayer of the Church, of the community of all the faithful.

In daily Mass the priest experiences in a new way the coming of the Lord and, in his coming, the continual renewal not only of his Body but also of prayer. In the Mass the Lord takes over the Church's prayers, imparting to all of them the fullness of his being. He is present not only to be distributed; he is there also in order to distribute. His being shared out contains the distribution of graces: graces of faith, graces of prayer, all graces whatsoever. And the same words which at the end of the day seemed to be a dull, powerless prayer will pulsate at the altar with the power of the Lord's being. His entire reality places itself behind these words and fulfills them. In faith the priest knows and feels this. The Our Father in the Mass is not only his and his people's: It is also the Son's prayer before the Father. The Son prays it at the altar, and the priest is allowed to participate in this prayer of the Son to the Father. And the Father hears the prayer as the Son spoke it on earth. When he said to his disciples, "This is how you are to pray", the Son was inviting them to share in his prayer; he gave them not only instructions but also something of the eternal, triune prayer of God himself. The reality of this gift is made newly present in each Mass. The priest cannot overlook it. He must be aware of it and allow his prayer for everyone to be taken up into the Son's prayer. The Mass is no mere "devotional prayer": The Son's prayer is present in it and provides its content. This prayer is more than human, even more than ecclesial. It has a dimension and a reality not possessed by prayer outside Mass.

At this point, then, the priest is, in a sense, overwhelmed. His vocal prayer, contemplation and breviary, by contrast, belong to him much more, even though the breviary texts are prescribed. They are prayers which draw their substance primarily from man and his faith. The readiness, the opening toward God which is expressed in them, can be determined and observed to a great extent by the person praying. But in the Mass, through the Lord's Presence, everything is borne away on a new tide. The Lord is bodily present: His being outshines all else. He has put himself into my hands to be sacrificed and to be shared out; what I do and what I am is now only a function of his doing and his being. I am flooded with a feeling of overflowing gratitude. All the day's labor and all the laboriousness of prayer is taken away; all monotony has disappeared. Of all the day's prayer, the thanksgiving after Mass is perhaps the most inarticulate. I can say nothing but "Thank you"; every prayer formula is inadequate, and all I can do is surrender myself. The more thanks I express, the more I see how great grace is and how insignificant my part. In the breviary, the priest knows that he is in communion with all other priests. In contemplation, he is in fellowship with his flock. This fellowship is realized in the sacramental prayers. But in the prayer of thanksgiving, any frame of reference and every purpose has been superseded. It is pure worship, with no other reason than that he has received the Lord and must give thanks for all that the Lord has given him through his coming, including his vocation and its burdens, and for his whole priestly life which has its foundation in this coming.

When the Lord appears in the Eucharist, no one can say how great he is. The little Host which is visible conceals his boundless being. From the insignificance of the Host to this infinity there is no transition but only a sudden reversal, a total overwhelming. The priest experiences this reversal in the thanksgiving, which sums up his whole priestly existence. He, a pitiful nothing, participates in infinite mysteries. He feels that he is almost nothing but a figure, a symbol like bread and wine, concealing the ineffable. The priestly office, too, is something clear and sharply defined, although the human being whom it clothes never fills it completely. But in thanksgiving there are no more defined outlines. In contemplation, too, all is open: It is left up to God to give what he will, whether consolation or aridity, a tangible answer or none at all or something in between. The priest knows, nevertheless, that everything which God gives has a purpose: An illumination must be applied to daily life or contribute to his subsequent preaching. Contemplation is still bound up with some purpose. In thanksgiving, the predominant note is the utterly free gift, the "gratia gratis data".

3. PRAYER IN MARRIAGE

A person who prays cannot look at marriage as a merely natural union of man and woman. He must see it as something that has its completion in God. Initially this supernatural element may be very obscure; it may seem only indirectly connected with the spouses' marriage relations and their daily life. One cannot get hold of this divine "something"; one only knows that it came into force in the sacrament of matrimony and surrounds their married life as an invisible accompaniment. Still, if the couple pray in a pure, childlike manner, if they approach God and give thanks to him just as they are, if they offer everything to God and commit everything to him, including their marriage and all that it involves, they will grow to understand that this accompaniment is not something abstract but a real, living thing that finds expression in their married prayer and is nourished and defined by it.

As soon as a Christian finds he is thinking of marriage he will go before God, revealing and offering his intention and the person concerned, to discuss his future marriage. And if this intention and this person find a home in his conversation with God, if prayer is enriched and rendered more decisive, if his nearness to God is not disturbed but on the contrary is encouraged, then clarity and perhaps even certainty about what he has in mind will be granted to him as well.

During the time of betrothal he and his intended will soon come to speak of religious matters. He will not do this until he himself has first prayed in quiet and has become clear about it. When he commits his beloved to God in prayer and talks to him about her, he will see her more clearly, and this will initiate a new stage in their reciprocal understanding and nearness. Most lovers have a certain reticence in speaking about their relationship to God. This spiritual reticence is like the counterpart of the bodily modesty of young people who are pure, and in fact there is a certain unity between the mystery of the body and the mystery of God. The former is contained in the latter. They sense that, as there is a bodily intimacy which is reserved for marriage, so too there is a similar spiritual intimacy; each is aware that the other knows of this, and can look forward to sharing it more at a later stage. Meanwhile each should be assured that the other's relationship to God is intact and alive.

In this matter men and women behave differently. The young man who feels and sees that he is mature also knows that he has new powers at his disposal. But he will leave them in God's keeping until he has chosen his state of life. Until then he will let his relationship to sex remain in abeyance. As a result, his prayer also will acquire an open, provisional character during this period. He knows that if he chooses marriage much will be fulfilled that, for the present, must wait. In the man's case there is a greater awareness of the sexual drive and its demands, and thus there is a clearer renunciation.

With the woman the contours are gentler and less clear-cut, and in this respect it is easier for her. She feels a longing, a need to surrender which encompasses both God and her beloved, but she is not at pains to fix the bounds of this surrender. The place which the man keeps within him for the woman is not simply empty; the fact that he senses it keenly is part of his renunciation. If it were empty, the young man would not need to pray about it. This place is one of the mysteries known at present only to God; as such they are full of promise. Simply to overlook them and take no account of them would be to impoverish and restrict prayer. To probe and dissect them would be to violate the integrity of the mystery. So the only correct attitude remains that of prayer, in which this awakening mystery is continually being entrusted to God. The woman does the same in a less conscious manner. Since her part in love will be to surrender, even now her prayer must consist in allowing herself to be prepared for every forth-coming surrender and—if marriage is chosen—to commend the man's faith to God, so that God may see that she expects to be made fruitful by his faith too. For as the man introduces the woman to physical love, it is also part of his duty to introduce her into his prayer.

Both of them should recognize more and more that the mysteries of their forthcoming marriage are also mysteries of prayer; they should give their prayer, filled with this recog-nition, to God. They should be aware that what they are intending will require much personal prayer and a great deal of personal grace from God, and yet they are not dispensed on that account from the prayer of the entire Church; indeed, they incur a new obligation to pray with the Church. It would be egoism if, having entered religious life, a person were to consider everything only from his order's point of view and not from that of the Church; so, too, it would be egoism if the couple at prayer were only to see their own family, expending, as it were, all their power of faith to make their family into a kind of miracle of virtue and piety, and forgetting the Church. Furthermore, as long as they live in the Church's faith and prayer, their love and desire for each other will not deteriorate. They will know that, as Christians, they will always need to make certain renunciations. In marriage, too, they will not lose the discipline which comes from prayer.

Prayer prior to marriage can have a special orientation to the saints and particularly to Mary and Joseph. For just as love becomes more concrete in prospect of its consummation in marriage—because it will be fulfilled in the coming together of these two concrete, physical beings—so the relationship to the Lord becomes more concrete through devotion to the Holy Family. The thought of these saintly persons in their relationship to the Son will help those who are betrothed to remain in God's sight and live within the requirements of the Christian family. Their prayer does not need to keep its earlier abstract form: It can develop along with the circumstances. It can even become much more childlike than before and regain something of the quality it had when one was introduced in prayer by one's own mother to the Child Jesus and his Mother, when one knew them both as if through some visibility of the Spirit. Childlike faith saw no difficulty in not doing something forbidden so as not to sadden the Christ Child. Now something of this childlike concreteness returns. What was more vivid than the life of the Holy Family? In order to know what to do, one only needs to look to them in prayer and model one's everyday life after theirs.

The clarity of this idea should first of all enter into that place set apart in the man and into the longing of the woman. It ought to play a role similar to that which, for the religious, is played by the life of the Lord, made concrete in his order and its rule. The person who would pray forever as a loner would be in perpetual danger of letting his prayer be distorted in two directions: into a false concreteness concerned only with the self and its relationships and needs, and into a false abstractness lacking a tangible framework, so that in the end it would be difficult to pray for the Church in concrete terms. The medium for it is lacking. The person who tries in life to avoid every genuine choice, who leaves it to others, feels that he is above it and wants to be wholly self-sufficient, and will gradually lose a sense of the gospel's true vitality until his existence is without any genuine Christian quality.

No time is of greater consequence for prayer than that in which a person is about to embark upon his state of life. The danger of inner alienation is seldom greater. If he were to use being in love as an excuse for praying less, he would soon notice that he has gone off the track. He would not be able to rediscover the rhythm of his inner life. Faith and prayer are so intimately interwoven that to give up prayer is to lose a part of one's faith. It could even be that such a neglect during the betrothal might never be made good again in marriage. If someone withdraws from God as soon as he begins a serious relationship and marries in this estrangement, how can it result in his drawing closer to God? During the betrothal, prayer must not be adapted to circumstances: Circumstances must be adapted to one's prayer. Otherwise the circumstances change so quickly that there is no more room for prayer. Many a person who has lost the habit of prayer in all the events and anxieties of his betrothal and in the early days of marriage tries to grope his way back, only to discover with horror that the whole situation in which he has placed himself and which he has built up around him did not take prayer into account. When prayer subsequently tries to regain admission, it finds the place already occupied. Having gotten into a routine apart from prayer, one is obliged to turn the wheel back, which is much more difficult.

At times in one's life when important decisions are to be made and when much is changing, one can least afford to give up prayer. When circumstances are calm and in balance, it is easier to resume what has been broken off; but if things are in flux, prayer must remain stable at any price. Its form may change, but it must not lapse. In marriage, furthermore, each is responsible for the other: By not praying, the one can rob his partner of her prayer life and can accustom her to living with him on a purely natural level. And the tardy attempt to get back into prayer could even bring about an estrangement between the spouses. The praying spouse could now seem to be a different person, a stranger. Experience teaches that those who do not at the outset put aside a definite time, however small, for prayer as a married couple, will be able to find it later on only with great difficulty. One's relationship to God cannot be put into cold storage.

In *marriage* the couple live in fellowship with one another before God to such an extent that they do not need to pray together a great deal. What prayer they do say together is more a means of reminding each other that they are leading a life of prayer. Each spouse should respect the other's prayer and let him pray as God inspires and as he prefers, without making any inflexible rules. There are couples who need to pray a great deal together, who find it a help, in times of decision or difficulty, for the prayer of each to be visibly and audibly united to the other's. But this will remain the exception. Prayer said in common must never be the exclusive form, just as it must never in principle be rejected. Communal prayer has a particular significance for the family. Couples who are used to praying some devotion or doing spiritual reading together will find it easier subsequently to let their children take part in it and thus to introduce them to prayer. The habit of prayer in common can often be a support in that it helps in times of crisis when personal prayer becomes difficult. The fervor of one spouse can prevail over the lukewarmness of the other. Something in their common prayer will remind them of the sacrament they received together and reunify their married life with all its joys and trials, strengthening their indissoluble bond. It shows that the marriage has its stability in the Lord, that the spouses' mutual bond in the Lord is so much part of each of them that they can together give expression to it, and that the Lord's word, "Where two or three are gathered in my name . . .", has a particular meaning for them. Each of them, however, remains a free personality before God and must therefore pray as an individual as well. Furthermore, their personal petitions should be limited mainly to private prayer, whereas prayer in common should have a certain chaste sobriety. The latter will generally not begin during the betrothal but within marriage.

From the first day of their marriage the spouses should pray simply and naturally, not allowing any tension or embarrassment to arise between their married life and their prayer life. No doubt they will have to overcome some inhibition. They should not be afraid of this, but take the first step in innocence and simplicity. It will be good for them to pray a little together precisely while the joy of their marriage is fresh; they should keep to traditional prayers and avoid extravagant words, so that their prayer does not suffer later in a more sober atmosphere. Both the husband and the wife should try to fashion their prayer—formerly private—into a real prayer of their state of life. It should contain not only the worship, thanksgiving and petition of them both but above all their aspiration toward the ideal of their state of life given by God in the sacrament. Once more the model of the Holy Family is relevant, imprinting its form upon contemplation and prayer. The man, with his concern for the newly-founded family, his work and his relationship to his wife, will keep the example of Joseph before him. The woman will look up to the Mother of God, to her relationship to her husband and to her way of managing the household and looking after the Child.

The marriage is to be fruitful not only in the physical sense, in begetting and bearing children, giving birth and bringing them up, but just as much in a spiritual sense. The physical must be rooted in the spiritual. Beyond the immediate concern for the children and for each other, the couple will always remember that they are a family within the Church: Thus they will be open to what concerns other families too. But it is prayer above all that effects this openness. The person who prays for his own concerns in a Christian way, that is, lovingly, will have to think of the related concerns of others and make his prayer available for them. One cannot nourish one's relationship to God in selfishness. Just as Christian parents do not think twice about sharing their surplus with the needy—giving to the poor the clothes their children no longer wear, for instance—so it should be natural to them in prayer to share with others the blessings of family happiness and peace that they have received in abundance. This will result in a kind of mysterious relatedness, partially dependent on them, since the prayer embraces those who have some connection with them, and partially dependent on God's good pleasure, for he distributes graces as he wills.

On the other hand, the couple will not forget in their prayers those in the other state of life. The vitality of the Church depends in large measure on a living relationship between the states of life. At the beginning of marriage the other state may seem distant and abstract; many spouses go to church and to the sacraments for years without having a genuine encounter with a priest. Then some difficulty arises, some tangled situation or some misfortune, and they are glad to be able to unburden themselves in confession or otherwise, whether they are the guilty party or the innocent one, seeking advice and strength. Now for the first time they realize how necessary the other state of life is to them, how grateful they should be for it and how important it is to pray for those in it. The same thing can happen when they are ill in the hospital, or when the mother is expecting a baby and they meet the nursing sisters, or when the children start to go to school, or when they visit some relative in the convent for advice and support in prayer. Openness to the other state and openness to one's own state are among the basic requirements for living prayer in marriage.

As the years go by, married life becomes more monotonous than life before marriage. The great expectations and surprises are in the past. The man is settled in his work, the woman in her housework and among her children. When everything is in equilibrium and there seems nothing to look forward to but the daily routine, prayer often seems to have lost something of its urgency. One no longer makes great demands of life; one is content, and, without noticing it, one has become less exacting with oneself. Then prayer is in danger of becoming a formality. Often husband and wife support each other in their lukewarmness. Left to oneself, one would want more, take more risks, attempt more. An individual who has to overcome the force of habit can pull himself together more easily than someone who must make the effort with another creature of habit in tow. With two people, there is more of a temptation to shift responsibility to the other. The spouse is blamed because life has lost its variety, because the world (and hence God) has become routine, because the couple has grown too settled and unimaginative, and because the world seems worn down and one has become hopelessly mediocre.

In marriage, children constitute the strongest impetus to renewal. They shape their parents' prayer to a large extent. At the start of marriage it is a prayer of hope, of asking blessing upon the marriage. Then both of them pray during pregnancy—the mother perhaps more than the father. She notices the changes in herself even before her condition is outwardly visible; she has a close relationship to the developing child, and in prayer she places it under God's protection. At the birth, while the woman lies in labor, it is probably the believing father who takes up the prayer. The woman is preoccupied with her physical pains; the father's emotions are in conflict, and he discovers, perhaps for the first time, genuine, searching prayer. He is deeply shaken; he has lost something of his everyday security. From now on he thinks more in God's presence of his wife and child and commends them to him, to the one who alone can always help. Then, again, husband and wife pray for the growing baby, and it will be the mother above all who introduces him to the life of prayer. Here the mother may encounter a danger: Her prayer could lapse into a kind of superstition. Her prayer will be specific and strongly motivated; she will be concerned with her child's welfare and will watch anxiously to see that everything develops normally as she thinks it should. The smallest things in the child's life are a cause of worry; the least fluctuation seems to accuse her of neglect or of some fault. The mother must of course pray for her child, but generously, not anxiously. Here, too, "Thy will be done" must be the sum and substance of it. Prayers of petition must not degenerate into a list of instructions for God. Where prayer becomes petty, there is the danger that later, when the child has grown away from his mother and his life is no longer subject to detailed control, the mother may continue telling God what to do while the rest of her prayer withers away.

When the child is going to school, good religious instruction can bring about a renewal of prayer for the whole family. Things forgotten or misunderstood are brushed up and put right; the parents too make more of an effort. Even where the tradition of prayer has not lapsed, new incentives are brought into the family. The child tells what he has heard at school or asks questions, and the parents must reply. Enriched by his classes, he will want to share these discoveries and might even want to introduce some new practice. If the parents believe and pray, they will be glad to accept these ideas. It might not even occur to them that their own prayer life could take a new turn; they are interested in the child and want to let him have the joy of creating something, something that will last when the enthusiasm for his lessons has evaporated. In this way the child will be reminded later that he himself was the instigator of this or that practice, and that will reinforce his fidelity to it. Although they may not notice it, the parents too will draw good from it.

If the parents no longer pray, the child will have a hard time. But parents often do things for the child's sake which they would not do for themselves. Perhaps the child unconsciously can bring his parents back to prayer. Initially they do it as a formality for the child's sake, and in doing so they are struck by grace and brought back to genuine prayer. Or at table, perhaps, the child speaks about the truths of faith, about receiving a sacrament, or he has to be prepared for first confession and Communion, or he has to recite from the catechism—things which, to the parents, are like distant echoes, recalling a childhood when they were in touch with God. Something wakens in them, and they begin to find their way back to prayer.

When the children get older and begin to have their own world, known to their parents only in general terms—their time spent at school and at work, their inner life which they keep to themselves—their parents' prayer accompanies them in a new way. It includes the unknown: what the children know but do not say, what the children do not know—dangers surrounding them—but the parents do, and finally those things that none of them can perceive, things known only to God. Thus, as the children grow up, prayer becomes broader and more all-embracing. It accommodates itself to the extension of the family, but beyond this, it creates in and of itself a suitable space for this extension. The children ought to know about this prayer. If they are at the age, however, when they have their own life decisions to make, then little should be said about their parents' prayer: They must not be aware of any anxiety in their parents, and parental piety must not be a burden or an inhibiting factor to the children. Their parents' prayer should be so much part of their personality that it does not need to be singled out; it can be observed in their robust and cheerful attitude. Finding the golden mean here is itself a matter for prayer and for supernatural, Christian tact. Parents should realize that the children can now draw their own conclusions; they do not need to have every single thing planned for them. It is enough to indicate a path discreetly. Sensitive parents will find ways of referring to prayer indirectly, perhaps by mentioning a childhood event associated with something religious. But they will make their own whatever concerns the child, discuss it in his absence, bring it before God in prayer, and thus come to a solution which is clear to the child and which he does not feel to be an imposition. They will trust God in this matter, knowing that not everything depends on direct dealings between human beings. It can even be an abuse of trust when parents assume responsibility for all the child's problems and thus reduce God's share. Many parents fail in this regard. The young mother has had to play the part of God, as it were, for the little child. As the child grows up, God takes over this role himself. At some point the mother must surrender the part; otherwise she will get confused and fall into self-righteousness under the guise of piety, and the family's animated life of faith will contract.

Once the children have become independent, life as a couple begins again. But everything is different. The future that the newlyweds had prayed about now lies behind them, with its plans and hopes, so completely closed and finished that the house would seem empty indeed if love and the constancy of prayer had not transformed this emptiness, in God, into a hidden fullness. No longer does one spouse see in the other the energetic idealist, but rather the tired companion, who, for better or worse, has accomplished his life's work, which has left its mark on him. So prayer too has changed; if faith and love have been preserved intact, the spouses remain the same before God, but they are in a different relationship to their fellowmen. They have become old and mature; the tasks which present themselves are those of maturity. Many an experience in prayer before God and in the Church which has matured through a long life was granted, not for the couple themselves, but for others. The young married person wanted his family to benefit from the fruit of his prayer; in old age one remains obligated to others. One must make one's possessions more widely available: to the children, who have the same right to their parents as long as they live; to the grandchildren, who can receive from their grandparents so much that only maturity can give; and to the many people, the poor, the neglected, the sick, whom one can care for now that domestic concerns are less time-consuming. These new tasks too, like those of one's own household, must be nourished by the strength of prayer.

At the beginning of marriage there was the danger of treating the family as a closed, self-sufficient circle. Prayer opened up this circle toward the Church. The children widened this opening by what they brought in from outside. Now in old age, the same danger returns. One seems justified in calling a halt. The end of one's existence is approaching. But it is in God's hands, and man is to be open to God and not preempt the conclusion. He must not fix times. As long as he lives he must try to stay as fully alive as possible. His powers decrease, and the demands on his time and effort are more limited, but as a result he gains more time and can pray more; and prayer, after all, is never heading for a full stop. Perhaps the material one brings to prayer has become less; there are fewer immediate concerns. Then it may again be time to turn more often to Scripture. One should not approach it in order to brood over things that are opaque; there is enough simple material in the gospel to strike a chord in our life and reveal to us the life of the incarnate God and his dealings with people. When one was young, one loved the parables which speak of sowing, growth and harvest. A whole life opened up in these words. Now these vistas are perhaps too large, and one devotes more time to final destinies: the life of Mary after the Lord's Ascension or the death of the Apostles. It is a fact that few old people are mentioned in the New Testament; this is part and parcel of the Lord's eschatological haste. "Let the dead bury their dead!" He will not overtax what is old.

One has more time for talking, but conversation must not turn into gossip. The grandchildren want to hear stories, and, since they love stories from their parents' childhood, they can be shown a great deal that is both personal and Christian.

Where there has been harmony between the spouses in the middle years, it will remain in old age. But perhaps the personality of one of them has changed through illness or a lessening ability to adapt; or perhaps both have to cope together with new difficulties. The burdens of old age can be hard to bear. All this will be less dramatic than in youth; they have been through so much together. All through one's life one has offered in prayer to bear whatever God sends, and now at the end God still takes one seriously. Perhaps this prayer had become a mere habit, but in every life God is inventive and infinitely varied in his demands. And nothing is such an antidote to boredom as obedience and docility to providence.

If one of the spouses has died, life will seem even more restricted for the one who remains. But "restriction" is never a Christian word, and so widowhood is for a Christian a new state of life, accompanied by a new wealth of graces. Its time is circumscribed and the person's strength is limited, yet this state offers the possibility of leading a perfect life in God. The tasks of this state of life will be preeminently those of prayer, and this prayer will perhaps be said primarily in church, where the Lord is present among the faithful. Those who pray belong here. If the younger people have to go about their duties and business, the old and widowed can all the better fulfill this ecclesial duty. They have time to pray. There is nothing anymore that is so urgent and significant that prayer would not be more important. What strength remains can be used simply to wait for the Lord according to his instruction, to wait patiently in prayerful faith, not only being there in an external attitude of prayer, but inwardly nourishing prayer and being nourished by it. Thus, in the end, the contemplative life comes into its own even in the secular state; not so much in the pondering of difficult truths of revelation as in the contemplation of well-known prayers. For many, the Rosary will be the right way of combining the vocal and the contemplative; it is suitable for the mind which is not as quick as it was. The beads between the fingers are like reminders; they prevent one from getting lost. One knows where one is, and one is glad to have a small task, something definite to do outwardly and interiorly. The life of the Mother of God unfolds with its unique fullness, yet it is not far away but familiar, as though part of one's own life. All the events of her life are reflected in the events of everyday Christian life. In this light, much of one's own life becomes clear. Then again, one sees how her life was so thoroughly determined by her Son's that through her one can learn to know the Son and the Father. Thus the Rosary becomes a bond between heaven and earth. One learns to see earth with the eyes of heaven, and heaven seems as near as earth. The Mother of God prevents one from looking at one's whole life as a failure, from grieving over the mistakes made, the opportunities missed, the many things not accomplished. Rather, one sees that she did all that God wanted of her and that one can share in her grace. And one is glad of that.

Many young people are annoyed when they find so many old people in church. They forget that the old people find in church what is missing at home; what they can no longer give to their relations, since they are all alone now, they are trying to give to God and his Mother. Often they have only small fragments of life left to offer God, but he accepts everything and sees love in it. Young people like to speak of totality. But they must learn to address their demands for totality to themselves; they should offer everything to God and learn a lesson from the old people who are trying to do just that.

V

THREE KINDS OF PRAYER

1. WORSHIP

The Christian who knows of the absoluteness of God does not feel that he has to come to grips with this mystery intellectually. He wants to contemplate God's majesty, surrender himself increasingly to it and pay it homage. Homage cannot be rendered, however, by abstract speculation, by enhancing one's ability to deal with concepts or to engage in dialogue or to consider things objectively, so as to establish a distance and to delight in it—whether because God is so great that, despite the distance, something of his greatness can be seen or else because, despite his greatness, he is so near. It is only in prayer that the believer can experience and bear the encounter with God's majesty, in that special prayer which is dedicated exclusively to God: worship. The worshipper renounces at the outset all attempts to evaluate the distance, any comparison between God and man, any thought of the creature's negativity before God. At most, man's smallness and inconclusiveness is a point of departure which is left far behind and is not a part of prayer at all. The person who worships has forgotten himself. He has no reason to return to himself. He is free to dedicate all his strength and love and attention to the greatness of God.

There is no question of measuring this majesty. All attempts to approach it and express it fall short of the reality: They indicate more than they can express. When the worshipper addresses God, gives him names, praises his nature and recalls his deeds, places all his hope for the future in him, lets himself be caught up by and filled with God's almighty power, he knows all the while that these are only childlike attempts, for God surmounts and surpasses every concept. Yet he is permitted to worship God with his feeble powers; indeed, God expects this homage, so much so that he accepts it not only from believers but also from God himself. The incarnate Son worshipped the Father on earth as a sign that in heaven he eternally worships the Father and that worship is a trinitarian activity.

In worship, the world of God opens up. Only in worship does God let himself be known. Most often, the believer, even as he begins to pray, will already have an experience, in faith, of the nearness of God and will situate himself in it. He sets out to contemplate God in a way that is fitting for him, the believer. He approaches God with his stammering words, taking the small first steps which faith and his knowledge of God offer him. He begins to worship according to the measure of his faith and his knowledge about God. But then he discovers that God, worshipped in this way, gives back to him what he has offered, transformed in such a way that he is enabled to worship better. His stammering becomes a word from God, filled to abundance by God himself. His attempt to conceive becomes a concept formed by God himself. He thought to bring to God the fruit of his own activity in faith, albeit immeasurably inadequate to its object, and he finds that God accepts this fruit and takes away all its inadequacy in order to reveal to him the sublimity of his surpassing and unfathomable divine nature.

Perhaps the believer was willing right from the start to renounce his own categories, applying them at best as unsuitable and provisional means and then putting them aside. He could not know in advance what would remain to him. He finds that, in demonstrating the uselessness of his categories, God does not simply reject them but replaces them by imparting from above new meaning to the delimiting concepts and words, and by fulfilling with immeasurable grace everything initiated by the believer. Whereas man was first active in prayer, now it is God who is active in man. The believer is like a shy girl unwilling to give more than a tender little furtive kiss, to whom the beloved responds with a full embrace. What he gives is a fulfillment of what was initiated, but a fulfillment beyond all expectation. The girl may know that such fulfillment exists, less from her own ideas than because the man has the capacity for it. She meant to show her love by this shy demonstration, but now she sees herself borne away in a torrent more powerful than she could have imagined. And as, in her innocence, the pledge of surrender and readiness which she offered was for her the utmost, and the prospect of what actually transpired would have meant *less*, so too the worshipper cannot anticipate on his own what will happen when God takes command.

Within every true prayer is hidden such a moment of "release" in God, although it is not necessary for the person to be aware of it. "Knock, and it will be opened to you"—to you, to me, to someone who believes, not necessarily to the one who knocks. The Son is empowered to initiate the Father's self-revelation at any time. And when, as man, he tries out what he has experienced in heaven, he knows how the Father will answer. But now, insisting on his Son's right—to which his Father in heaven has always responded—he wants to exercise this right as man also in order to make it available to his brothers, so that the Father's response may become a gift to believers. From God's point of view this happens with a kind of infallibility: Whoever knocks on the Father's door in the way the Son intends is sure to receive an answer, if not for himself, then surely for someone else. God does not put off the answer to some indefinite later time; he answers immediately, in an infallible event here and now. This is a communication of the Son's rights vis-à-vis the Father which takes place as worship and which always becomes a revelation of God, since the Son's vision always leads to the Father revealing himself. The essential thing here is that the actual movement of worship is initiated by God, that God takes the incipient human movement of faith and replaces, refashions and converts it. The worship of God has nothing whatever to do with self-knowledge. The self is neither its origin nor its goal. God is both the origin and the goal of worship.

We ought to learn to worship God at the point where he created Adam, where we cannot pride ourselves on human nature and human experience, since it has not yet been demonstrated. If I set my "I" beside Adam, I am setting a limit to God's possibilities. I am regarding myself as a fixed entity, even if "I" am a worshipper. Our starting point should be what God does to bring man into being (and God's actions are part of his being); or God's relationship to man as it is objectively, as it is known to him for instance in the Church, but which is not accessible to the individual man and cannot be controlled by him; or the relationship exemplified in God before he created the world and Adam. Even then, God was greater than his creativity. One cannot reach his greatness by starting out from limitation; one cannot attain the objectivity of his surpassing nature by starting with the subjectivity of one's awareness of oneself and one's condition; to arrive at God one cannot begin with self. There is in worship a certain impersonality, just as in listening to music attention is paid only to the content of the symphony and not to the act of hearing and feeling.

All that man is and all that the creation around him shows are reasons prompting him to worship: It has all flowed from God's creative power. In itself it is limited, but it points to a divine activity which is boundless and unlimited. In a finite way it reveals the providence of God, which is in itself infinite. The worshipper looks through everything to the infinite God beyond in order to worship him. God is all that matters. Even when God worships God, he sees that which is worthy of worship. When the Son worships the Father, he has a proof of the divine glory in the Father's generative power. Or when Father and Son see how the Spirit allows himself to be brought forth, how in his readiness he matches their active sending forth, what they see in him is worthy of worship. It is as if the prime cause of worship lies in the revelation of that which is worthy of it, in a self-manifestation which can be found both in deeds and simply in being. The Father is always revealing himself to the Son, continually and increasingly calling forth the Son's worship. So God, too, has reasons for worshipping God, reasons which lie in the manifestation, in God, of the absolutely other. All worship has its primary basis in the other's otherness. Where there is mere oneness, worship is not possible. The Son does not worship the Father because the Father is like him; that would mean that the Son found himself worthy of worship and that he worshipped himself. Worship is a relation to a Thou, a relation so strong and pure that only the Thou is of any account. Thus worship does not rest on a need but in the being (and the "being-thus") of God for God and for creatures.

The worshipper always has the most varied reasons and at the same time one single reason for worship, for God's revelation is always both manifold and unified. He proceeds from the Many to the One. As he approaches God, from whatever side, he immediately beholds the unity that makes

God worthy of worship. The prayer that the Son teaches us begins with the word "Father", which is a word of worship. Before presenting our various petitions, we must remember with whom we are dealing. We must begin by beholding God: All that follows must develop as part of this vision. When the Son says, "My God, my God, why have you forsaken me?" these words create the situation for worship. Distance is a constituent part of all worship, but the extent of it is realized only if one is drawn by God in faith and allowed to come close to him, only if one discerns how great he is and who he is. In being begotten the Son is taken into the Father's power, to experience there the distance between Father and Son. Worship's distance has nothing to do with a repellent fear or anxiety, nor with the distance of indifference which wants to be left in peace. It is the acknowledgment of a distance that already exists, a consequence of the other's majesty, in which nothing is visible (not even the distance itself) except the other's greatness.

In love, distance is not everything, but it is an essential condition which has to be continually recreated. I behold you because I have been endowed with eyes that can see you. I come close to your face and feel cheek against cheek because skin has been given to me that can feel you. But in feeling your face against mine I cannot see you, and so I take two steps backward in order to look at you. Love needs this play of closeness and distance, and both are gifts from God to love. Both come from God, who has created a whole spectrum of receptivity, and both are also represented in the relationship to God. Worship is of the parts as well as of the whole. It is of the whole because God has created us out of his will as a totality. But so that God can "see" what he has created, he takes us out of himself and places us, as it were, over against him. From this position we worship God; and to that extent worship is a part. And yet, at the same time that he projects us in this way, he gives us the desire to return to him. This return, however, does not overtake and cancel out the departure. Each act of worship contains material for new, increased and deepened worship. Each return calls for a new setting-out, just as, in physical love, no gesture can become obsolete since, in the interplay of attraction and withdrawal, everything keeps returning to its place.

When God worships God, he does so, not in a kind of jealous, divine exclusiveness, but in a way that includes all his thoughts and plans. When the Son worships the Father, he is in the presence of the one who has it in mind to create the world. And when the Father worships the Son, he sees in him the one who is willing to be sent to save the world. So from all eternity the world is included in God's worship, and one of the preconditions for human worship is grounded in God himself. Something of the communicable, mutual worship within the Godhead is granted and commended to men so that they may emulate it. When Adam is in conversation with God at the beginning of creation, he knows how to speak with God. And he knows this because he has received a definite share in the divine worship.

God wants our worship. That is why he renders himself and us capable of it. He makes himself perceptible and gives us the opportunity of perceiving him. The relationship was established in Adam. Sin obscured both our potential for perceiving and God's perceptibility; now, in order to pray, one has to grope and stumble over sin in trying to return to the pristine relationship. But the sinner cannot worship as though he had no sin. Sin makes his worship wither, spoils his joy in it and clouds God's image. That is why the Son had to come with all his ability to worship God, to show us what is really meant by worship. Adam was so quick to fall into sin that his abilities had no time to manifest themselves. We do see him conversing with God, but we do not see the rapture of worship. It is as though God first wanted to create things in a certain order; before revealing himself to Adam in all his greatness and glory, he first gave him the woman, so that, from experiencing the distance between like and like, he might more easily grow into the relationship with God. But the woman led him astray, and so it was not possible for earthly love to expand into divine love. The Son had to appear in order to teach us worship as it is in heaven.

2. THANKSGIVING

Surrender in love is a token of gratitude. In being begotten, the Son sees first the Father: his greatness, his worthiness of worship, the act of his love. In worship, however, he sees that worship itself contains and calls for something beyond the sphere of knowledge: an initiative, an offer, a response not of mere words, something which he and not the Father has to achieve and which has no other name but surrender. Recognizing this, he immediately puts himself at God's disposal; this recognition thus contains not only the disposition of gratitude but also the actual thanks rendered. The necessity of this response is inherent in the necessity of that recognition which worships, and this in turn is rooted in the necessity with which the Father generates the Son. Without this generation the Father would not be Father, and therefore without his surrender the Son would not be Son. The Father reaches out toward the Son, and with the same necessity the Son reaches back to the Father and surrenders to him. The Son's return to the Father's possession creates a unity which is always welling up, alive and fresh. The force with which the

Father generates the Son is, as it were, counterbalanced by the force with which the Son surrenders to the Father. Their unity is a unity of giving and taking. Moreover, since there is no temporal succession in this unity, the Father already receives the Son's surrender in begetting him, just as the man takes in order to give and the woman gives in order to take. Yet this simultaneity in God does not abolish the priority of the Father's act. The Father really begets; from out of his contemplation of the Son he performs this act in order to let the Son share in his vision. He cannot hold the Son back within himself. His very act of begetting is an act of surrender to the Son, to which the Son replies with his surrender. And gratitude is contained both in surrender and in its acceptance. The Father's act of begetting contains a gratitude to the Son for letting himself be begotten, just as the Son's willingness contains a gratitude to the Father for his wanting to beget him.

In God, the act of worship and the act of grateful surrender form a perfect unity; in man, the acts must strive increasingly toward this unity. In worship man gives to God complete dominion over himself once and for all; he gives himself away radically, and as a response to this he receives himself back from God in such a way that now, concretely, he can abandon and surrender himself to God bit by bit as time goes by. The response on God's part to unreserved worship is the wealth of his act of self-revelation, which manifests his glory in many aspects and wills that men take account of these diverse aspects. It is also that grace which comes to man in his multifarious temporal existence, making it possible for him gradually to realize the surrender which is latent in his worship. Even if someone were to be converted with the speed of lightning like Paul, and were to acquire faith, love and perfect worship in an instant, he would still have to arrive at an understanding of this act in all its human implications; he would have to recapitulate it so as to make it come true. Having once uttered an initial consent that embraces and implies his entire existence, he has to imprint this consent afterward on every single phase of his life and rebuild the totality of his Yes out of its individual parts. Otherwise his situation before God would be entirely approximate and indefinite; his will to surrender would be unconsidered, enthusiastic, unreal. To realize this will and to prove its genuineness requires an experiential knowledge of God's demands and of the ways of meeting them. It is not enough to say to God, "Your will in everything"—this must be proved true by obedience in every small detail. To say Yes and to be willing to surrender oneself without at the same time intending everything that this involves would be nothing more than ingratitude. For man has received his gifts from God: He must put them at God's disposal in all their variety and uniqueness, just as they were given to him. Therefore, in order to deserve the name, gratitude must always become concrete thanks.

When a woman loves perfectly, she gives herself without any mental reserve, and it is the man who awakens in her the response to his desire. What was unconscious and un-experienced in her up to then now becomes conscious, in order to take on the form of surrender. All this, however, takes place in, through and for the man's love. It is as though step by step, wherever the man goes, he causes the woman's love to blossom, as though he had made a dwelling place within her in advance so as to lead her, by his presence, to surrender. It is as if he imparted to her a substance which had lain so dormant within her until now that it seemed to be absent, but which now takes up more and more space in her until everything is totally surrendered. It is similar when man worships God: God awakens in him the will to surrender; he fans it into flame and clarifies it for a more definite, particular purpose. The substance of this will to surrender is given and molded by God himself; it is the perpetual response which God is always placing inside man. On his own, no man could surrender himself to God. He is able to do so because God, in accepting his worship, forms this surrender in him. He experiences how God takes possession of him, refashions his will and conforms it to the divine will, and in this experience he can only be thankful because, by God's power and according to his plan, he becomes a new person. At the most intimate level of his faith he senses this transformation. Before, he always felt a lack of unity in himself, as though he were divided into many parts. He had longings, the need for love, abilities and gifts, fragments which all seemed to have been created for some totality which yet eluded him. Prayer acts like a magnet, giving all these fragments the same orientation, guiding them toward God; or like a furnace, it welds them all together and puts God's fire within them, imparting God's order and unity to them.

When the Son becomes man, the Word of God acquires human form; a man, the Son of God, bears the Word of God within him. Since the Son, the Word, was prior to the man, in becoming man he was a unity before becoming a human multiplicity, and his multiplicity is permanently rooted in the unity of the Word. The sinner had destroyed the divinely willed unity of his life. Now it can only be restored by the Word of God made man. But this Word is prayer. In the Son it has been from eternity the prayer of the Trinity; in us, through faith and the knowledge and worship of God, it becomes the unity of surrender in gratitude which God grants us through the Son. Adam was, at the beginning when he communed with God, a unity. He allowed himself to be turned away by the serpent from communion with God and lost his unity in God. Through the Son, and more precisely through the eucharistic word of the Son, the Father restores to mankind the possibility of becoming a unity in God. Eucharist means gratitude. It was the Son's gratitude to the Father that caused him to become man and give his flesh for mankind, and hence there is in him a perfect unity between Eucharist and prayer—Word as flesh and Word as prayer—and through this unity he leads men back to the unity of God. The believer who receives the Eucharist can experience very strongly the element of gratitude in eucharistic prayer.

The one who surrenders himself does not feel that he is doing anything extraordinary: The surrender arises simply out of his gratitude to God and increases it in turn. If he sees that God takes everything from him, he understands that it is done out of pure love for him and for mankind, and so he can only be thankful. The grateful person who surrenders himself must not dwell too long on the thought that God loves him so much that he accepts his self-surrender. He must remember that God loves all the others in the same degree and that his self-surrender is a sign of God's love for mankind. Though he be one of the chosen few, he must regard and fulfill his election together with the others. This is what continually unites the private prayer of thanksgiving with the prayer of the Church. In the gospel the Lord calls his disciples and they follow him; but the movement of calling continues so that those who are chosen then have to share their vocation with others. (Only Paul is in a certain sense an exception, insofar as he considers himself to be one set apart and chosen by God alone; he was not among the original Apostles and does not share automatically in the fellowship of the later ones.) Thus in the grateful self-surrender of Christians there is something of the Eucharist of the Son, who thanks the Father for his unique mission by distributing it among all those on whom he pours out his life.

3. PETITION

Man's concerns are manifold: There are those which arise out of his human nature, his private life, his family, the Church, his country, the world, some in which he himself is involved and which correspond to a personal need of which he has become aware, and some that are much greater than he, in which he participates because he is alive at this particular time, but which extend far beyond his individual life: These are the concerns of the kingdom of God and of the Lord himself. When he encounters God in faith, he meets him with his entire existence, with everything that makes up his life. He cannot open himself to God, he cannot yield a space where God can work within him, without also trying to interest and involve God in what concerns him and what constitutes his life. There is a reciprocal invitation: Man invites God into his life, and God invites him to join in his work and to seek, as a believer, the cooperation of God.

If man's faith is weak, he will see in God primarily a support and will go to him with his little personal troubles. He will perhaps find it difficult to give way to God in everything and to trust that God understands things better than he. The more he believes, though, and the more firmly he is anchored in confidence and love, the more impersonal his petition becomes, not because he has lost interest in his own life but because he has to live it out in the service of God, and hence all his needs are dependent on God's will. In some way or other, all his petitions will be concerned with the will of God. He will use all his power of prayer to beseech God to carry out his divine will, to have mercy on the world and the Church so that they will be conformed to his will more and more and serve his purposes. His petition will become more and more a means of returning to God all the things that have ever been his or that ought to belong to him. It will be like an attempt to involve

God afresh in his creation, his Church, his people, his faithful. But in this asking he will not forget thanks and worship. He will recall that he is only showing God one side of the relationship, and that world, Church and mankind must not cause him to forget the sublimity of God, his goodness to all beings and his desire to be worshipped by them.

To pray for the will of God is to ask for it to be done everywhere, not only on a large scale, but in the smallest particulars, even in situations hidden from the one at prayer; and again prayer is concerned not only with individual matters but with the total picture. A person who prays for something particular should pray in such a way that his petition may find a place in the realm of the divine will. All "influencing" of God must always be conditional on man's being influenced by God's will. Every true petition is an expansion. If one's prayer is heard with regard to some detail, it becomes a cause of thankfulness and worship of the divine will; if it is not heard, then that provides an opportunity to realize how much greater God's will is than one thought or wanted to perceive. Anyone who petitions the Father in the Son's name will be heard, according to the Son's promise. But his name itself is an expression of his obedience, and as the Son only asks in the context of obedience, so do we when we ask in his name. To ask in the Son's name influences the Father who loves him, but it also influences us according to the mind of the Son.

When, in eternity, the Son lays before the Father his plan and resolve to become incarnate and to redeem the world, on the one hand he desires from the outset to do the Father's will in this—for the Father wishes to hold his world back from the abyss—and on the other hand his own personal will is involved since, as God, the Son has a personal divine life at his disposal which he can dedicate in his human form as well to the service of the Father. So he lets the Father's will become his own, lets himself "be influenced" by the Father; but he also "influences" the Father by prompting him to permit the work of redemption in accepting the Son's proffered service. The Son is at the disposal of the Father, who manifests his will in the Son's work, but this manifestation is itself an expression of the Son's will. Moreover, when the Son has become man, he possesses as man a new freedom of personality, and in it he desires to know and do the Father's will more and more, thus dedicating his own life to service. He freely commends himself into the Father's hands as his instrument, and he shows us this path of surrender that he has taken in perfect purity and invites us to follow it as he did. Even as a man he has an influence on the Father. The Son's influence is necessary so that the Father will permit the work of the Cross, so that, in his own will as it has been shouldered by the Son, he will recognize the full extent of the Son's will and consent to it. In some way the Son derives his influence as man from his trinitarian influence on the Father and then confers it upon us in the Eucharist.

This influence involves a movement contrary to that of sin. When Adam sinned, he went away from God and, as it were, compelled God to increase his efforts on man's behalf, to raise his voice so that it could still be heard, to go the extra mile in the order of grace. In the surrender to God there is a conversion: Man seeks to draw closer to God; he turns to face God and moves toward him. The Son exemplifies how man can approach God: It is as if the Son spares the Father the trouble of approaching man by going himself as God to man. But God cannot dispense man entirely from the effort entailed in drawing near to him; seduced by the devil, man fell by his own free will, and only by free will can he return to God. The Son accomplishes this movement, too, in that he approaches God as man. By his Incarnation he takes on both tasks: bringing God to mankind and mankind to God. He does the latter not only by placing himself in the position of Adam prior to the Fall but also by taking upon himself sin and its estrangement from God. The acceptance of this burden of sin contains a petition to the Father: that he redeem the world. In his redemptive work the Son is not acting independently of the Father but is in constant touch with him, a contact which consists first and foremost in a petition: that the Father prosper the work, make it fruitful and acceptable and abide with it, so that man's conversion to God may really succeed. The Son petitions the Father not to reject him even though he has now taken sin upon himself, not to remain far from the world at the distance created by sin. From this point of view, the whole course of redemption is a prayer of petition, and hence one can see the intimate connection between petition and sacrifice. Even as he looked down from heaven, the Son saw that he must sacrifice himself so that his petition would be granted. That is how it will be for believers also: God gives them a mission, but he takes something away from them and imposes a sacrifice upon them so that their petition for their mission's fulfillment can be granted.

The Son's petitionary prayer imparts a new meaning to worship and thanksgiving: He gives thanks for his suffering, and as a sufferer he worships. Worship has undergone a kind of amplification, residing less in the Father than in the Son, less in the one worshipped than in the worshipper. In the glory of heaven, the worship within the Godhead has, as it were, outbidden and outshone every possible prayer. The prayer of petition, strictly speaking, always rests on an experience of suffering, on knowledge gained through some deficiency. The Son's worship on earth proceeds in suffering, in the night: "If it be possible, let this cup pass from me; yet not my will but thine be done." The two things are united in the Son: heavenly worship and the earthly prayer of suffering. With the saints, the night of worship is always close to the day of vision.

VI

DIRECT AND INDIRECT

1. THE SAINT

The saint is the person who seriously lives only in God, who has God as his only aim, who seeks God in all that he does and tries to stay in his presence. He knows that he can do nothing by his own power, and so he endeavors to do everything by the power of God in such a way that he does nothing other than what God wills, and he expects neither more nor less from this power than what God wants to give him. His desire to live only by the power of God does not lead him to call upon it unreasonably and indiscreetly; he is humble enough to lay claim only to what God wishes to grant him. In his prayer he tries to understand as much of God as God wants to reveal to him. It is a prayer which ascends directly to God and hears him directly. And yet, precisely because the saint has a low estimate of himself and his powers, he is probably the very person who would be naturally more inclined to indirect than to direct prayer. He is not importunate. His knowledge about God's direct dealings has shown him how weak and unworthy he is. And since he is always a solitary soul, he likes to look to other solitaries, to see how they lived by the power of God. In the company of the saints he learns to pray. Thus he himself would sooner have recourse to indirect prayer; direct prayer is given to him by God. His vocation is bathed in the light of the other saints. So it was with Ignatius during his illness. Searching for true prayer, he reads the lives of the saints and continually finds there a "test" for his own life. He sees how the others prayed and asks that, for the greater glory of God, a similar prayer may be granted to him. He feels so clumsy, though, that he turns to the saints for their help as he prays. The Curé of Ars looks out from the unholiness that he hears about in confession to the holiness of the saints. In cases of specific sins, he always considers how a particular saint acted or would have acted in that particular situation. When saints are facing difficult tasks, it is very important for them in prayer to contemplate other saints who had to deal with similar difficulties or trials, and here contemplation must also mean being schooled by the saint concerned. This can be seen very well in the case of saints who lived at the same time, such as Teresa and John of the Cross. Their spiritual discussions are always like unformulated, latent prayer. They ponder their questions together before God and commend their concerns to each other's prayers, and each is grateful that the other "is taking care of things". They embody the Catholic form of friendship in which God is the center and where each knows that the other is right with God. If the saint who intercedes is already in heaven, this is no obstacle to their fellowship. It is simply transposed, and the dialogue becomes at the outset an open prayer. Instead of saying to someone, "Remember my intentions in your prayers", one says it to a Thou who is a saint in heaven. The intercession is thus all the more certain. And the dialogue becomes more "prayerful", since the heavenly partner already enjoys the vision of God. He can judge the importance of the concerns and knows what power is needed for each. The dialogue has become more wide-ranging be-cause the heavenly partner is involved in God's providential decrees and in the distribution of graces. There is the certainty that what cannot be resolved on earth will be dealt with properly in heaven. In this mediation, too, there is a connection with the Lord's word, "Not my will but thine be done." Each word spoken by the Son on earth was a prayer. The more Christian and holy a person is, the more he will seek to integrate his words into Christ's words of prayer. In faith he knows that he shares in the grace of the dialogue between Son and Father. Still, trying to pray constantly is one thing: Knowing about it is something else entirely. No one, not even the saint, should try to know whether he is praying constantly. Hearing confessions and, indeed, the whole life of the Curé of Ars was a single prayer; but he neither knew this nor wanted to know it. His role as a confessor continually drew him directly into prayer, and thus his prayer life was more evident, whereas in the case of other saints it is less easy to observe. Like Ignatius, for example, they had to live more in the "spirit of prayer". The Curé of Ars stands between God and the penitent: He stands at the point where the Lord is working, where Mary Magdalene accepts him and lets him perform his work; he stands face to face with sin and with the process and the ministry of pardon, in the midst of that event for the sake of which the Lord came into the world, in the encounter with the sinner. With Ignatius things are far less obvious; the founding of his order places him in a whirlpool of secular events, in a confusion of plans, projects and human relationships which may be useful to him in carrying out his mission. Much of what he does is expressly prayer; much is in the spirit of prayer.

The saint lives his life under the sign of that word from the Cross: "Into your hands, Father, I commend my spirit." It is abandonment of the self to God. On the Cross the Lord gives his spirit back to the Father, to suffer finally as a naked human being. Yet this does not mean that he ceases to be God-Man and becomes merely human, for the Father accepts what has been commended to him so that it will be efficacious in the spirit of the Son as the Son would wish. The saint is one who tries to hand over his entire being to God, and this surrender is essentially prayer. There is an ongoing journey, starting with

223

the sinner, who may believe in God but for the rest desires and seeks himself, and leading to the saint, who has given himself away totally and who, in commending his spirit to God, has entrusted all earthly and material things to him as well. God will look after him; he obeys the Lord and is following the one thing needful. He can live free from care, he can be almost completely passive and carefree, until suddenly it becomes necessary to be absolutely exact: at the point where vital issues of his mission are concerned. Then it will be seen that he has lived in God and that his life was the spirit of prayer.

The life of the saint is always characterized by involvement. The saint lets himself be involved and knows, too, that at some point he is involving others. In his indirect prayer there is a necessity that corresponds to a law of the communion of saints. This necessity not only arises from himself and his feeling of unworthiness but is also provided by the other saints, to encourage him and give him a share in their prayer of holiness. To some extent, moreover, they accept his particular contribution, to apply it to their own intentions. The patron saint is not restricted to watching over those who have entrusted themselves to him; he draws them into his affairs. It is as though the saints in heaven simply cannot wait to involve in their work those who pray on earth.

Moreover, the saint who is acquainted with God's immediacy will continually be thrown back into solitude. He is like a person who knows of all the world's riches and yet has to live in poverty: He is even more acutely aware of the contrast between rich and poor. He is rich because a direct insight into the fullness of God's grace has been granted him—whether in heaven or on earth—but then the treasure is closed to him, and now he might well doubt whether he ever really experienced that wealth. Or he wonders whether it is right that he is now excluded from it. His faith could falter. So, again, he holds fast to the experience of other saints; he needs to see what God demanded of them, which paths he led them along, how they managed to persevere through poverty and darkness. Thus, when through indirect prayer he sees that the saints experienced again and again God's direct intervention and yet had to go back into the darkness, he finds reassurance in this prayer and is encouraged to face the direct encounter, just as a person finds the courage to face a serious operation in knowing that others have gone through it before him.

From the example of the other saints, the saint learns that he must live also in the immediate presence of God precisely because God may have prepared a path for him which is not entirely parallel to the paths of others, a path which is unique to him. So he must be alone with God, and alone he must worship him, letting go all mediation, so that God can be sure that he is with him in solitude and so that God can say what he has to say to him. Maybe this solitude in the presence of God seems more exposed than before because now he stands before God in all his poverty and inability. Earlier his inability was covered by the ability of the saints, and since they are not God they provided an introduction for him: Thus his miserable condition was extenuated, and the depths were made level. Now that all mediation has become imperceptible, it is more jarring to stand before God. His certainty about what God is has become much stronger, more concrete, more massive. It can be almost oppressive. Nothing is left but the certainty of God. To achieve this, it was necessary to sweep many things out of the way through an earlier uncertainty, many of his own things that otherwise would still be there. The certainty he now receives has little to do with him and his inabilities. It is a certainty which goes right through him and strikes the core of the mission within him.

And God gives him grace to be united, in his presence, with

his mission. It is not as though God neglected his saint in favor of the mission. God wants the mission to bear the saint's mark, quite personally; that is why he illuminates not merely the mission but the man too, so that the saint can transmit this radiance to the mission. And in the lives of the saints there are always moments when they are overpowered, blinded by the glory of God and his grace, as if a vessel were suddenly to know of the wonderful substance it was privileged to contain. Peter experienced something of this when he cried out: "Not only my feet, Lord, but also my hands and my head!" It was above all in the confession of sin that he felt the ever-greater grace of God: "Depart from me, Lord, for I am a sinful man!" And again: "Lord, you know that I love you." The saint is overwhelmed in prayer when he catches a glimpse of what has been entrusted to him and also sees that it remains in God's protecting hands; that the mission is not something isolated and free-floating but a function of divine life in the world; that God exists at all and is as he is, and that he is so today, not only in the past when there were still saints, but now, here, in a human being who can scarcely grasp that he has been gifted in this fashion; that all this is still possible after so much sin and in spite of so much sin; that one has not already ruined everything a hundred times; that one knocked, with a weary and perhaps semiroutine prayer, and the door opens in a blaze of light. . . .

In the life of the saint it will often happen that he is considering some matter before God, trying to arrange it as best he can for God's greater glory, when he suddenly finds that God has taken up his whole idea and transformed it and brought it into a greater dimension, turning everything into glory. And he understands that God is using him, that God is alive in the ideas and actions of his servants and that something is really moving. . . .

The saint knows when he is in the presence of God. He also

knows that he must always be in God's presence and that at any moment he can break off from what he is doing to be tangibly summoned before God. But like the ordinary believer, he too must reserve particular times and hours in which he can be free from everything else and deliberately place himself in the presence of God. He must perform this act regularly—if not every day, then at least from time to time. He feels it within him, like the need for confession. And there comes a time when he must, as it were, dismantle himself, in order to place before God both himself and his mission— separately—and receive them both back from God, ratified. Perhaps his mission has several branches, and he is not sure when to do something and when to entrust it to someone else. In such a case he will make what amounts to a technical analysis of the situation in the presence of God, and he may have to show himself not only as he was from the start but as he is in connection with a particular mission. He will contrast his difficulties, lack of strength, ill-health, preferences and antipathies, achievements and failures, with the various things he has to do in his mission, so that God may tell him whether he must continue on all fronts or whether he could or should set aside this or that, whether certain modifications here and there in himself or in the details of his mission are in order so that he and it may once more be in harmony, as God expects.

In doing this he must give up looking at himself. He is not to observe and analyze himself: He is to let himself be scrutinized. Perhaps he should not even look at God in this moment so that he can be perfectly free to receive God's scrutiny of his soul, like a patient who, with his eyes closed, shows himself naked to the doctor so that he can examine him. He himself does not look. He feels the doctor's hand but does not see the significance of the various movements. And the mission is like the clothes he has taken off. Now he puts them on again and notices that this or that has changed; he will have to make some changes in himself here and there if he is going to fit. These adjustments, however, are by no means an excuse for looking in the mirror and taking pride in the improvement: Everything is directly for the benefit of the mission. He will never reach a point where he is satisfied with himself or his achievements. He is always aware that God's demands are much more exacting. The need for confession, too, never results in complacency but rather in pardon, in grace alone, which makes all calculation impossible. The man who has made his confession will never try to "make up for" his previous failure to love; he will simply try again to be more loving. It is not a matter of filling up or compensating for what was negative but of going forward into the positive, of looking and proceeding in the opposite direction, into God's fullness. The negative side will automatically be counterbalanced in the process. Thus, whenever the saint is in the presence of God, his mission rather than his person is primarily concerned; for in dismantling himself and his mission before God, he was not acting for his own benefit but for God and for the mission. He himself is only an instrument.

Even his longing to be alone with God must always serve his mission. He must never neglect the latter in order to have more time for the former. If, for instance, his mission is the apostolate, it must not suffer through his personal need for contemplation. Of course, this does not mean that prayer or even God has become only a means to an end, for the whole mission is to be carried out in the attitude and spirit of prayer. Thus the apparent conflict is resolved. And God is always the one who fashions love, whether the saint communicates it to God directly or indirectly by applying it to his task among people.

2. THE PRIEST

For the priest, who has to say the prayers prescribed by the
Church—the prayers of the Mass, the breviary, meditation
and many other devotions—prayer is already divided into direct
and indirect prayer in a way which is not left to his discretion.
He knows that through his ministry he is placed directly
before God; no one is more immediately in the presence of
God than the priest at the Consecration and at Communion.
And his awareness of all the time which his calling requires
him to spend in God's presence is mixed with a personal
feeling for the encounter with God. There will be moments
when he is permitted to sense the presence of God in a special
way; at such times it will often be up to him whether or not he
brings his prescribed prayers into this area. At certain times he
will have such a longing to speak to God directly that it will
burst through his tiredness or even his resignation, and he will
put everything aside so that he can get to God without any
intermediary. At other times the power of his office will seem
so vital to him that by comparison his personal powers will
seem minute, and he will not have the courage to turn to God
so unveiled; and so he will gladly seek the assistance and
mediation of the saints. It is no accident that litanies are most
often prayed in the evening; the faithful commend all that they
cannot do themselves to the Mother of the Lord or to "all the
saints".

The direct and the indirect are inextricably woven together
in the priest's prayer. The priest is a person who, because of his
studies, has a great deal of knowledge about God and, through
the grace of his office, a special supernatural illumination and
certainty. In prayer he has an insight into his relationship with
God. He is aware of his vocation and his priestly faculties, but
he is equally aware of his unworthiness in general and of his

personal sins and failings in particular. In this situation he is always having to face new tasks. Alone with God in prayer, he will meditate on them, reflect on what he has to do and try to achieve clarity and find the way forward. Finally, there will be a surrender not only to God but to the saints. They must guide him. They are to cast these tasks and their execution in a worthier form than he can. It is quite clear to him that, to achieve this or that, he would need to be purer than he is. A better man would have to take his place. Yet now he himself must take this responsibility. Then he remembers how much the saints had to go through before they were fit for their task. So he commends himself to them for purification, and on his lips the words "pray for us" also mean "work in us".

On the other hand he knows that, by virtue of his office, he has a task that puts demands on his whole personality. Therefore in his prayer he will leave a great deal of room for his direct personal relationship with God, so as to learn from God what must be done and so as to let it be accomplished through God. For him, everything can be a signpost pointing to immediacy. When at his official prayer, for instance, he may feel that some sentence is not as true on his lips as it ought to be: This inadequacy and this longing bring him into the presence of God, where he can plead and struggle for what he lacks. Or he observes certain qualities of the saints—the strength of Paul, the devotion of the beloved disciple—qualities which God gave them and which he so painfully lacks. In his pastoral work, in the confessional, in his conferences with people, he comes up against much that is beyond him and that only God can change. He sees not only the blatant sins of some believers but also the general dullness and lukewarmness, how the prayers of his flock to the saints are often close to superficiality and superstition and how they only pray to God directly when they are looking for tangible earthly results. He must replace and correct all this through his own direct prayer. Or perhaps he sees how he is lacking in charity in various ways, how he lets cowardice, weariness or ill-temper get the better of him, how he fails to give in his own house the example that he preaches in the pulpit. This too causes him to have recourse to direct prayer. Again, after having asked the saints to help him—all the more, perhaps, because other people have let him down, or because he has received their help in a tangible way—he will turn from them directly to God, to pour out his soul before him alone, to recollect himself in prayer's innermost chamber and to receive his own self back from God once more.

His direct prayer may also be one of thanks to the saints for their intercession. One prays ten Our Fathers in thanksgiving to St. Anthony in the belief that he can use them, that they are coin for his purse, that he can go to God with this fresh prayer and receive new graces for some matter currently on his mind. This kind of mediation depends not only on the personal prayer of the believers but also very specially on the Church's office. This office can put something at the service of the saints, thereby broadening their sphere of influence: through the prayer and the trust which the Church gives them, and hence also through the help which is asked of them. When the Son says, "Everything you ask in my name, I will do", he clearly indicates that through petitionary prayer God's power is increased—not in itself, but in its effects in the world. The same is true of prayer to the saints. Notwithstanding the freedom which belongs to grace, a saint can indeed accomplish more when he is called upon than when he is forgotten. God has given the saints tasks and commissions; he has shaped their spiritual countenances, and even in heaven there are areas and matters which are properly "theirs". No doubt Christians have arranged many things here to suit themselves and have assigned duties to the saints on their own, but there is a fundamental truth beneath these naive distortions. On account of his office, the priest has a particular responsibility to see that the saints' respective missions are clearly outlined and that in the awareness of the community they may become more vital and effective. Above all, this calls for his prayer.

Often the priest, whose ministry requires him to look after the saints' ministry in the Church, is aware of his dependence on a particular saint. Perhaps he became a priest because the little St. Thérèse pointed out and prepared the way. Or, as a priest in a religious order, he serves under the banner of the founder. The character of the saint in question will affect and color his whole life in the ministry; they will be linked in a relationship of mutual gratitude and reverence. For the saint, too, will draw profit from the priest's office. He can rely upon it when he asks something of God; it increases the power of his intercession. Thus, for instance, the power of Theophanes Vénard was no doubt enhanced by the veneration which St. Thérèse had for him, as was that of St. Philomena by the Curé of Ars. Holiness on earth is involved with sainthood in heaven in a mysterious interaction; although those in heaven cannot grow in the earthly sense, they can accept with gratitude whatever is offered to them in love because they themselves are animated by love.

Ultimately the priest's direct prayer expresses discipleship of Christ. If he has consecrated his life to the Lord and is trying to walk in the footsteps of the Master, then the best of what he achieves will come, not from himself but from the life of the Lord. When seen through the eyes of faith, encounters of a personal nature and seemingly private events are like things repeated from the gospel. For the most part this is not apparent to him, but occasionally he becomes aware of it to some extent. He recognizes and reverences the power of the Lord, and this throws him back upon direct prayer. He knows that he must live in the sight of God, just as the Son lived in the vision of the Father. For the redemption of the world, the Son renounced everything that was his own in order to be obedient to the Father alone. The priest tries to do the same by living entirely in the strength of the Lord, who was able to learn perfect obedience. However, because the Lord instructed his disciples to follow him, because together with them he founded the first Christian community, the first religious order, this direct prayer is once again transformed into an indirect one. The person who wants to follow the Lord directly finds himself in his community together with the Apostles and the Lord's Mother. Through them he becomes a member of the community of all those priests and religious who have followed the path of discipleship. The first, the eyewitnesses, continue to have a special importance: They are the ones whom the Lord, through direct earthly contact, made into saints. Since the Lord's Mother and the Apostles have direct experience of the Lord's requirements and know what forms they take, they can provide the best introduction to discipleship.

3. THE BELIEVER

A believer can often pray for years or decades without noticing whether his prayer is direct or indirect. As a child he learned the prayers his mother taught him and the ones he learned later in religious instruction, and now he repeats these prayers. It may be the Our Father, which is addressed directly to the Father, or the Hail Mary or a prayer to his guardian angel or to various saints, in which he leaves it up to them to bring his thanks and his petitions before God. In church he participated in the prayers just as they were recited. For him there has never been a serious question of how and when he ought to turn to God or to his saints. Perhaps his prayer was not sufficiently alive to permit the question to be raised. He may have had certain saints ready for particular needs—St. Anthony, for example—and may have remembered them and implored their intercession. But this was less a matter of deliberate resolve than a kind of habit, something which may once have had a more vital meaning for others and which he has simply adopted. It has never occurred to him to get to know the saints' actual areas of responsibility or to approach them in a livelier spirit of faith than the unbeliever who knocks on wood or recites a formula.

But if his faith is still alive and he is a thinking person, sooner or later he will consciously distinguish the two kinds of prayer. He will comprehend that there is a difference, interiorly, between going to God directly and going to those who lead us to him. This awareness does not mean that he has to opt for only one or the other; both forms of prayer will continue to go on side by side. Regarding the same intention he will sometimes turn to God directly, in childlike candor, and on other occasions tend to conceal himself behind the saints, aware of his unworthiness and therefore sending those who have God's ear ahead of him. This may express a certain faintheartedness and lack of trust; his complete trust in God may only be awakened when he finally comes to see what great things God has given him through the mediation of the saints and what confidence God has expressed in these gifts.

Once he becomes aware of his faintheartedness and lack of trust, he must try to counteract them by placing himself directly before God and speaking openly with him. It may encourage him to recall that at the creation it was God who first spoke to man and that even after the Fall he did not stop searching for man, sending his word to him and even putting the correct reply on man's lips. In this way he sees how much God cares about this dialogue. He also remembers the Lord's promise that the Father grants every request made in his name. And because of God's triunity, praying in the Son's name is part of direct prayer; thus it contains an injunction of Christ to pray directly. But the believer will not forget that, since the Church recognizes the saints' mediation and the different works to which they were called, it is appropriate for a member of the Church to remember the saints, not in some vague way, but in order to honor and support them in their respective missions.

By way of advice to the simple believer, one could suggest that he use both forms of prayer but try to reflect a little, from time to time, on what he is doing: to become more aware of the distinctive qualities of prayer to God and to the saints and the particular workings of each. In other words, he should take into account the life of heaven: the being of God, the being of the saints, their unity in faith and in their readiness to hear and to help those on earth.

Moreover, each time that a Christian takes stock of the kind of help he expects from God, he must recognize again how limited his hopes really are. They correspond more or less to the extent of his needs. He restricts God's almighty power to a human measure. Here, too, the saints can be of assistance. He knows something of their earthly lives; he has some idea of how they prayed, what they expected from God and how God fulfilled their expectations in a way intelligible to earthly man. At the same time he will remember that these very saints now participate directly in the fullness of eternal life; in heaven, though, they are still the same people they were on earth. Their earthly characteristics have become heavenly ones. The grace they received, the miracles they wrought, the help they rendered and received from God while on earth—none of these things came to an end with their death and their entry into heavenly joy; on the contrary, everything has reached fulfillment. The graces that were granted to them on earth were given with a view to heaven and so were already theirs in heaven. All graces received on earth remain in heaven and continue to have their effect. The "halo", visible or invisible, which surrounded a saint on earth was the radiance of a heavenly totality and an eternal vocation. Thus the person who prays to the saints is brought by their mediation nearer to the immediacy of heaven. Every grace that he receives on earth is the expression of a greater grace which is alive for him in God and in his heaven. This is guaranteed by the life of the saint on earth: If he was privileged to follow the Lord so closely on earth, to have even here an insight into the mysteries of God, how much more fully now in heaven will he be conformed to the Son and share in the vision of the Trinity! And how much more of all this will he be able to communicate to others! If the question arises to what extent earthly conditions impose limits on the saint's heavenly mediation, the reply is that one should think more in terms of the kind and quality of the graces entrusted to the particular saint than in terms of "quantity"—a category, ultimately, which does not apply in this area.

The believer will somehow seek out the saints whom he will call upon according to his own spiritual bent, his needs, the answers God has given him up to now and the things that God expects from him. This mediation is a help toward what is immediate; it is something fluid, something in motion, the opposite of a restraint or limitation. A prayer to a saint which did not have God as its goal and its context would not be a mediatory prayer. Every friendship between a saint and a Christian on earth is to serve the greater glory of God. The saint may not keep anything for himself, nor does he want to;

it is his part to bring people and things to God. From the example of the saints the priest should understand the meaning of his ministry: all for God! And the believer must do his best to follow him and must try to do what the saint does: He must open himself up entirely before God, communing with God as directly as the saint has done, both in heaven and on earth, letting himself be taken up into the direct prayer to which indirect prayer leads. Herein, finally, a relationship is established which is not unlike that between Christ and the Church, since, in founding the Church and in his relationship to his Mother, the Lord prepared a place for indirect prayer within his direct prayer. He could have been the Son of God on earth without choosing the mediacy of a mother, a *viatrix*. She, however, prepares the way, the *via*, for him; indeed, it is the way, almost more than the Son, to which she gives birth.

VII

BEFORE THE FACE OF GOD

1. THE DEVELOPMENT OF THE ENCOUNTER

The faith which the child learned from his mother is all of a piece, yet it is full of mysteries which can be unfolded. New facets are continually being discovered in school lessons, through experience in the Church and in everyday life. God reveals himself ever more fully, without our really having to seek him. He is like a permanent fixture: Just as one's parents and brothers and sisters are simply there and constitute the family, so God is there too, and dealing with him is what constitutes the life of prayer. He has power over everything, and the child need not reflect or wonder about his presence. If he were to think what his own father means to him within the family, or if he had something very special to ask him, he would gain new insight into the Father's being: He would go to his father and ask him for this favor; the latter would say yes or no and give reasons, and suddenly the child would have a totally new experience of what a father is and how it is possible to call upon him personally. As a result of this particular concern and the resulting conversation, the idea of "father" would have become much more personal. Similarly, sooner or later, the child will start to go to God about a particular matter that concerns him personally. He feels that only God can clear up this difficulty or confusion by stepping in personally. So his requests become much more conscious and explicit than before. Now, moreover, he is much more alone when he is in the presence of God: no longer wrapped in his mother's prayer, no longer simply a part of this praying family, no longer using only the ordinary, familiar words. This is something new, different and unique. He has to emerge from a shell of habit in order to take this step. He must seek God. He is more naked and exposed before him. When the young person puts aside the cloak of habit and dares to venture forth, God too seems more strange, more remote and greater. He has to enter into a new I–Thou relationship with him. And he may well be shocked to discover his own poverty, to see what condition he was in when he formerly called upon God, and to realize how little he appreciated the grace of being permitted to speak to God and how little he thought about what it means for God to make himself available to a human being and listen to him. Now, perhaps caught up as in a whirlpool by the starkness of this encounter, he will experience something of the grace destined for him personally; he may gain a new sense of the responsibility and the demands which God is placing upon him. An entire lifetime cannot make this kind of encounter grow old. It will recur again and again in the same or similar form, and each time it will be new and unique. This aloneness in the presence of God can never become a habit; this seeking God and being accepted by him is so dependent on him that it is forever breaking through the monotony of one's existence. It may be that this new experience shows that one's prayer up to now has been carried along by family and Church to such an extent that it scarcely carried itself. It was not supported by any personal decision, any desire to turn to God, any effort to enter his presence. It was more an inclusion in the order of the Church and in the order of grace than a meeting with God. It was not therefore wrong: It was an introduction to faith's ambience and atmosphere and a precondition for the new way of appearing before the face of God.

Once a person has experienced what it means to stand alone before God, he will want to repeat the experience as often as possible, not to accumulate experiences, but because every meeting with God carries within it the necessity of meeting again. On each occasion God opens himself like a beginning that calls incessantly for continuation. And each time the Christian can see more clearly that in these meetings all he has to do is simply be there and be ready, divested of all that might be a hindrance, that God himself wishes to take full responsibility for the encounter and that he himself shapes it. All the person at prayer can do is offer his emptiness so that God can put his fullness into it. Yet he is not empty; again and again he becomes filled with what is not God, and so first of all he must put aside what is improper. Again, he cannot do this prior to the encounter; it is God who turns him around. God must set him right before he can begin work with him properly. For instance, if he comes to prayer with anger in his heart, the image of God remains hidden. He is out of alignment; he must look to himself, quickly put things in order, ask God for forgiveness and make ready for him. He must do this in God's light, in his grace and according to his intentions. If he neglects these preliminaries, if he remains stubborn and brings his ill-humor and lack of tenderness toward God into his prayer, or makes his plea for forgiveness a mere formality, his relationship with God will soon lose its freshness and authenticity; God's light will grow dim, and there will no longer be any true encounter. As Adam became conscious that he was naked, this awareness already contained a reproach to God: Why did he make us naked? This nakedness, furthermore, becomes man's pretext for no longer appearing before God; he no longer feels that he is in a position to come into his presence. If he settles for this disproportion and becomes resigned to this condition, he allows the estrangement from God to take over. He becomes too dull and too comfortable to put his house in order for God, to take the trouble of making a "confession" to God or of coming into God's presence clothed only with grace. In every encounter, God asks: "Adam, where are you? Where do you stand? How is it with you?" To answer this question, a person must be willing, lucid, transparent. Once someone has left behind the habitual prayers of childhood and has entered into the personal encounter, there is no way back. He must live in the light of God and expose and entrust himself to the light ever more unconditionally.

2. BEING FORMED BY GOD

If a man is genuinely in the presence of God, it is never something colorless: It is always an event, a process of becoming. It can never be weighed and comprehended in advance like some mere situation, and the man who comes back from it is never the same as the man who went. Even if he tries to abide in God's presence and to maintain his attitude of prayer, this abiding is nevertheless full of life and fruitfulness which come from God. It changes the person who prays as pregnancy changes a woman. Her body shows that it is being transformed for the sake of fruitfulness and made to serve that purpose more and more fully; her task is to be the vessel for her child given to her by God. So it is with the soul before God: Observing the soul, God should see that it is bearing fruit for him and is adapting itself to this task as the fruit requires. The person himself should sense that God is transforming him. This is not to say that he should be thinking about himself or striving for his own personal gain; rather, he should devote himself more and more to what is demanded of him, abiding in it and serving it. When he first came before God, he was the person that he was by nature. But the longer he is in God's presence, the more he is despoiled of everything that cannot be used by God. What is bad or superfluous, all that does not lead to God, is left behind. He is like a tree exposed to a mountain wind: Gradually it takes the shape that the wind gives it and disposes its roots accordingly. God molds the man who stands before him until he has the attitude that God demands of him. This conformation to the will of God has nothing to do with self-knowledge. The person will certainly have to gain insight into his sins and shortcomings in order to rid himself of them. Primarily, though, he must see God's desire for him and the task or mission that God has intended for him. It may be a very limited mission. Yet because it participates so thoroughly in God's all-embracing plan and has its place among the myriad forms of mission, the bearer of the mission must not himself become limited in outlook. The workman who always has to repeat the same action with one arm gets overdeveloped muscles. God, however, wants balance and harmony in those whom he sends, and this is gradually achieved by standing in his presence. The person may notice that God always makes demands on one particular part of his being, but at the same time God gives him a love for all the other vocations. A person may be a theologian and have to pursue a difficult course of studies; yet if he does this properly, he will be interested in everything that goes on in the Church. This is a further argument against "self-knowledge". The disciple might try to limit and define himself according to his mission: I am a person who does this and not that, who loves this and not that, who is interested in this and not that. Such a fixing of limits is impossible in a mission, for here each person puts himself totally at God's disposal, for the sake of God's entire will and of his whole Church; he offers himself for service in a total plan which is far greater than the individual; he is assigned to a place within the service of a totality that he cannot fully comprehend. Starting with his particular area, therefore, he must remain aware of the totality and continually participate in it in a living way. God will not let the man who stands before him waste away or lose himself in specialization. He wants the man who stands before him—including the specialist—to love him as a complete human being, with all his abilities, not only with those which are currently being put to work.

Being in the presence of God is both something permanent that is not interrupted for a moment and something that has a unique quality at particular moments of the day. These two forms are reciprocal: Power flows forth into daily life from the moments of solitude before God, and faithfulness to God in daily matters produces its effect when one consciously places oneself in God's presence. This standing before the face of God, something which is full of movement, has its foundation ultimately in the heavenly Son's standing before the eternal Father.

The Son stands before the Father as a little child stands before his father and looks up at him and his unlimited capabilities. The child who is beginning to walk from one chair to another can see how effortlessly his father can walk from room to room, disappearing and reappearing; the older child, slowly joining one letter to another, observes how his father can fill whole sheets of paper; at every little goal that the child undertakes to achieve, he imagines that his father can do everything. The child who has some plan of his own—here we see the Son before the Father most clearly—goes to his father with it, expecting him to carry it out. The limitations that exist for the child are no longer there once the father acts. Thus the Son stands before the eternal Father: in boundless, loving admiration and surprise, desirous of being surpassed by the Father at every point. It is as if he had no other experience than that of being surpassed by the Father, as if he were bound by limits and wanted to be bound by them, as if, from all eternity, he has lived within the limits which he will accept as man on earth, as if he were representing man before the Father, while the Father remains God forever. But he stands before the Father in such a way that he does not contemplate himself, but the primacy of the Father whose power is boundless. It is as though he regards it as the greatest gift, that the Father should reveal himself to him at all, as if this gift is so precious that nothing matters but experiencing the Father as the Father offers himself to be experienced. His own being, his work and his mission also concern the Father, and at particular times he will have to discuss them with him, but he does not use his most intimate being in God's presence for that purpose. Here there is no room for anything but his relationship to the Father, in ever-new variations which depend on the Father and arouse in the Son wonder, gratitude, love and worship. His own being is only a function of his capacity to perceive the Father.

And so that men may learn how to stand in God's presence, the Son shows them what he does when standing before him. His demonstration bears the marks of the Incarnation as a coming reality, as a reality taking place and as a reality achieved. For mankind, too, it is true that their standing in the presence of God will bear fruit in their own being and in the development of their mission. But when they stand before God, nothing is of any importance except being itself; all else that flows from it is in the background. It is not to be despised, but neither is it to be taken up without a specific commission; it is enough for it to *exist*—in God's sight. It is what it is as a function of the Father's being, for at this point only one thing is important: to see God as he chooses to reveal himself. It is not that something in man has to be silenced or weakened: What is necessary is for man himself to be still, not wishing to change himself or increase his stature, so that God alone, in manifesting himself, can change and shape man as seems good to him. By showing himself, God causes man's becoming. By manifesting his being, God causes this becoming to appear in man as his standing before God. And man must receive all this in the measure in which it is shown him. What he does with this gift is subject to instructions, which may follow either immediately, after a short time or much later when he returns to ponder on this experience of being in God's presence.

3. ALONE AND IN COMPANY

In the presence of God, one is both alone and in company. To understand this, we must return to the Son's eternal generation and the eternal procession of the Spirit from Father and Son. The divine processions occur in eternal simultaneity: The Father begets the Son eternally, and Father and Son cause the Spirit to proceed in the same eternity, so that, while the Son is being begotten, he and the Father are already causing the Spirit to proceed. On the one hand he stands alone before the Father in a solitude which springs from the Father's solitude, for if the Father were not solitary he would not beget the Son, and the one begotten is never more alone than in the act of begetting which brings him into existence. But on the other hand, this solitude is subsumed into the community of the Trinity—since, while allowing himself to be called forth, he participates with the Father in a community which gives rise to the Spirit's procession. So the Son stands alone before the Father in company with the Holy Spirit, which presupposes a community with the Father. Standing before the Father, the Son shows his relationship to both Father and Spirit: Father and Son united in the common act of calling forth the Spirit, the

245

Spirit united with Father and Son through the unity of his procession from both. And if the Son shows his distinctness as a Person in order to stand before the Father, he can show the Father the Spirit's procession and the community of Father and Spirit which originates in it: In the Spirit he can show the Father a mirror image of his fatherly being.

During his sojourn on earth, the Son founds the Church. He comes to bring redemption through his death and through his Church, which he brings forth through his life (which includes his death). And he cannot separate himself from his mission. Within his mission, therefore, he comes before the Father both in solitude and in company. Just as he was begotten in God before the Spirit and yet had always breathed forth the Spirit together with the Father, so as Son of Man he stands alone before God and yet has always borne the Church within him, showing her to the Father. All his solitude before the Father stands as if in the shadow of the Church because he cannot separate himself from his mission. Even in those moments when he beholds the Father alone and the mission recedes to the background, he is still accompanied by it.

Like his, therefore, our solitude before the Father must always have the community of the Church in the background. We can deliberately summon this community to the fore-ground and present ourselves before God together with it. We can also move it back in order to be alone with God, and yet it will still be there. The Son is both head and body; we remain his members and cannot separate ourselves from the company of the saints. If we are alone before God and are being shaped and fashioned according to his pleasure, then the Church is also being shaped and fashioned indirectly. The Church is not only present as a witness to this shaping of men; she herself participates in it, and she must receive something from the process. In prayer one need not think about the Church;

indeed, one ought not. One ought to be able to be really alone in God's presence without any thoughts of profit for oneself or the community. Being alone before God is not a form of egoism. In allowing this encounter, God is honoring man, not treating him as a function of some general law. When, in the Church, believers become nameless, it should be an act of their personal freedom and decision. And the individual's conversion is by no means merely for the sake of improving the Church. Here, too, the moment of solitude is essential: The Church, which molds the individual, is also to be molded by him, and this requires a certain distance from the community, a distance created by God in solitude.

4. THREE WAYS OF STANDING BEFORE GOD

There is a quality in love which at first appears to apply only to infatuation but which is a part of every genuine love: the ability to gaze at the beloved and never grow tired. It is something very tender which is not to be misused. You are away, and I think of you; perhaps I imagine the sound of your voice and immediately I see you before me, whole and entire. Or you are hidden, and I look for you, full of the expectant joy of finding you—and if there were no sin, nothing bad could ever happen to you—for love's expectation is always joyful. It is like the expectation of the little child when mother is playing hide-and-seek: His joy is as great in seeking as in finding because the seeking is only a prelude to finding. This element is most pronounced, certainly, at the stage of infatuation, but since infatuation is itself a prelude or an accompaniment of true love, in love itself this game is good and Christian and divine. Say I want to know what your favorite fruit is; if you say, "Apples", your answer will tell me something and will delight

247

me. Your preference will be revealed to me, and I will rejoice to know that you prefer this fruit rather than another. The very fact that you have said so is enough. In the same way, the lover stores up a thousand details which fill out the picture of his beloved and speak of her. He believes her in all matters: He anticipates her reply as confirmation of something which already exists unconsciously in him. In his innermost being he knows that the beloved's answer will delight him and render her even more beautiful in his eyes.

This quality of love has its prototype in the Son as he stands before the Father. There are moments when, in love, he seeks the Father in order the better to find him, when his finding and delight in possession acquire the features of the joy of seeking. It is a kind of game of love where the play deepens love's possession, reveals its infiniteness and renews its own sense of wonder. And it is a genuinely Catholic aspect of love. The Puritan Protestant has stripped love of this quality, made it a strict and clear relationship, removed all superfluous ornament and reduced it to its "simplest form". But God is eternal abundance, and he has also given man imagination so that he can enjoy this abundance. No love is complete without it.

The implication for prayer is this: If the Son, who stands forever before the Father, sees him in a new way each time, he also worships him in the most diverse ways. Precisely because he knows that from whatever side he approaches him he will reach the whole Father, he does not scorn to contemplate him continually from new aspects, continually seeking him in an eternal finding. Similarly, every human prayer, even the most well known and most often used, even the Our Father, can be completely new each time it is prayed. In prayer God can seize the person at the most distant point and suddenly cause everything to open up toward the center. Thus a Christian can be attached to a particular devotion, and it is quite all right so long

248

as he knows that, starting from here, he must seek and find the whole, and so long as he knows that every other particular path can lead to the center too. The "little way" of St. Thérèse is especially fruitful here, since it starts from any detail, from things that seem to be insignificant and yet mean everything where lovers are concerned. Nothing is superfluous, since everything leads to the whole; nothing is superficial, since it points to the depths. Thérèse has that childlikeness which is fundamental to the game of seeking and finding, the attitude of the innocent child with his mother. She is all love. In love, nothing grows dull. So long as no estrangement occurs, every game in love is new and exciting each day.

We can think of the eternal Son's seeking and finding of God on three levels: the level of the child, the level of the man and the level of God. At the level of the child, the game is played for the game's sake and for the joy of finding. At the level of the man, it would be an anticipation of his humanity in order to know what mankind would have been like if it had not sinned but had continued forever to seek and find God. Even in heaven, the Son is able to appear before the Father as a sinless man; not as the "begotten" man that he will be (because his Incarnation will be an extension of his divine sonship into the world) but as any "created" man like us. He has acquired this ability by dwelling among us and in us. For he has the power so to purify us that he can be at home in us, and on the basis of this power he has the further power to take us up into himself, so that in a certain way we dwell in him and make our home in him. That is why in heaven, because of this substitution and adoption, he can live and can be as if he were us. He reconnoitres, as it were, the manner of seeking God that he will learn on earth, and tests it out in heaven in a transition from the childlike to the manly stage, in a way suppressing his godhead but not in the same way in which he will suppress it on the

Cross. This is no pretence: It is perhaps part of his truth which he wishes to show us on earth. Just as now, in heaven, he knows that he was an earthly man, so before the Incarnation he had prior knowledge of his coming humanity. Above all, however, it is as God that the Son is together with the Father in heaven. And the Father would not permit the Son to seek him only as man and to experience the joy of finding him only as man, seeing him from a kind of distance. It is rather the reverse: Precisely because he is God and as God eternally finds the Father, the Father allows him to become man, so that he can find him also as a man among men. But it is not through possessing the nature of God that he finds the Father; instead it is insofar as he is the Son that he continually experiences the Father as Father. Otherwise there would be no point in seeking, for God would always be only with God, and the Son would see only himself in the Father. What the Son seeks is not just God but the Father. Let us imagine a boy and a girl who have grown up together in purity. Now there awakes in them the love between man and woman; they seek each other, not as human beings, but in the complementarity and correspondence of man and woman. The relationship between Father and Son in God is also one of reciprocity and complementarity. Of course, this complementarity among human beings and in the Godhead has meaning only within the context of a shared nature. If man forgets his divine destiny, he will seek in the opposite sex only what is sexual and "other", missing the true unity of the sexes in God. Then the relationship will quickly be exhausted, for it can only last if it is in contact with the unsearchable mystery of human nature which lies behind it. Where the Son seeks and finds the Father in God, he encounters his personal Father, but in him he also encounters the whole of God, the Father's divine infinity and inexhaustibility.

Just as the Son is able to encounter the Father as a child, as a man and as God, the Christian too can do so through him. The one he encounters is God: Father, Son and Spirit. He can seek and find God *as a child*. This presupposes that he has remained childlike and innocent in his soul, or has become so. It presupposes that when he stands before God he is not obstructed by any serious sin; he may be a saint or simply a person who is faithful and truehearted, someone who may have been in serious sin at one time but has become transparent again through confession, or someone who is plagued by problems of faith and unbelief but yet has the grace to be simple before God and to leave the difficulties on one side, not mixing up his personal faith with his intellectual problems. He sees the questions of faith and wonders about them: What is predestination? How can we believe in the Trinity? What effect does the baptismal vow have on the sinner? But all these obscurities do not touch the security of his faith, which remains congenial, childlike, trusting. If one of these issues were to be resolved, he would simply adopt the new insight into his childlike faith. Even a great scholar and theologian can exhibit this childlikeness in the presence of God. Part of his mystery would lie in the fact that the core of his faith cannot be touched by any problem, that he loves God just as much and is just as ready to serve him whether this or that point is cleared up intellectually or not. This is the childlike way of seeking and finding God; it is a seeking which contains within itself the confidence of finding, secure in the knowledge that all is well.

The second way in which a person at prayer can stand before the face of God is as a man. Here he knows that there is some part of him living in the Lord, that in spite of his unworthiness an exchange has taken place; and within this knowledge he has two possibilities.[1] The first possibility is that he can meet God in the way the Son does, but concealed, perhaps, within the

[1] Cf. the section "Consolation and Desolation" in the chapter "Nature and Grace".

Son, standing before the Father in a manly way in that part of him which is entrusted to the Son, but without experiencing the Father in himself. The other possibility is of a manly experience of God through the senses, as it were, by that part of him which remains his after having handed himself over to the Son. All that he experiences is done in the certainty that it is the Lord who provides it by addressing some part of his self which cannot perceive what is done to it. It is like a person who keeps his money either in his own purse or in his friend's, for they enjoy such mutual trust that it does not matter who pays or gives alms. The person who prays like this finds God in the Lord's dwelling in him or in his dwelling in the Lord. The one who receives the alms (God in this case) has the same joy in either situation; but whether the person praying experiences the joy of giving, or whether his friend, the Lord, experiences it, is almost a matter of indifference: It is not discussed.

Finally, there is a Christian way of standing before God which corresponds to that of the Son insofar as he is *God*. This too has a remote reflection in man, not within the seeking for God itself, but in the fact that what is received is superabundant. This overflows and irradiates the seeking, which becomes a superabundant seeking. The image is that of the believing man who, on the basis of his vocation, his task, his very being, is aware that the Son has stood as God before the Father and therefore asks to catch something of this attitude of the Son, not for himself, but so that his faith in the task committed to him may be increased. In some way he lives by the mystery of the Incarnation; his borrowing from it is, in a way, the counterpart to the Son's borrowing in becoming man. The purpose of this borrowing does not lie in himself: It is to give more to the Church, the Bride, and through her to the Bridegroom. Its meaning is absolutely mystical. So each time the priest says "Domine, non sum dignus", he is aware, in sober fact, of his own unworthiness and yet lives in the worthiness which the Son lends him; for the Son was the Lamb of God and desired to stand before God as unworthy, maintaining a distance even while standing before God as God. This way of acknowledging one's inadequacy and at the same time borrowing from the Son's adequacy is foreign both to Protestantism and Pharisaism. It is the search for God who is ever greater, but in the perspective of finding that is enjoyed by the Son as God. Whenever such a priest seeks, he knows that the Son will find. And when this finding is received, it immediately goes through and beyond; it is given in such a personal way that it is immediately depersonalized, and it is clear that the only thing possible is to pass it on at once. It is the awesome point at which one is so dazzled by God's superabundance that it becomes unbearable. First, perhaps, comes the trembling awareness: Can it be that I am the one who is meant? It is such a personal experience that there is never any question of stressing or getting stuck on the I. Then, the clearer the call becomes, the more obvious it is that I am the one meant; yet at the same time I am given the opportunity to let everything go for the sake of this vocation. This is like a reflection of the Son's experience: The Father surrenders himself to the Son, who experiences this surrender in such a way that he must pass him on in the Eucharist, must share him out until everything has been given away. And the joy would remain, even if the sharer were left with nothing.

Augustine lived at this level, as did Francis de Sales, although in his case there is a kind of misunderstanding: He tries to style himself in the childlike form and then allows the "child" to taste a little of the third form. Francis of Assisi was first of all a "child"; then, when he was perfect, God translated him into the third form, which, however, retained features of the first. Those who experience the "dark night" belong preeminently to the second form, where exchange and concealment occur. Hildegard also belongs to the third form.

5. PERSON AND OFFICE BEFORE GOD

When the Son stands before the Father as a man on earth, it is his endeavor to be only a man, even in his silent prayer and turning to the Father. In doing so, he is trying to help the Father find joy in his creature once again. He is at pains to give to him in a new way the man of faith, of love and of hope, while effacing himself, the giver, in the process. He forms a community with his fellowmen which will be prolonged in the Church but which in the meantime has the purpose of presenting perfect man to the Father, man who has not attained goodness through the Son but through the Creator, the Father himself. The Son represents the two things simultaneously: He is the Son eternally begotten of the Father and the man who stands at a distance from God, and under both forms he is the one, beloved and perfect Son, in whom the Father sees him who is truly good. It is as if he manifests to the Father his origin from him, yet in such a way that he masks his godhead with his human loving, believing and hoping in the Father.

A husband presents his wife with a pearl, and she wears it so tastefully that she gives the impression of having been given a whole necklace. And the pearl really is so magnificent as to represent a whole necklace. Perhaps he says to her what a pity it is that he could only give her one pearl; he would like to have given her a ring. She replies, "Look!" and shows him the pearl on her finger. If he says what a pity it is that she cannot wear it as an earring, she says, "Look!" and shows him the pearl at her ear. She uses the pearl wherever he would like her to be adorned. This is an image of man's goodness as shown to the Father by the Son. The Son is one, yet to the Father he seems to be "everyman". On the Cross, the Son will gather all the sins of humanity, in order to bear them himself. But now, in his prayer before the Father, he gathers together all the goodness of which men are capable, all their love of the Father and hope and faith in him, in order to concentrate their radiance as intensely as possible. It is true that all men's goodness comes from the Son, and they receive their goodness through this very radiance; but where the Father is concerned the Son wears this goodness as man, to show him the human side of it. The Son's giving is so radical that it looks as though men have taken over what he imparted to them. In his love he represents them to the Father as if they were already lovers. He so burns to give them what is his own that he acts as though they had already accepted it, presenting them to the Father as if they were already converted.

This is the Son's quite personal prayer. But at the same time it is also a prayer in and for the community, a community which for the moment is still located exclusively within the Son and for which he alone is responsible. In his person he is the primary supporter of the community. But his character as a community-forming personality will pass over to the members of his Church: to the saint with his particular vocation, to the priest in whom person and office are united, and to all believers. They all stand before God as exponents of a community, and their personal prayer leads to community as and when God so wishes.

The Saint

A saint's standing before God with a community within him is no plain and simple fact. He can be in God's presence in such a personal way that, involuntarily or even voluntarily, he forgets his mission. And between these two poles there is a whole spectrum. It may happen involuntarily when God alone wishes it so because he wants to have his saint to himself. It happens voluntarily when the saint himself feels it right on this occasion to be alone in God's presence, leaving his mission out of focus in the background. There is another extreme in relation to these two forms of prayer, namely, the prayer of those saints who never appear before God except in the very midst of their mission, whether because God wills it so or because the saint himself will not have it otherwise. Here too there are gradations. One is inclined to a certain suspicion of those who always do everything completely deliberately and of their own free will, choosing whether to go before God with or without the mission entrusted to them, whereas there can be no grounds for suspicion in the case of the saint who, involuntarily and only as God requires, is always standing before God in one sense or another. In general, however, there is an alternation: There are times and moments in which the saint is more important to God than his mission, and others when the mission itself is the most important thing. If the saint himself makes no choice, God can work in him or in his mission or in both, within the relationship he chooses. But if the saint and his mission constitute a single unity as willed by God, God's shaping influence on the one will always benefit the other. It can happen, then, that when a particular mission begins to make itself felt it brings difficulties for the saint in his standing before God in prayer. But these difficulties and their mastery contribute to his fruitfulness. They never take the form of insuperable obstacles but of a gain at a higher level, be it a deeper insight or a better adaptation to God's will or a closer integration of saint and mission. Mission here always means an embodiment of the community. It is what, in the saint, is of and for the community: the seed of community, a task within the community, a fruit entrusted to the community. This fruit is greater than the I; it is the Thou, in all its manifold forms, which has been entrusted to the I. Ultimately this multiplicity belongs to the Church and indeed can be the Church.

Ignatius Loyola did not choose: He made himself available. He stood before God just as he was. He wanted to serve the Lord, but for him his idea of the Lord and his love for him were always linked with his idea of the Church and his love for her, although the Church as a totality only developed in him slowly. Then there was the Society of Jesus, which for him signified community. When he went into solitude in the presence of God, in a touching fashion he took his still un-formed community with him, just as later on he could take the existing Society. Many times he was unaware of taking it with him, but it was there all the same. He entrusted it to God so totally that God always had every freedom to act. The great St. Teresa chose to a certain extent. But her choice was less between herself and the community than between the com-munity and the Church. In some measure she set boundaries to the development of her community, stopping, in a sense, once she had reached the Carmel, whereas Ignatius, as soon as he had begun to move toward community as commissioned by God, although this community was very differentiated, never saw it apart from the Church. Little Thérèse never chose while she was in the world. In the convent she was often close to making a choice before God; this choice was often a matter of some common concern or a part of her vocation within the community, and she would then define that part. Where she would like to experience martyrdom in all its forms, integra-ting them all into her mission of love, she chooses deliberately and radically: She compels God, in a way, to see her in the form of vocation she has chosen. And she would have been astonished if God had suddenly decided to do something with Thérèse Martin, instead of with "little Thérèse" in her vocation, if it had pleased God to reveal in her some imperfection not demonstrably connected with her vocation in the convent or in the Church. Where she desires to be nothing but a ball tossed about, she does not choose, although it may appear that she does. She is simply there with her love for the Lord, and at that moment it is utterly unimportant to her whether the Lord wants her love or something else (or even spurns what she offers), in the Church or apart from her, in community or outside it. But this is one of the last times that she is found in this state.

The Priest

The man who wishes to be a priest has already met God and offered him his life in a personal encounter. Above all he wants to serve God in a form which is both official and personal. But, not having had the experience of office yet, though he can offer God service in a general way, he cannot foresee in detail how his personality will fit in with priestly office and how, through the office, it will adapt itself to God. He knows that it is the same God who encounters man in the sphere of office and in the personal sphere but that this encounter acquires a different face through being incorporated into the priestly office: So he cannot anticipate subsequent encounters with God. The person who remains in private life will always encounter God as the individual he is (including all that life in the Church, in community and meeting with the Lord in the sacraments brings); the scope of his encounter is more limited. God remains free to reveal himself in this way or that, but these revelations will always take place within a certain personal framework. The fruit of this encounter enters into the Church, but even if he has a distinctive vocation, the recipient at the moment of receiving the revelation remains an individual;[2] his knowledge of himself gives him a kind of outline of possible encounters. In the case of a person in priestly office, this framework is expanded and shattered. The personal and the official merge in a new integration: the sacerdotal. And even where the two elements seem to be autonomous, they are not independent of each other. The better a priest is, the more his personal encounters with God will bear the mark of his office, not in the sense that his inner life shrivels, but so that when he stands before God as a priest, God can do him no greater favor than to view him in the context of his office, never separating him from it even where his most personal development and guidance are concerned, which are destined to enrich his office. There is something unyielding in priestly office to the extent that it is subject to ecclesial law; but it is also a gift of grace from the Lord. The Lord, who lived his life entirely in the presence of God, equipped as man with a fully formed personality, was also the first to take ecclesial office upon himself in the New Covenant, the office of redeeming the world. This took place within his teaching, but, like his personality, his teaching was always in the Father's presence; because he was always receiving and accepting the Father's will, there was a continual living flux of offering and being accepted, of growth and development. It is not as if the Lord modelled his office on his personality; rather, he shaped his distinctive personality according to his office. But his office was ultimately only the expression of his divine love for the Father and at the same time the expression of his possession of the Spirit, and, to that extent, of his sharing with the Father in

[2] This refers to lay persons. Religious, including those who are not priests, occupy a kind of intermediate position: In their case the place of office is taken by their rule, which God uses to shape a new, superpersonal framework of encounter.

bringing the Spirit forth. In a way it was a continuation on earth of what he had done in heaven from all eternity: together with the Father causing the Spirit to proceed. And as this Spirit was a kind of Rule of personal life in heaven for Father and Son, he became the principle of his office for the incarnate Son. The Spirit was continually returning to the incarnate Son, and the Son continually received him back in order without any interruption to bring him forth in conjunction with the Father. Thus what is official in him always participated in his eternal *exitus* from and *reditus* to the Father; through this involvement the official side participated in all that was personal in the Son, and through him in the Father, and finally in the Holy Spirit. Consequently, office and person were inseparably interwoven in the incarnate Lord. But since the Lord wished to pass on his office to the Church, since it had to be made an exemplar, capable of transmission—not only for the first disciples but for all who would come after—he gave it a letter, a law, in the teaching of the New Covenant. At the same time the office had to remain so personal that whoever offered himself in total service to the Lord should discover his surrendering love in the office itself. The office, in its lived reality, had to be able to reconcile in itself the rigidity of the law with the mobility of the Lord's love and of the priest's love for the Lord.

The prospective priest knows about the reciprocal relationship between office and person and the personal factors which are part of the office. If he holds fast to this knowledge, his encounters with God will stay alive. But he will also need continually to offer himself entirely to God and be accepted by him. As soon as a man thinks he has arrived and that his relationship with God is permanently settled, as soon as he thinks he has nothing more to expect from God and God has nothing more to expect from him, as soon as he thinks that he has sacrificed everything that he could or that was required of him, the office retreats behind the letter. Personality becomes its own center, instead of interpenetrating with office; an abyss opens up between them, all reciprocal stimulation ceases, the person shrivels and the office becomes a dead husk.

The Son, who from eternity offered himself to the Father for his redemptive work, abides forever within the terms of this offer. It is manifest in his eternal resolve (which constantly wells up during his earthly sojourn) that God the Father is always accepting the Son because he, in turn, is always making himself available. And, beginning with the Cross, the Son continues to offer himself to men in the Eucharist; that is why mankind can continue in the reception of the Eucharist. This point, where the Son is perpetually accepted by the Father and perpetually offers himself to men, is the locus of what is personal in the priestly office. It is also the central point of the priest's standing before God.

As long as this standing before God was purely personal, time and place could depend on the person praying: It was he who decided when to go apart to pray, and where. In priestly office he is bound to prescribed occasions in what concerns his standing before God: He is bound to Consecration and Communion. He offers the Son to the Father and, in offering the Host, is himself offered. He is offered in order to translate the Son's office into ecclesial boundaries. Again, the Son is offered to him in Communion, and he receives him just as any other Christian does. The range between these two moments represents the center of the priest's existence in the presence of God. And if office predominates here, as it does, that is only because he has personally offered himself to the triune God for that very purpose. His personality is, as it were, enclosed within his office; and this enclosure is the salvation of those priests who no longer seek God personally because they do not want to find him. Out of his love for the Son, God makes it possible for them to perform their office completely and effectively in Holy Mass in spite of everything; this grace is included in the indelible sacramental sign. We can also see the predominance of office at this central moment in the fact that, subsequently, the priest officially administers Holy Communion. Communion signifies the whole glory of personal encounter, but this bliss is contained within the office, in the objective performance of Holy Mass. (In a similar way, lovers engaged in a project together can make some swift demonstration of love without interrupting the work in hand.) Since the priest's personal Communion takes place within the framework of office, he is, as it were, lifted up at this moment, borne through the personal into what is divine. The effect of his personal standing before God in Communion is so dependent on the Son's standing before the Father and on their reciprocal give and take that he is unable to assess what personal transactions are taking place. It is conceivable that a layman might have a communicable notion of his existence in the presence of God. For example, he might say, "This encounter brought me this or that as its fruit", and whatever he had not grasped would be simply the remainder that is ungraspable because God is always greater. But where a priest stands before God in Communion, it is impossible to put things into a personal framework of this kind. As soon as he becomes aware of something personal, it transcends the personal sphere and is passed on to others. This does not mean that the priest too cannot "experience" his Communion profoundly. But such experience does not reach the innermost reality: It lies beyond the priest's office and person. It is by no means impersonal but superpersonal, so personal that it cannot be confined within the limits of created personality but is oriented to the infinitely personal nature of God.

The first time Adam sees his wife, he is utterly amazed to find that he is no longer alone. What he sees in her is not, initially, a reflection of himself but—although she comes from him—the first human being. Certainly he recognizes much of what he sees, hands and feet and face. But above all he sees a totality of humanness, a total human being whom he does not know in spite of the fact that he too is human. This is a source of endless surprise to him. If he had not fallen into sin, this surprise would have recurred at every encounter; familiarity would not have blunted it, and every occasion of being together would have been a new and unexpected fulfillment. This first condition of mankind was part of their genuine imaging of the triune God. In spite of all knowledge and experience, the Son's eternal standing before the Father is eternally new and eternally different, for throughout all its love and surrender the divine tenderness of the relationship is constant and self-renewing. And the divine exchange of both in the Holy Spirit is like an eternal communion of the one God in the three Persons. It is a communion of surprise, for each fulfillment is more divinely fulfilling and fulfilled. In God, this being fulfilled by the Others is at the same time a being opened according to the measure of the Others, so that the particular Person is not restricted to his own particular measure of fullness, but is always being refashioned into a vessel for an overflowing content. In Holy Mass the priest experiences something of this law of divine Personhood which is beyond all personal and particular measure. He experiences it all the more personally, the more detached he is from personality; all the more in its differentiation, the more indifferent he is; all the more fulfillingly, the more he places himself naked and empty-handed before the Host. At the moment of Communion his person and manhood, although he stands at the altar, are elevated above the altar in accordance with the invisible proportions of the Host which he receives, containing as it does the Son before the Father together with the Spirit.

263

He is taken up into a triune encounter and shares in an infinite fulfillment; he knows this in his spirit and soul, as on a mountain one fills one's lungs with the fresh, unused air of a boundless atmosphere. One can only drink in the tiniest amount, yet one experiences the totality. This is not an experience of the senses; the priest participates in heavenly things whether he feels and experiences them or not, whether he is in a condition of consolation or of dryness.

When the priest seeks the face of God outside of Mass and his exercise of priestly office, he will probably do as he used to before he was ordained. He needs to be a human being, to have an individual relationship with God based on his former private existence. He suffers from a kind of official weariness arising less from physical than from spiritual causes, from his awareness that, in the continuing process of receiving in order to give, power is going out from him. Certainly, it is given back to him in the Mass, but its quality becomes more and more official. Nor is he meant to be subsumed under his office: Here too he should remain the distinct person he is. The strength he receives from the community and its prayer and from what he himself administers in the exercise of office accrues to his office first of all and then to himself within it. So what he is looking for in the solitude of his room is like what the Son was looking for in his prayer on the Mount of Olives, when, as it were, he appeared before the Father for the last time as an individual, private person before entering upon the purely official path of the Cross. In his daily solitude with God the priest experiences something of this "last time" as he finds the strength to carry and do justice to the cross of office. To do this the Son recalls his eternal offer, the resolve made in heaven to redeem the world. And he makes a totally new offering of everything, now that his will no longer exhibits primarily a divine quality but is increasingly colored by what is simply human, now that he can evaluate with his human will the importance of the office of the Cross. So the priest puts his will—which is both personal and official—into the Father's hands, recalling his act of surrender at his ordination before he received the office.

Toward his wife Adam played both a personal and an official role: personal as between fellow humans, official insofar as he mediated God. Again, Christ also is both person and office: person in his life among men, office as the mediator of the Father. And through him the priest is both office and person. But all three must hand over their dual nature to the Father so that he can increasingly produce unity in a lucid, unconfused, living interplay. Renunciation of what is personal in office is not something achieved once and for all; man must always have a personality to offer to God so that its renunciation keeps its freshness within the context of office. Just as one cannot be emasculated in order to be virginally chaste, one cannot become impersonal in order to be official. The Son renounces his divinity without ceasing to be divine, and on the Cross he renounces his human form without ceasing to be a man. He makes a double sacrifice—the Son of Man to the divinity, the Son of God to the humanity—and in his doing so, his official character as mediator, his very unity as God-Man, is built upon a heightened renunciation. His unity is based on an indifference which is the opposite of apathy, namely obedience, the surrender which is ready for anything. The priest, too, as he stands before God, must renounce what is personal for the sake of his office, and as a person he must renounce the privileges of his office so that God may take him as an individual and remodel him unreservedly. He must be offered to God as a whole and undiminished man.

The Believer

The ordinary believer at prayer has the whole range of possibilities open to him, from prayer in complete solitude to prayer in full community, in any place and at any time. Generally speaking, however, he prays according to a narrowly restricted pattern; he keeps to a minute selection of prayers until the day he dies. For the most part he does not grasp the fact that God's grace is more important than his own understanding and preferences, nor that the whole plan God wants to realize in him is infinitely greater than the petty scheme he has put together in his daily timetable. Very often his family life and his work seem so important that he can always bring them into his prayers in all their concreteness, but all the while he is afraid that God might take them from him and change them. Somehow or other he cannot quite trust God to guide him. If his prayer in solitude is so often a colorless affair, it is primarily because he seldom opens himself entirely to God, seldom puts himself at his disposal, rarely has the will to encounter God in utter nakedness, and for the most part thinks it enough to rehearse his own opinions and concerns before God, tacitly assuming that they coincide with God's point of view. And if, for the time being, God does not make some move, he takes it as a sign of his agreement.

Really to stand before God in prayer would mean quickly revealing one's life to God and then letting go of it, trying to be so genuine in his presence that he can manifest himself to one. It would mean looking at him and not at oneself, not using words in one's own sense but in the original sense they have as used by God. For the believer, the hardest thing is perhaps really to stand before God in *faith* and not as a secular man full of his own notions and plans. The definition of the saint is a person who wills what God wills; he is forever leaping into the abyss of God. The priest is continually being compelled to do this because of his office, because of people's expectations and also, to a small degree, through the many prayers he has to say. For the ordinary believer, prayer is something freely taken on, but in the main it is not really free because he is so entangled in worldly concerns. If, in spite of this, he makes the attempt, he will immediately see how much God has to say to him and how the difficulties which he regarded as insurmountable can change, loosen and be resolved. If he really prays stripped of all externals, he will recognize that God has something serious in store for him. He may even see this more quickly than the saint and the priest because God makes allowances for his difficulties and goes to meet him. When he actually achieves something, the average pupil gets quicker praise than the exceptional one.

A man lives his life with his memories and with his estrangement from God through sin; and if he takes the trouble to think about his past, he knows that there were times when he stood before God, that he did try at one time to make a promise, that once he did experience some special grace, that on some other occasion his prayer was heard. But between these isolated points there is again the estrangement from God. To find his way back to God a decision and an act of the will are required, more than a fleeting thought or a throwaway remark, a pseudoprayer, if he is to return to the place where he reaches God with his desire to let his whole will be done.

Because of his calling, the priest has so much to do with God and divine things that he simply has to surrender himself and return to prayer. He has a stock of grace in God's sight, and God will recall him all the more quickly. The layman may have to apply more effort to travel the greater distance from his everyday life back to God. If the priest is in danger of praying in a habitual way, the layman is in danger of no longer praying at all and of forgetting about the path to God.

The layman's prayer life, too, is shot through with tensions: between personality and community, where community is embodied by the supernatural Church but also by the natural bonds of society. Thus someone may sense a strong tension between his private life of prayer and his professional life among unbelievers; the necessity of being an upright Christian in this milieu obliges him to cultivate a particularly intensive prayer life. To live and exert influence as a Christian, he needs constantly to be sustained by the power of his prayer. The tension between Christianity and the world must impart a fresh vigor to his prayer. He is light of heart in the presence of God in quietness; but this changes when he goes out and enters into dialogue with his surroundings, where he may find scarcely a trace of grace. He needs redoubled strength if he is to shine in the world and to bear the fruit of his prayer into such a situation.

Moreover, the saint knows exactly what his proper place is. Little Thérèse is in Carmel, in a clearly delineated vocation, whether she stays in France or is sent to the missions. The great Teresa, founding her convents, is unshakably sure that she is doing what God wishes of her. The Curé of Ars must be in his village, and every time he tries to flee to the monastery he is inevitably brought back to it. The priest and the religious similarly know from their office and rule that they are in the right place. The layman lacks this precise certainty, since he lacks the framework of office and rule. He is somewhere in the world; as far as his faith is concerned, the particular place is to a certain extent fortuitous. So his prayer will retain a certain personal tension of searching. Of course he has a kind of "mission", but one that he can partly choose and shape himself and adapt to his possibilities. The saint is and must be naked. The priest has his habit. The lay person can tailor his coat according to fashion. The saint is the one who is most defined by his framework: He must at all costs remain within the space allotted to him. With regard to the strictness of his framework he stands above the priest. Paths like the "dark night" of John of the Cross, the darkness experienced by little Thérèse, and John Vianney's struggles with the devil are utterly personal and unique; the saint pursues his path not without freedom (indeed, his cooperation is expected), but it is a path on which he becomes the person he is to become, and none other. The path, the vocation and the obligation are so objective that the saint must pursue and realize them at all costs, even at the cost of his life, just as a mother in childbirth gives her life, if necessary, to save the life of the child. The ordinary Christian, with no such unequivocal vocation, is not pushed into an ultimate decision of this kind. As a layman in the world he can do this or that to please God more. He can advance his spiritual life here or there; he can pray more and do various things to improve. What the saint does is irrevocable, for it is part of an irrevocable mission. If a person comes to his confessor and says that he is desperately wrestling with God, there may be a vocation at stake.

In a way, the lay person's position in relation to the Church is also somewhat vague. Of course he is a member of the Church and has his place there as a layman; that much is fixed. But this position is not clearly defined. The individual layman may have a particular area of operation (Paul accords charisms to the laity as well) in response to the needs of the Church. The vocations of the saints are dispensed by the Bridegroom. But there are vocations within the Church which are dispensed by her as the Bride: personal tasks within the community. For the most part, the Church today has forgotten about this; in place of personal charisms she has erected the associations which tend to the lowest common denominator. The Church should not be concerned with those who try to avoid rendering service but with Christians who are willing to accept personal responsibility. She ought also to decide the distribution of tasks somehow according to the vocations of the saints which God has given her. If a particular saint had the gift of healing, others should arrange things so that the sick could be brought to him in an appropriate manner. It is a question of distributing the balance. The priest would play a mediating role between the person with the charism and the layman, and by virtue of his office would fashion, structure and build up the community.

Since the Christian has an indeterminate position in the Church—although the community itself has a fixed structure—all his prayers and good works and thoughts are invisibly and very quickly absorbed by her. He gets no general picture of what is achieved through his work and prayer. He does not even know where he stands with regard to his own prayer, nor what is his locus in God. We can illustrate this by a comparison with Adam. God spoke with Adam in Paradise, but not in the sensory, adumbrated form as subsequently through his incarnate Son. He placed his word deep inside Adam, and Adam was in touch with God in a kind of innocence and nescience which was no longer present after the Fall. The layman moves in the plane between the Adam who sinned and the Adam who did not sin. He proceeds from Adam the sinner to reach what lies in fact behind him. But he will never quite reach this goal on earth. Although the triune God has opened himself and sent his Son to earth to speak with Adam a second time, the goal is unattainable. The first Adam did not listen to the word within him. The second Adam, who is God, bent all his senses to God in order to be the manifest Word: the Word made perceptible to the senses for the benefit of sense-bound men, the Word which performs in the Host the miracle of being sensible flesh in a spiritual manner for all who come after. That is how obliging God is, coming to meet the sinner as the Word perceptible to the senses. He also comes to meet him by obliterating original sin in baptism, thus shortening the path back to the sinless Adam. Adam had gone the whole length of the way from God's word to the commission of sin—which was potentially in him ever since he failed to make a firm resolve not to sin. Not until he was seduced by the woman did he make a definite decision; she, seduced by the serpent, took his failure to decide into her own sin and thus, in effect, decided for him. And as it was more in Eve than in himself that Adam decided to sin, so it is in Christ that he decides to repent and believe. He is caught in a tension between Eve and Christ: This is no peaceful middle position but a state of continually being pulled back and forth between opposite decisions. But just as he could not see that his failure to decide made it easier for Eve to seduce him, so now he cannot see that he needs to make a total decision to follow Christ and must choose what Christ has chosen. From his impossible halfway state he is still trying to get back to the state of Adam prior to the Fall, which is unattainable on earth; but he is deprived of insight into the difficulty of his situation. A return to Paradise is impossible simply because that which, in the sinless Adam, was a kind of priestly office has become explicit after the Fall in the form of ecclesial office. Even the most childlike priest will never be able to have that paradisal naiveté for which the layman strives in vain. The priest and the religious have already made their choice. Adam was the one who did not choose. The layman is somewhere in between. Eve should have taken the place now occupied by baptism: She should have prevented the slide into sin and prevented Adam from coming into contact with the serpent. Over against her is Mary, who took the incarnate Word into herself, just as Adam took to himself the word of the serpent.

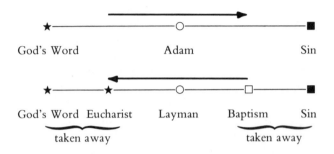

VIII

NATURE AND GRACE

1. PRACTICE AND SURRENDER

We start praying properly when faith becomes important to us and when communion with God becomes a real necessity. Prayer reveals its meaning and we try to pray in such a way as to realize this meaning. No longer is it a time to be filled out somehow, with an eye on the clock; it is a central point, focusing all preceding and succeeding time. To prayer belong both a preparation and an aftereffect which span the time intervening between actual praying. That is why it is very important, especially for the beginner in the life of prayer, to grasp prayer's objective meaning. We must examine ourselves to see how far we have understood this meaning and to what extent it has been realized in our own prayer. We do not do this by trying to analyze the grace of God in detail or discover how his grace has answered or affected us; indeed, we do not do it by concentrating on our own prayer at all. What we should do is become aware of the greatness and extensiveness of prayer in itself and then see how far we are from appreciating it and in what areas we need to make special efforts, or even to learn all over again. By deepening our understanding of faith we receive much that is new within prayer also. We see how much we have neglected in our communion with God so far. We resolve to do better. This new awareness results in a new adaptation to God in prayer; and this transition from understanding to its fulfillment in prayer is fundamental to faith. It is an adaptation of human nature to the supernatural God. We do not attempt to appear before God with our natural reason and our personal capabilities, as if we were confronting some object to be researched: Our approach is that of a striving toward surrender, which is in itself the beginning of surrender. Nor must we forget that our spirit's orientation toward and contemplation of God are themselves effects of divine grace, and that our very thinking about him is dependent on the objective influence of his revelation. My unaided reason can reflect profoundly on God, but for the most part this only results in a new distance between us; the insight gained is constricting instead of being content with the simple truth that God is with me and accepts me, and that I may accept him. In prayer, of course, we are not, as it were, hypnotized by God; the fact that God is so near to us makes us freer, and what we do together with God is done better and more productively. There is a kind of communion and collaboration that expands man's horizon and freedom. When two artists work together on a project they do not inhibit each other, but each creates an area in which the other's work can come to fulfillment: Thus the goldsmith's tabernacle has a creative effect on the architect's church. They both operate within a relationship of trust which is founded on a common will and a common love of the work in hand. In the same way there is a relation of trust between God and man. God does not overpower man; he does not oppress man in his role as the "Absolute". He helps man toward his freedom. Man can invite him and ask him to fashion the good in him. Protestants largely misunderstand this relationship, seeing God in terms of an enchanted circle: Once one has entered it, God alone takes over.

At the same time man must not take up prayer with the idea that it is the meeting of two somehow equal partners. The fact that there are two sides and that there is cooperation must arise as a new discovery within every prayer. Primarily it is the creature entering into the presence of the Creator. The being

274

that is not God, that is infinitely other than God and yet has his
origin in God, whose whole nature is solely dependent on God
and only intelligible through him, enters the presence of God
who is not a pious notion but the highest reality, and he is
exposed to this reality in all his nakedness and transparent
poverty. At this point the very idea of cooperation is utterly
remote. Even if the idea had suggested itself during the preparation for prayer and in prayer's realization, it must now be
suspended within prayer, to be recreated out of the encounter
with God: out of the clear relationship of God and his creature.
It is true that prayer will consist in God's increasing and my
decreasing in order to let him become everything in me (as he
is in everything else), and I certainly cannot push God into the
background in the encounter and give prominence to myself;
yet, in all truthfulness, I must stand before him as an "I", even
if only for a moment. Initially, before one has acquired the
habit of prayer, an effort may be needed to free oneself from
the world in order to stand naked before God. But sooner or
later it must be done: I must leave myself open to God. Later
on it becomes easy and natural. This nakedness also provides
the guarantee that, in the important decisions which occur
within prayer, prayer's results are not being influenced by
one's own will but come purely from God.

Part of this separation which leads to nakedness before God
lies in freeing oneself from everything that exercises one's
mind—later it can enter again into the content of prayer. Every
prayer is under the guidance of God, and hence the person at
prayer cannot determine its subject matter. In any case it is by
no means certain that God will take up the subject which I
present and suggest to him. I may have some burden to bring
to God, but he may leave it aside and introduce another topic
without causing the least distraction. In a similar way, God
may alter the mode of prayer (except in the case of prescribed

vocal prayer): I decide to pray vocally, for instance, and God replaces it with contemplation. The praying person offers himself to God in such a way that he can be led.

This is the origin of all supernatural (extraordinary) paths of prayer. All they presuppose is perfect indifference in prayer. The man who wants to fashion his own prayer himself, deciding in advance what may or may not take place, restricts God to one path and prevents him from undertaking any supernatural work. But if he tries to be ready for anything, God can mold him in prayer as he will. The more plans he makes himself, the fewer opportunities he leaves for God. If he is content with what he has done and experienced so far in prayer, his prayer is more a memory than something present or future. To want to fashion prayer entirely oneself, refusing to surrender to God, is to be blinkered and to obscure one's view of him. Conversely, the man who is really open to God will find that God reveals many forms and variations of prayer to him.

It often happens that, as he prepares for prayer, the beginner grasps its meaning and eagerly enters into it. Then, as he tries to accomplish it, he finds that the meaning is withdrawn from him. He has expected something which did not materialize. He thought he had understood something, only to find, as he prayed, that it had become obscure. Suddenly prayer has become empty and even boring, and he is tempted to regret having spent so much time on it. An abyss opens up between preparation for prayer and its fulfillment. This phenomenon is not what is known as "dryness", but arises from a general insecurity. The whole thing was conceived in too intellectual a manner. He did not consciously intend to give God instructions, yet now he is puzzled to find that God does not correspond to his unconscious expectations. He did not intend to calculate results, and yet, covertly, he was speculating as to what should happen. In such a situation the best thing for him to do is to turn to quite simple prayers that suit his taste at all times, to vocal prayers which he finds stimulating as he recites or ponders them. He uses these reflections to enliven his prayer. And setting out from the familiar and congenial meaning of the words, he tries to go on to their meaning as perceived by God, not praying the words as fixed statements, but in an open and receptive spirit. For instance, a mother may like to address a prayer to the Mother of the Lord. In doing so, she can certainly bring into the prayer her own maternal experience and love, yet she must be ready to experience the meaning of the greater motherhood of Mary which is latent in the words and to let the words be filled with Mary's spirit. This is a simple way of learning to pray properly in the presence of God without doing him violence. This expansion of prayer involves a renunciation of one's own experience, although it served as a starting point and a basis. A bridge has been built, but, once one is across, it collapses. It is an attempt leading toward the sacrifice which is absolutely essential if God is to control events. This bridge may also consist of my occupations, responsibilities and tasks. Everything can be a means of access, provided that prayer does not cling to it rigidly. The ultimate goal is always to allow God's free operation in the soul, an operation which alienates the soul from itself in order to move it toward God in the state he wishes it. Things which concern the praying person may smooth the path, but they are never conditions. It may be that God wants to use one of these things as a way to him, setting it aside once it has performed its service. An artistically gifted person might try to approach God through works of art, drawing them into his prayer, and God might indeed draw nearer to him through them. But subsequently God may visit him with blindness or put him in a situation where no beauty is to be seen. There too he will be grateful to art for having brought him where God wanted him, to a place where God has become infinitely greater and more important than all art.

When God inspires someone to pray, the desire to pray is itself due to God. But in prayer itself God works more extensively and more profoundly. What led him to pray was something external, a shell; now comes the inner content, the reality, which is the transformation of the one praying into the person God desires. Initially God takes him just as he is: with his ignorance, hesitation and doubts, his more or less goodwill, with what he offers and with what he withholds. Then gradually, in a timescale which man cannot calculate, God begins to fill and complete him. The man tries to separate himself from whatever prevents his coming to God, and God takes over every empty space thus made available, filling it with his grace and will. The more a man is to be filled by God, the more he needs to have emptied himself and to have died to all that is not of God, so that the life of God can pour forth and take the place of his dying. God's fullness can express itself in such a way that the person never again lapses from the attitude of prayer: He remains constantly attentive to God, endeavoring to do his will, remaining within God's purposes, trying to perform in a spirit of surrender whatever God shows him and asks of him, in virtue of the inspiration and strength which he gives him. When God takes things away he does not leave a wasteland behind. Right at the beginning of his prayer life a man can see in detail how God replaces what he sacrifices to him with something better, something divine. He discovers that what is sterile in him is supplanted by God's fruitfulness, an experience that contains the germ of true humility: He sees that he can do nothing of himself and that God does everything. At the beginning he can pick some visible new fruit of prayer almost every day. He discovers this in the changes he is undergoing, in the things he can do, in the feeling of being continually accompanied by God. He can almost give an hour-by-hour account of what God is doing with him. But since the real relationship with God lies in God infinitely more than in man, this tangible aspect of grace is mostly given as an encouragement at the commencement of a life of prayer. Later it withdraws more and more into God, and the person may experience barrenness and desolation; he may fail to discern any progress because now everything is taking place within a surrender which lays down no conditions, and all fruit is now to be found on God's side.

At first the life of prayer can fire a man with enthusiasm like a new way of living, almost like a new game. This initial enthusiasm contains much impurity that must be refined if the prayer is to become something permanent in his life. In prayer there are certain experiences of God which can arouse a great thirst for more experience, a thirst linked with the pain of realizing how much of one's life has been frittered away in bad prayer or no prayer at all. He wants to make up for lost time, but to have as much as possible too. And he wishes that what he now desires should last forever! He does not want to see that there can be an exaggeration in this thirsting and that there is prudence in moderation. Excess is human, and it provokes a human backlash—sated distaste. In this condition, borne along by blind fervor, with very little experience and with no true estimate of oneself, it is essential to have the guidance of a priest. The person praying knows that prayer is nourishment, but in order to profit from it, he needs to be shown the proper measure and method. And here he must adhere strictly to the advice given, even if it does not address his situation perfectly. Perhaps he might like to do more or to do things differently, but obedience contains a fruitfulness for prayer, especially since even the most intimate prayer and the greatest thirst for it are not merely matters between the soul and God but immediately flow into the sphere and experience of the Church.

When prayer begins to take up more room in someone's life, it is all the more important to keep a check on it. The particular mode of prayer must also be examined, for in an excess of fervor it is possible for someone to select a form which is either totally unsuitable for him or one that is too elementary and does not allow him to progress as far as God wishes. The Church's supervision of prayer is not intended to make it subject again to human evaluation or dependent on mere obedience. Rather, the Church's experience is to help the person to recognize obstacles and grow into a genuine readiness for God's will. It should give him the proper balance, which is liberating, not restricting. Anyone who tries to pursue a life of prayer according to his own lights will generally overestimate his progress. His assessment will be superficial, in terms of perceived quantities. He cannot evaluate the deep effects. The Church's official representative can evaluate them far more objectively and thus is also better able to tell whether what he is doing will have lasting results. For instance, since he has begun to pray responsibly, he may have eliminated some fault only to have become more proud without noticing it. Or he may have forced God into his system of prayer: God has become smaller for him, and he himself has grown bigger in his own eyes. So prayer must come under direction as soon as human fervor and effort begin to show themselves, as soon as prayer becomes prominent and starts playing an important role. For the most part this occurs when someone is facing important decisions in his life, which of themselves call for supervision and guidance—all the more so if the decision seems to be going in the direction of discipleship of Christ in the religious life. In such a case the Church's appointed director will have to guide prayer particularly carefully; by observing the effects of his advice, he will seek to discover what form of discipleship God wishes and what rule corresponds best to this particular prayer. At this point, spiritual direction merges into an introduction into the prayer of the religious life.

***

No prayer can do without discipline. One prays in order to come nearer to the truth which is God and to be grasped by it. The believer knows that the words of the gospel, inspired by the Spirit and interpreted by the Church, are truth, truth of the Son who referred to himself as the Truth. Truth is the Word which was in the beginning, and to pray is to expose oneself to this Word, to seek for it and let it exercise its power. Discipline is necessary if there is to be a vital encounter with the Word in prayer, and if prayer is to be fashioned according to God's objective word in the gospel and the Church.

In prayer itself there must be nothing vague; I must know that I am in the presence of truth, that I am beholding truth. But I behold truth in the word. Thus if the word stands in clarity before the soul, if prayer is active within the gospel revelation and is being drawn closer into it (instead of operating in a closed circle designed by man), if this movement flows into the word more and more, truth becomes visible. The person at prayer senses that he is held by it, but he also sees more and more of it, his acquaintance with it improves, and his knowledge of it grows deeper. For God's truth is a truth which reveals, unveils and proclaims itself; it provides firm ground, expands horizons, reveals insight, removes obstacles and generates an objective light. As a result the person praying can see that he is part of a movement created, not by himself, but by truth and that his knowledge is not imaginary, originating in himself, but comes from the word of God, which, for him, increasingly has the character of divine truth. His active contribution in prayer is only a preparation for what God does. He prays for truth; he takes into his prayer the truth he already knows, so that it can be expanded and made more true by the truth which will be shown him, and which is the pure action of God.

Step by step, however, he can test this path of prayer by comparing what he has received privately with what he receives through the Church from the gospel; he can compare it with the truth which is valid forever, which acquires a new and living face in every prayer and yet is the truth which, from all eternity, consists in the Son. To carry out this test (which can be itself both active and passive, both a testing and a being tested by the Church and her representatives) he needs the same qualities as in the case of prayer: a desire for objectivity, a genuine readiness to make himself available, an unconditional faith, but also the will to be corrected, to admit mistakes, to be so seized by the true word of God that he is ready to put away everything that is found to be daydreaming or unproductive personal speculation.

Under both forms the word of God has a clear visibility: as the subjective word which prays in me and as the objective word which is proposed to my faith. There can be no contradiction between personal experience and the Church's teaching. Perceiving the truth is an act of faith which evinces an inner submission to the encountering word in both prayer and the gospel. Provided the believer's personal experience is genuine, it cannot distort the word of the gospel; on the contrary, the better he learns to pray, the more radiant and convincing this word becomes. He is like someone who has learned a foreign language at home and then hears it spoken by the foreign people and understands it, confirming that he has learned it correctly.

2. CONSTANCY AND PERSONAL MOODS

God is unchangeable, yet he is always revealing himself to man in different ways. At times he makes himself known in an almost unveiled manner, and then again sometimes knowledge of him is totally enveloped in faith and nothing apparently happens to move this knowledge forward. But it leads to the strengthening of faith. Man is by nature changeable and his moods alternate; but in his prayer he should endeavor to acquire certain features of God's immutability, mirrored primarily in a constant availability, a regularity, a firmness of obedience, a resolution to be at God's disposal and to think only of God—things which affect his fundamental attitude. Of course, some exterior aspects of prayer are influenced by one's mood. The prayer of festivity must be different from the prayer of sorrow; prayer made in weariness will be different from prayer in the morning. If God permits something of one's exterior life to show itself within prayer and influence one's attitude, one should conceive it as God's way of encouraging man lest he falter through a too oppressive evenness, a way of taking something of one's personal tension into the tension of prayer. The sublime example is that of the Lord: He is always equally obedient and attentive as he stands before the Father, yet he lets the exterior conditions and moods of his life influence him as he does so. His festal prayer, his prayer of joy, is different from his prayer of fasting in the wilderness or his prayer on the Cross. It would be a sign of ingratitude to try to compel oneself to lay aside the hues of one's personality before coming to pray in order to come before God neutral and colorless. It would be to forget that personality is itself a gift from God and that no event of everyday life is without its connection to him. In the prayers of the Church it is otherwise, for here the individual at prayer embodies part of the Church. Here it is largely the Church herself who sets the atmosphere, and the individual's task is to fit into the ecclesial form, renouncing his personal mood.

3. ACTIVE AND PASSIVE

The prayer which man undertakes for the most part actively, on his own initiative—as in the Divine Office—is the easier kind. The prayer in which he is primarily receptive is harder; he tires of it more quickly, or else he becomes discouraged when he imagines that he is not getting anywhere. Active prayer carries one in such a way that one is prevented from slipping; in passive prayer it is essential to begin anew from moment to moment, to keep offering oneself and to let oneself be carried. In active prayer the duration of time is felt as something supportive, something one has conquered in advance; in passive prayer it is an obstacle which must continually be faced and overcome. In active prayer one is borne up by the governing and compelling law of action; in passive prayer one is left much more to one's own devices, situated in a vacuum and obliged to set off through it anew each time.

In contemplation the person is led willy-nilly by God and his Spirit. Here there is a form of guidance which can only be experienced when he is really being led passively; he grasps its direction more than its nature, and it is continually re-fashioning him. He may imagine that, with his initial readiness and his attitude of listening, he has done enough. But this was at most the starting point. Only now can he be required to abide in the attitude of listening. It is prolonged indefinitely and is apparently endless and without any contours; it may be the cause of pain, the pain of uninterrupted mortification, self-exposure and self-renunciation. But that is not the issue:

The central point is not here but somewhere else, exclusively in the goal of his readiness and his listening. The essential thing is to wait and let things take their course. Often one does not know the way forward or what is supposed to happen, yet one must not look for any consolation or any support. When pain comes, one thinks, "It will pass" or "It could be worse." Or one thinks of others who are suffering much more. But here this kind of distraction is inappropriate. All that is required is the quality of one's abiding, in this precise form, devoting attention to what is before one now. There is a certain abasement and humiliation in the fact that one is completely expropriated and made available. No "observations" are allowed; not only is one not to say anything, one may not look for things to express. What is revealed is a gift to such an extent that one must attend to the gift in its entirety. What is required is participation in what is happening *now*, in this quite particular event which one can neither perform nor control. There seems to be a contradiction in the demand: not to be concerned with the way things develop or how long the situation lasts—i.e., not to engage in reflection—and yet not to relax the tension and the attention, remaining quiet until all has been revealed, abiding within the framework provided, attending to this picture, these points. Contemplation is not measurable in terms of temporal duration. In half an hour's contemplation one should not have the feeling, after twenty-five minutes, of being nearer the end. If one is really paying attention to what one is doing, time no longer plays a role. Or if at the commencement one gets some inspired idea, one should not think, "Now I've got it." One's attention and readiness should remain perfectly constant whether one finds inspiration or not. A feeling of superiority should never be allowed to insinuate itself. Actually one should always offer oneself to God from the lowest place, remaining there and never rising up with the feeling of being adequate to the situation. Contemplation always retains a mysterious, inaccessible side, particularly in what concerns God's influence. This influence can never be concretely ascertained; often it remains entirely indirect. This hidden side is just as fundamental as, or even more fundamental than, what one feels and understands.

All this is different in the case of active prayer. Here there is progress to be made. There are achievements to support me, there is a plan, I can see where I am—for instance, how many psalms I have prayed and how many are left. In passive prayer it is God alone who has the plan. The person praying has no awareness of time and no calculations. But he knows that everything is in God's control. If he contemplates properly, in the spirit and the obedience of contemplation, peace and calm reign even where he is deprived of an overall grasp.

Someone contemplating some joyful mystery, perhaps because its feast is celebrated today, can bring his mood of joy into the contemplation and try to harmonize it with God's joy. And God can accept this mood and lay emphasis on it, making the feast even more festive. But he can also mingle some serious and grave element with it, revealing the side of the festal mystery which calls for response and responsibility, a side that the person at prayer had forgotten about. In this way he can mold the praying person. Here, too, the most important thing is this process of letting oneself be molded in passive prayer; any anticipation is forbidden, for it interferes with God's work.

4. CONSOLATION AND DESOLATION

There are two possibilities when the soul enters into prayer. It can come as it is or it can adapt itself somewhat to contemplation before prayer begins. If it comes as it is, the soul may think that the good mood and the desire to contemplate which it brings with it are something essential which must be maintained during contemplation. This is not quite true. But perhaps the soul knows no better; perhaps it lacks direction and thinks that God must accommodate it in this point. Perhaps the soul is looking forward to conversation with God and to being in a joyful mood in his presence. Assuming that God has nothing extraordinary in store for this soul, he may leave it in its mood of joy, enriching it to a certain degree with which it must be content; and the soul leaves contemplation in a largely unaltered state, as far as mood and readiness for God's will are concerned. If God has other intentions, he can break the soul's mood. He may let the soul see what he is doing, or he may act so that the break arises like a wall right in the middle of the soul's contemplation, causing the soul to take fright at this change because it does not understand what is going on. In certain circumstances this lack of understanding is the whole fruit of contemplation. But if the soul is already initiated into contemplation and adapted to it, it will enter into prayer with a certain reserve, in whatever mood it happens to find itself. It knows that its tangible joy is not of the essence of prayer and will only think of this joy as a gift of God for as long as God wishes to grant it. It is willing to adapt and be adapted. When such a soul comes before God in joy, it makes this offer from the very beginning: "Joy belongs to you, my God; you can use it in your service, but you can also bring it to an end." Joy enters the relationship only conditionally. Now the soul's overall attitude is readiness for service and joy in prayer. Contemplation has its place as something special here, but the fundamental attitude outlasts the individual contemplation, forms a bridge from one period of contemplation to the next, and only permeates contemplation when God wishes. If a soul enters full of fervor into a contemplation which then develops

287

into desolation, this should not result in the soul being discouraged until the time for the next contemplation. Nor will this happen if the soul has the correct attitude. If it does occur, it means that a mistake has been made somewhere. The soul was not flexible enough, not passive enough under God's shaping hand. The soul ought to be like a naked body before God: God can cover it up, removing all embarrassment, or he can merely cover those parts which are embarrassing, or he can leave it as it is. In any case it is up to God to make any change with regard to the soul's nakedness. And the subject of contemplation is not one's own nakedness but what God reveals while one is in this condition. Nakedness is only the expression of the fact that the soul is leaving behind everything which, at this moment, God does not permit.

If the soul is sad or dejected at the beginning, it must surrender this mood to God for the contemplation. If the material given in contemplation happens to match the soul's own dejected mood, it would be wrong of the soul to mirror its own dejection in that required by contemplation. It would only be right to engage in contemplation in the same downcast mood as one had prior to contemplating if God specifically requested it for this particular period of prayer. Before contemplation all moods must first be relativized by indifference. This sacrifice must be made, and it will be accepted even if God leaves one's mood intact.

***

The source of consolation is the fact that the Father accompanies the Son. On earth the Son beholds the Father, feels his guidance and his company and is constantly in dialogue with him, and this conversation gives him courage, helps him and shows him the way even in difficult situations. In fact he would be able to find the way himself, but he wishes to do the Father's will, and in answer the Father shows him his will. Thus in all his actions, his readiness and his planning, the Son is consoled by the Father's company.

The source of desolation is the Cross, where the Father, accepting the Son's will, has withdrawn from him, leaving the Son forsaken. While the Son abides in this contemplation of the Cross, in perfect obedient passivity, he calls to the Father and hears no answer. From this point of view, one would be inclined to conclude that desolation is more fruitful than consolation, since it springs from that most fruitful of all things, the Cross. But consolation and desolation correspond to the same will in the Son, and both are signs of his Incarnation, his saving will and his saving action. They are two phases of the same process which he is undergoing. Therefore, if they are genuine gifts of God and not self-fabricated, consolation and desolation are both signs of the true following of Christ. Within this discipleship no one thing has any more weight than another; everything is comprehended in the one obedience. The awareness of either consolation or desolation is the response to accepted obedience and the sign of the Father's will in operation, a will that is realized in the Son and in the person who takes the Son's path.

Since desolation is harder to understand than consolation, God sends consolation to souls that are beginning to worship him rightly more often than he leaves them in desolation. Desolation, genuinely and properly borne, demands more sacrifice of the soul. Few can bear it in the right spirit; thus, humanly speaking, a greater share of the Cross falls to those who can. The disconsolate individual has more to bear than the person who experiences consolation: Accordingly, his influence, participation and fruitfulness are greater. At the same time it would not be altogether correct to follow this thought to its logical conclusion; it is complemented by the most hidden of God's mysteries.

God consoles beginners more than others in order to encourage them, help them and show them how near he is. He can also give more consolation to those who, apart from contemplation, have a hard path to follow and need to gain strength for it through prayer. But one cannot establish principles for God's granting or withholding consolation; all depends on his will, which to us seems arbitrary. Perhaps one can say that he leaves those people more in desolation whose main mission is within the efficacy of the Cross. It may be that absolute desolation is more often to be found where someone's mission is not so much a matter of communication, or where distinction between the mysteries revealed to him is less important because their interpretation is less necessary. Religious founders who receive their order's rule through prayer and contemplation cannot be plunged into desolation for long because they need to experience and search the mysteries of God's nearness so that they can communicate them to others. Conversely, there are sacrificed souls living in the obscurity of the cloister that experience utter desolation for a very long time; God then distributes the fruit of this all over the world, without the sufferer necessarily being involved in this result of his suffering.

***

There are two ways of standing before God in prayer where the genuine encounter with him is guaranteed: one in feeling and the other in not feeling. The man who goes to prayer knows from experience that he can encounter God, the God who has something to say to him personally; he knows that this encounter is most likely to occur in the solitude of prayer and that he receives answers, instructions and guidance from God. This knowledge is habitual with him. And when he attempts to pray, equipped with this knowledge, it may be that, in spite of being certain of standing in God's presence, he experiences nothing, feels nothing, hears nothing. His certainty is not shattered, but it does not console him; he is not aware of being enriched by it, and it does not expand into a central position in his spirit. But it can happen that his habitual certainty is confirmed in an actual experience. He senses that God is here, hears his answer and thus gains a new security—either a general one which brings him happiness or a quite specific one referring to a particular point which may or may not have caused him problems, an answer to a specific question or some other issue. At all events, he cannot doubt the genuineness of the answer.

In the second case, standing before God is like the meeting of I and Thou, and grace fashions this supernatural encounter into something quite natural, like an exchange between human beings. In the first case, the encounter is like a subordinate making a report to his superior: The latter listens, but no expression of his betrays his own reaction or what he intends to do as a result of the report. Yet the subordinate has spoken to him and knows from experience that he was listening.

***

It can happen that in the middle of prayer a person becomes disconsolate because he is given no vision, no clue and no light, and because his expectations are not fulfilled. And as desolation envelops him and he lets everything be withdrawn from him, a great vacuum is created in him as he stands before God. Previously he assumed that the goal was to make progress in prayer: by the practice of virtue, making efforts in prayer, growing in the knowledge of God. He forgot that true progress is made by God, whereas the progress he himself can engineer is only intended to empty the soul of all that obstructs God's action upon it.

God may say something which, to him, is utterly clear, whereas man cannot find the connecting thread. He understands individual words but not the context. So all that he has understood remains in flux, and his prayer cannot get a foothold. Possibly the meaning may not become clear until God has finished speaking, and humanly speaking this may take a very long time. Trying to decide on the meaning prematurely would be disobedience and constriction and can lead to a complete misunderstanding of the message. It is essential to hold on when the meaning will not yield itself up, even if it means emptiness, blind stumbling and desolation.

Or a prayer begins in consolation. Perhaps it is a question of love: I become aware of new demands, and I affirm and embrace them with enthusiasm. But then the consolation is withdrawn, and all that remains is barrenness. It would be wrong to want to summon the consolation back again. Being acquainted with the fullness of consolation, I must be prepared to accept desolation. At the moment when the Son says to the Father, "If it be possible, Father, let this cup pass from me", his confident hope in the Father is infinitely great. But at the same moment he is required to renounce this hope, and forsakenness is laid upon him. Increased forsakenness can be the direct consequence of trust.

A man may have prayed for a long time simply out of a desire for service, experiencing neither special consolation nor desolation. God may wish to test him by means of desolation. Thus he will give him joy in prayer, fervor and longing, for only after experiencing this will he be able to appreciate real desolation. Otherwise it is not possible to test obedience, for if a man has not experienced desolation, it is hard to tell whether he prays out of pure love for God or for the sake of the joy he experiences. The novice, for example, who is bored with his studies, looks forward to prayer time, since it is his recreation: His desire coincides with his obedience, and the danger is that he may make God into the compensation for his ennui. He is not seeking God as he is, but the God who determines his joy.

In daily life man is largely able to induce his own moods. He can read either a humorous or a sad book. He can start reading a book, decide whether it suits his present needs, and put it down if it does not. Or he can hold himself aloof and not be influenced by the mood of the book. To a great extent he could do the same with God. He could draw back from what God shows him, "switching off" or only following in an external sense, not participating internally. He could try to skip some experience that he ought to undergo, nullifying a time of desolation, for instance, by trying to live entirely from a future consolation. But it is a mistake to try to withdraw from God's "moods" (provided that they are his and not one's own!); we should learn more and more to be at peace with whatever he sends and to let go all the bonds which keep us from going along with him, even where there seems to be no end to what may be demanded of us.

God's intention may be to empty the soul of everything, and each individual demand is for him only one rung of a very tall ladder. But man stops at each rung, feeling that he may take a rest since he has got nearer to his goal. But the real goal is for man to let himself simply be led and carried by God. God has asked him to put away some failing or to sacrifice some habit. Now he asks more and different things, and ultimately man feels that the chain of demands extends into infinity. He is seized by panic, which his consciousness interprets as desolation. But it is simply because he will not let go and will not be led. If he would only submit to the will of God, his desolation also would come to an end. Nor should he expect the reward of consolation after every accomplishment, some kind of tangible satisfaction from God. Carrying out God's demands is something totally objective; it is a service, intended to call forth in man neither a feeling of sadness nor one of relief.

5. GOD'S PREDOMINANCE

The Christian lives on two planes: that of his consciousness, in which he knows what he is thinking, willing and doing and which seems fairly fixed and intelligible, and that of the Spirit, which is always causing him to do things which are beyond his horizon of understanding, a plane on which he simply obeys: This latter plane is that of the reality of his faith. He must try to integrate these two planes by the one Spirit who governs both the natural and the supernatural, who issues the commands which come from the invisible realm and also indicates the course of things in the natural realm. Fundamentally, being a Christian means, not subordinating the divine Spirit and his supernatural guidance to the laws of the human spirit and its disposition of the natural realm, but letting the divine Spirit govern the natural realm as well as the supernatural. This applies especially to prayer. In prayer man is to be introduced to the world of God, of which his "I" is not aware, yet in which his "I" and the whole natural world take their place and play their part. The unreflective Christian believes somehow that the world of God is open to him, but he lives in the everyday world to such an extent that he subjects the laws of the divine world to those of daily life, trying to keep control himself over what God may or may not demand. But if a Christian really prays, he sees that all control and disposition are God's and that, through genuine obedience, he can bring God's world into his daily life. When, in supernatural obedience, he does something that is contrary to his will as a natural man, he enters the world of God and gives it power over his nature. And the desolation of his sacrificed nature is a token of the fact that he has come nearer to God, nearer, in fact, than in obeying without really noticing it. As long as there is no pain in the renunciation, a kind of parallelism exists between the two planes. One may perhaps have obeyed, but without God's world having won a victory over nature. These two worlds must be separated sooner or later so that they can unite and interpenetrate by God's power; thus it will be evident that man is not doing his will but the will of God. If this is to occur, active obedience must be taken up into passive. But in prayer the world of God is opened up; man is led into regions unknown and closed to him in ordinary life, and he gives the predominance to unseen reality, as did Brother Klaus on leaving his family, as does every Christian who, in obedience to God, delivers a puzzling and painful blow to his nature. What once was right and good is now committed again to God, and this time God does not give it back.

From here it is only a step to the law of visions. Up to now I have believed my eyes to be my faithful servants; like others, I regarded what I saw with my own eyes as clear evidence. Now, suddenly, God gives me a new mode of sight, and the criteria of my former eyes are of no use. When God wants to reveal something, he creates the appropriate organ with which to perceive it. Suddenly it seems that the world is breaking in two: One law contradicts the other. Or perhaps I think that I have been praying up until now, but God says, "That was no prayer; I never regarded it as such." All is contradiction. But then, through grace, God's world comes down into the world of nature. And God's world has the preeminence. "I saw you when you were under the fig tree": Nathanael stood in God's sight before he knew it. Man's deeds have echoed in God's world in a way he never guessed. And now, perhaps, God tells him what he, man, has done; what he knew without knowing it; what he has perceived, not with his natural senses, but with senses that only obey God, with that part of his "I" which stands before God in heaven. But what takes place in the supernatural world is never without an echo in the natural. Each grace from God is like a seed planted in the soul which must sprout in the course of daily life. God opens up his plane so that the natural plane can be seized by it. (The denial of this possibility is a Protestant denial.) Even where this opening of God's plane has a mystical quality, it always implies a fertilization of the earthly world. Through and in his saints the Spirit speaks to the Church in order continually to enliven her. The saints are an opening into the divine world, and as such they belong to it and cannot be completely governed by the earthly sphere. They are a form of the Spirit's blowing where he wills. Every believer whose faith is alive must live on both planes; in the saints the energy and tension between the two planes is more visible and vibrant—all the more so, the more distinctive their vocations are.

***

Each person brings himself along when he comes to pray; and if he is inexperienced in prayer, what he brings with him will mostly bear the stamp of his personal problems and daily life. Then he will learn that, in prayer, even if he asks for something or for clarity in a matter that is important to him personally, a reorganization always takes place. What he regarded as essential may become quite unimportant from God's point of view. What seemed easy he may now find difficult. He cannot calculate how this change is going to take place, so he must be ready to fit his arrangements in with God's. In prayer he will learn what shape God now wishes to give to his nature, his abilities and his current situation, in the context of grace and supernature. Even if this nature is already Christian, if prayer is properly cultivated it will continually be exposed to the reshaping power of grace and will be subordinated to God's nature—which, for us, is always supernatural—as its rule of life. The supernatural possesses the orientation, the importance and the countenance of God and his truth. So in prayer it is crucial that nature should be in a state of indifference regarding grace in order to be open and accessible to God's nature. The person who perseveres in the attitude of prayer will experience the effect of grace on nature as the real constant in his life. He will enter each succeeding prayer with an ever-growing renunciation of what he thinks of as his own and of all he has preconceived, planned and explained, letting himself be led by grace more and more. In his own affairs he will experience the blowing of the Spirit. He will come to see that he has been handed over as a victim and that in his sacrifice and his desolation (which may be subject to very natural causes) he has been permitted to know the consolation of the experience of God. He will realize that consolation does not consist in seeing his earthly life pursuing its course according to his will and expectation, but in God adopting him into his providence and fashioning his destiny. On earth he may have to drag the same problems around with him to the very end; yet, from a Christian point of view, he may continually enjoy God's consolation, which is to experience his truth. Prayer becomes renewal, and renewal becomes truth, and truth becomes the presence of God. As time goes by he will learn so to long for this presence that he will mention his own natural affairs less and less, until he almost forgets them when he comes before God, letting God alone speak. No longer will he try to force God in some direction of his own: He will leave the whole area open for the divine direction, for the Spirit.

IX

LOVE AND FRUIT

1. LOVE IN PRAYER

Out of love God creates the world and man. And out of love he enters from the start into a reciprocal and companionable relationship with Adam. Initially this is simply something given, a matter of fact. To Adam it is quite natural that God should wish to be with him; he does not reflect about it. Only after the Fall does he discover himself to be a stranger standing opposite God. By his self-concealment he has broken their life together and no longer knows what God has in mind. And God seeks him out and calls him. God reties the broken thread, showing that his love and care for Adam is greater than the latter's estrangement.

Man at prayer is always Adam, sought out by God. He himself would never have hit upon the idea of starting a conversation with his Creator, but the Creator searches for him and is concerned about him out of love for his creature. So every conversation with God is enveloped in God's love; it is a consequence which flows from love.

When God speaks out of love, his word is a word of love, and the person praying will try to receive and return it as such. It is remarkable that he often tries to speak a word of love to God, but rarely realizes in his heart that he is also hearing and receiving a word of love. In prayer he fulfills a kind of duty, forgetting that the deepest meaning of this duty is love. Many people had the joy, as children, of praying with their mothers. Later on, life knocked them about, and they have forgotten how to pray. In some time of need they recall the warmth and security of their childhood prayers; perhaps they use their mothers' love as a bridge to get back to the love of God. But somewhere they get stuck in human emotion; they scarcely touch God's sphere because they have forgotten to listen for God's word of love.

If the man who prays knows that the essence of prayer is love, his attitude in prayer will be one of openness to love. He will try to be accessible to love: not by straining to catch special and extraordinary signs of love, but in a simple attention, not letting slip any proof of love which God gives, refusing nothing, misunderstanding nothing, whitewashing nothing, reinterpreting nothing. If he is a beginner in prayer he should be so inspired by the thought of love that he is never in a hurry, but takes his time. He may pause a while after each prayer, picking some thought, some idea, some word out of the world of love: However small and insignificant it is, he takes it into his daily life in order to fill that life with the love of God. In many ways modern man lives his life automatically. He at least ought to learn not to pray automatically: He needs to re-discover a sense of wonder at the love of God, going on to impart a sense of eternity to his world once again.

***

God's love is offered to men like an overflowing vessel from which they may draw. But there are different ways of en-countering the love of God in prayer: Some are more central and others are more peripheral. Believers know that God is love and that the closer we get to him the closer we get to love. They know that, since he is love, this love is found at his very core, in the innermost being of his godhead, because in him this love is the very heart of truth. They also know that they too can be taken up into this central core. But as well as this—and perhaps in a more experiential way, through feeling—they know that they ought not only to become acquainted with the innermost center of love (indeed, they are probably not strong enough to resist this rushing torrent, this intense heat) but should also get to know all the scattered drops and rays which this love emits. Every genuine life of prayer manifests two experiences: that of the central fullness and that of deprivation or aridity which, regarded as experience, seems peripheral. At some point the man who prays will be touched by some knowledge or experience of love which causes him to desire to come nearer the fountainhead and awakens in him the longing to be cast into the center. But in terms of tangible experience the center is the exception, an exception that becomes the rule that one can return to and live from the memory of what one once received. Such was Paul's Damascus road, Ignatius' conversion, Pascal's "night"—and, on another plane, John's Apocalypse, which is perhaps one of the deepest explorations of God's center and which John himself found inexhaustible. All that he saw, heard and experienced here, all that he merely indicated as a background, was the center of the love of God, a center into which he was cast by his prayer. So the Apocalypse remains *the* experience of prayer *kat exochen* for all succeeding Christians, not *because of* its mystical quality, but *in spite of* it: Where the center is concerned, transposition into the mystical is only *one* possibility; but the Apocalypse belongs by right to everyone who prays, to such an extent that everyone can find nourishment for his prayer, and direct experience of the love of God, in the Apostle's mystical experience.

Every praying person who loves and strives toward the love of God has his share in it. The love of God becomes everything to him, to such an extent that from it he can form his life decisions. Because God loves him he can take the risk of some particular surrender; because God loves him he can follow this or that path; because God loves him he can put up with a life which would be otherwise intolerable; because God loves him he can renounce the world and lead an apostolic life; because God loves him he can die as a Christian; because God loves him he can daily love his neighbor as himself. Everyone who prays is given such a share in love that it becomes his center, and his whole existence manifests traces of this central experience.

Then there are the peripherals: the smaller experiences, including prayer's attraction, contentment in the presence of God, longing for his truth, the desire to live in the shadow of the encounter with God, perseverance in a Christian attitude and the will to acquire a Christian attitude in prayer and love. There is the determination to keep faith alive through the power of prayer in order to learn of the mysteries of the sacraments, to know and preserve the whole range of Catholic experience, to remain discriminating in all the multiplicity of available things and possibilities, to discern love's form in everything and to be led through everything to love, particularly to a love of prayer, of dialogue. For example, one of the reasons why God has created the Eucharist and the other sacraments is in order to maintain love's dialogue with man, a dialogue that is saturated with meaning, to speak words that are full to the brim. Through the sacraments the matter of the conversation between God and man has been infinitely expanded: This matter is pure love in all its most diverse forms.

***

The average Catholic may pray, but almost always with a fundamental reservation. He excludes the possibility that God means him, that God could have something new and personal to say to him. For him prayer is an act of worship, but he does not expect a response to this worship. Worship seems to be a monologue. The most he expects from God is that he will accept his worship and not bother him further, or merely look upon him with a general benevolence. It can happen that he is wakened out of the reserve he has imposed on his prayer by some surprising experience. It may be today's Mass that has struck him forcibly. Or he may have felt a momentary warmth during his evening prayers. Or parents may be filled with a sense of gratitude to God at the sight of their children. The experience is peripheral, not because it relates to God's periphery, but because of the Christian's peripheral Christianity. He gives God his hand but not his whole body. Even this degree of contact can be a wonderful experience, but it has an inner limit which has its origin in man.

To experience the love of God in a central way presupposes that the man is no longer concerned with status. Since God has no status, the man who loves him also has no status if he belongs to God and is hidden in him. For him there is no longer any up or down. As soon as a man gives up making conditions, God encounters him more frequently and in different forms, for now the soul is open, and far less of what God wishes to say to it is lost. The more open the soul is to God, the more he uses it, and for that very reason he has more to say, so that it will know how to carry out its tasks. And when such a person has a life decision to make, since it is a decision of faith, it will be made in prayer and, indeed, in that central love which comes from God. This is also why a person who has chosen the path of discipleship of the Lord is understood by so few: Earthly categories by which people judge have ceased to interest him. It is also why one cannot know anything about such a path in advance. God's visibility has outshone that of material things and the laws which govern them. The perspective has become that of eternal time and of the love of God, and here nothing seriously counts except love itself.

***

In his relationship with those close to him, every person prefers clarity, candor, agreement and the elimination of mis-understandings. He wants to know how far his conversation partners are in agreement and what objections they raise. He feels the need to explain and demonstrate what he means, not going into every detail, but keeping to the main issues. Sometimes his partner in conversation will raise some point in praise or criticism on his own initiative. It is similar with man's need to speak with God. It is the need for agreement, encouragement, protection, acknowledgment and correction. Here God is the one who can point out details.

Provided that this need to be clear with God is not simply the expression of mere habit or lethargy but a genuine need which is cultivated as such, God will very soon take it over and control it; then the person will no longer pray merely on his own initiative but in strict obedience. His need will intensify and his prayer time will increase, and prayer's dialogue will become easier to initiate. But if all goes as it should, this is to be explained by supernatural rather than natural causes. It must not be produced by a certain religious loquaciousness. Prayer's correct development is always in the direction of that central meeting with God in which words retire more and more into the background. Initially contemplation had to use external things, for two reasons. First, it had to build the bridge from the known and familiar to an understanding of Christian truth, the Lord's life and the mysteries of God. Second, especially later when prayer had become more established, contemplation also had to lead the person out from God's center back into everyday earthly life. In the apostolate, people cannot suddenly be confronted with the mystery of the Trinity: One must start from everyday things which they understand. Thus in prayer the person will return to quite simple things, for they too belong to God and can lead him to God by smoothing the path to his neighbor. Nonetheless, the peripheral factors indicate the center and help to simplify issues, just as a man who does not know another person first has to express himself in considerable detail but can be more brief as the acquaintance proceeds because their mutual understanding has grown; ultimately a mere look can say everything. So it is in our relationship with God. When two people who love each other are doing their own work in the same room, in silence, and one of them gets stuck, it can be enough for him to look up and see the other at work: He is strengthened and encouraged to persevere.

2. THE EFFECTIVENESS OF PRAYER

One of the first effects of prayer is that the person has a growing need to be involved with God. This takes effect in him, but it does not stop there, for its goal is not the need but what the need results in: listening to God. Prayer's first fruit creates room for God's purposes in the one praying. In intensifying his thirst, God increases his receptivity, his faith, his allegiance, his obedience. This initial effect is not aimed at the person at all but at the task to be done, the coming mission. The need for prayer contains the germ which will grow into an awareness of vocation, of the life decision, of the Christian's place in the world. At first he does not notice this; all he knows is that he is becoming firmer, without understanding in what way. His interior space is being put in order, but not to give him deeper self-knowledge; rather, he is learning better how to forget himself so that he can know God better. He learns the beginnings of obedient passivity. This is not yet surrender in its fullest sense; it is a desire. He lets himself be prepared for something, he knows not what. Thus it is an effect of prayer itself, within prayer, oriented to prayer. Prayer's goal is prayer.

Only then does he observe that his attitude is being changed, that he is being educated from prayer to prayer. His absences from prayer become shorter and shorter, and his strength becomes more and more concentrated on prayer. Slowly God is drawing his attention to himself, even apart from the time of prayer. This new effect is connected to his longing for more prayer. It corresponds to his aim, his wish. This second effect is more conscious and complements the first. The second reveals God's intention to do something with man, so that the longing for prayer opens up a new field of influence for this intention.

Prayer has its own matter, and this is always God: God in everything that connects man with him, such as the Lord's life, Scripture, the Church, the traditional prayers. This matter is effective substance; it can initiate man deeper and deeper into God and into what, as God's creature, he is to become. And the matter of prayer, which was initially a thing outside the person praying, is changed through prayer and becomes his interior possession. By prayer this matter is shaped; it comes alive in the person as a result of God's response and the surrender which the person invests in it, and slowly it changes into the person's Christian substance. At first he had looked on prayer as a purely personal dialogue with God, the exchange between two identities. But now something else places itself between them: the sphere of the immutable Word. An example of this is the Son's word expressed in the Our Father.

It is a word which can be taken to oneself personally, but it cannot be wrenched and twisted, for its meaning is original and inalienable. The expression "Our Father" can be interpreted either in a banal or in an incomparably sublime sense, but it will always mean that God is our Father. And when a man takes up this word in his prayer, the objective truth sinks deep into his heart, leaving its effects there. As well as the personal and subjective effects which the man primarily sought and experienced, there are objective effects which in many ways work contrary to them; these are meant to open up to him the whole truth of revelation, doctrine, Scripture, the Church's kerygma and the Church's prayer. He is to absorb this truth, while realizing that it is he who is being more profoundly absorbed into it. It is a reciprocal incorporation. His "I" is to remain "I" as God wishes, but an "I" that is penetrated and refashioned by prayer and its grace, an "I" united to the effect of the living Word. The growth in genuine personality on the part of the man who prays is also his growth in ecclesial and Catholic existence.

The first effect of prayer has nothing to do, as yet, with this dispossession. But the two are only opposed if they are conceived psychologically, if the thirst for prayer is thought of as a quantifiable spiritual experience. In that case, certainly, the man praying would be deceived if, once he had reached God on the basis of his longing, God were subsequently to lead him into the totality of truth. The initial desire for God is part of the mystery of creation. Here man stands before God like Adam in his creaturely dependence on and need for God. But God already knows what he will do with man. For example, it may happen that, from the very first day of a retreat, the retreat master can see that a particular young man is called to the religious life and that he must try to help him to see it. He gives the unsuspecting man some guidance in prayer, and as a result of his subjective experience of prayer the latter gains objective insight into God's will. This is no psychological game, for the retreat master was also basing himself on objective evidence of the will of God, and the retreatant does not work himself up into something but, in prayer, comes to know the truth. And as for God, he appeals, not to the man's soul, but to his being. It is a man's being that is capable of responding and of corresponding to God, for it is man's being which is seized by God's creative purpose. The evidence shown to me certainly addresses the man I am today, but to a certain extent it ignores the conditions of my life up to now and my more or less expressed wishes, plans and preferences, and puts me back in the state of being that I had when God created me. If it were a case of psychology, one would have to examine my experience, the quality of my spiritual awareness and the course of my development, and not this absolutely primitive state of being in its origin from God. If a person goes in for a lot of psychology he will no longer be able to practice obedience because he will always be observing and measuring his reactions and the states and habits of his soul, unable to place himself in that pristine being as it came from God. The impersonality which is the basic approach of the entire retreat, laying aside all personal experience, indicates the proper way to achieve the fruit God wishes, namely, accepting his divine truth into oneself and living by it.

* * *

But prayer also has an effect on the environment, on the Church and on the world. If a person has such faith that he prays a great deal, his prayer is absorbed into his environment in two ways. First, externally: His family and friends notice something of his life of prayer. He is seen going to church, and at home too he withdraws to pray. Those who observe this have to come to grips with it. They may see in it a kind of help or insurance when they have problems or troubles; he may make them feel secure; they may expect things of him. No doubt God uses the prayer which encompasses those around the person praying in such a way that they do benefit by it. And, conscious of being involved in this prayer, they will try to imitate their praying friend in their behavior and ideas. They will try to interpret his words and actions by reference to his atmosphere of prayer, and thus in a human and natural way they will try to approximate his prayer life. Straightway we have the tangled interplay of nature and supernature, merit and grace: In an exterior way they are made open to prayer by the presence of a man who prays, and simultaneously, through the inner effectiveness of his prayer, they are opened up to all that God intends to give them through prayer. The man who prays, as well as those around him, will discover more and more how to bring the demands and decisions of everyday life into prayer, to test them and to shape their lives through prayer. And whatever his situation, the actions and decisions of the man of prayer will bear witness to the fact that they have their origin in the world of prayer; thence, enriched and amplified, they exert their influence on the everyday world.

Prayer's influence can extend to everything: to what the person explicitly includes in his prayer and to everything else as well. It affects what he specifically offers or requests in prayer insofar as he is manifestly granted his desire, so that here it is not hard to recognize the grace of God. But many things are granted in quite a different manner from that anticipated; yet the grace of prayer will enable him to recognize God's love and answering fulfillment here as well. The effect of prayer is often quite invisible, and it is precisely the invisible fruit which binds the man of prayer more closely to God, draws him more surely to him, and makes him increasingly God's instrument. If he knows, in prayer, that all is well between himself and God, he will be drawn onward by the absence of visible answers. He learns no longer to apply his own will, his own calculations and his own standards to things, but to submit to God more and more, seeing the will and power of God even in areas where his reason is no longer adequate. If his prayer is in order, he will have the certainty, even when he sees no results, that he is abiding in God and is carrying out God's will and that his prayer has brought forth fruit, though intangible to him: It belongs to God, and somewhere or other it is tangible to him. He is initiated into further mysteries, spiritual realms that otherwise would be closed to him. He learns to worship the will of God even when it is impenetrable. Thus he grows more deeply accustomed to the world of prayer and becomes more confident in his relationship to God, in his surrender to him, in his whole sense of God and divine things.

From this vantage point we can begin to understand something of the influence of prayer in the Church and the world. Every praying person belongs to the company of the saints; as well as his personal concerns, he takes to himself the concerns of the Church. He is to bring them into his prayer and regard them as his own. Indeed, he must consider all of God's concerns as his own if he wants to be God's creature and in touch with the Creator. So he will make it his custom to pray for the Church and all her concerns, all of which he cannot possibly survey. He is not bound to them, but the Church is, in a bond which involves him since he is a member of the Church—a bond which he scarcely feels and understands, since, as he belongs to the Church, he himself is not the Church. He will remember that the Church is the Bride of Christ and that there are many secrets between Bride and

Bridegroom; in a mysterious way he is privileged to participate in them, but he cannot penetrate to the details. These are mysteries upon which he has an influence through his prayer, on the basis of his participation in them, yet without being able to work out what that influence is. This participation of his is perhaps the most concrete thing he learns of the mystery between Bride and Bridegroom. Much of this he can put into words: He can pray for the well-being of the Church, for the conversion of sinners, for the spread of the gospel. God and the Church count on his praying for these tangible things. God also, however, counts on his not stopping there, but going on to pray for what is not accessible to him. If he is aware that, when he prays, he has a share in the entire mystery of the Church, he will renounce from the start all attempts to test his prayer's effectiveness or to restrict its scope. Aware that he is participating in a mystery that must remain such for him, he will not be inclined to put the effectiveness of his prayer to the test on those things which are accessible to him. No longer will he see prayer as a limited activity—be it vocal or contemplative—but as an act of *trust* which does not demand to be informed of its own consequences. It is an act of trust which generates new acts of trust, a prayer which spills over into new prayer without any generation and transformation being perceptible. And this applies to all kinds of prayer: to worship, thanksgiving, petition, formulated and contemplative prayer, personal and community prayer. Where prayer's results are invisible, the man of prayer grows into a more powerful faith.